Conversations with Ilan Stavans

W9-BGP-652

12/06

Conversations with

Ilan Stavans

The University of Arizona Press   Tucson

For Ofelia, mi mamá

chá-chá-chá

The University of Arizona Press
© 2005 Ilan Stavans
All rights reserved

♾ This book is printed on acid-free, archival-quality paper.
Manufactured in the United States of America

10 09 08 07 06 05   6 5 4 3 2 1

Library of Congress Cataloging-in-Publication Data
Stavans, Ilan.
Conversations with Ilan Stavans / Ilan Stavans. — 1st ed.
p. cm.
ISBN 0-8165-2264-2 (pbk. : alk. paper)
1. Hispanic American authors—Interviews. 2. American literature—
Hispanic American authors—History and criticism—Theory, etc.
3. Authors, American—20th century—Interviews. 4. Hispanic
Americans—Intellectual life. 5. Hispanic American artists—Interviews.
6. Hispanic American actors—Interviews. 7. Hispanic Americans—In
literature. 8. Latin America—Intellectual life. 9. Authorship. I. Title.
PS153.H56S73 2005
868'.6409—dc22

2004023662

Publication of this book is made possible in part by the proceeds of a
permanent endowment created with the assistance of a Challenge
Grant from the National Endowment for the Humanities, a federal
agency.

A man's life is like those geographical fragments with which children learn "the contiguous countries." The pieces are a puzzle; but put them together carefully, and lo! they are a map.

—Charles Reade, *The Autobiography of a Thief*

Contents

Introduction

Over the years, I've spent hours engaging others in public dialogues. It is an essential aspect of my role as critic, and the pleasures are manifold. To squeeze the juice out of the tête-à-tête, it is best to remain spontaneous. But spontaneity ought to be approached with caution. I usually bathe myself in everything I'm able to put my hands on related to my future interviewee: books, films, CDs, Web sites, and published conversations. But I make no notes, nor do I decide at a premature stage how the dialogue should evolve. It is only during the encounter that spontaneity takes its course: the weather, the hour, and mood of the day—these are aspects that impinge on the development. The conversation is generally in front of a TV camera, or else with a tape recorder nearby. Then comes the transcription period, which, in a subtle fashion, even more emphatically defines the course of the material. I let words stamp themselves consecutively on the screen, but the actual structure of the talk is still up for grabs. To edit an interview isn't only to eliminate some of the "ahs," "mms," and "likes" but to give shape to the stream of consciousness. I add a question, or else I divide an answer in half. Next the interviewee gets a draft, which he or she may make substantial changes to. This exchange, done more often than not by electronic mail, is repeated until the two participants are comfortable with the final result. Only then does the interview go to the printer.

My hope is that the outcome will somehow survive the mercilessness of time. I want the transcription to go beyond the immediate present, to be read not as journalism but as history. I also want it to be a collaborative essay. These goals aren't always easy to achieve, since the reason for the encounter is often occasional: a new book recently released, a controversy still in the air . . .

Why do I enjoy these tête-à-têtes so much? The answer is simple: a conversation can push my mind in unforeseen directions, to the extent I find myself surprised by its course. To let my thoughts loose, not to know where I'm going, is a thrill. When I draft an essay, I alone am in control.

But a conversation is a tango, for it takes two to dance it. My choice of interviewees is based, first and foremost, on empathy, although availability in the end becomes equally important. In spite of the fact that my role as interviewer pushes me to the foreground, in the talks I seek to remain as unobtrusive as possible. Equally, I refrain from pushing my own ideological agenda. My purpose is to let the political and aesthetic views of the company I keep emerge unhindered. Consequently, these talks seldom become full-fledged dialogues: it isn't what *I* believe that is at stake—not overtly, at least.

In this volume I've collected a selection of interviews done over a period of twenty years. The majority have been published in periodicals and aired on PBS. Some have more depth than others, yet almost none took longer than forty-five minutes. In harvesting them for *Conversations with Ilan Stavans*, I haven't given in to the temptation of retouching them: they are a product of the imperfect present tense, so to speak, and should be read as such. My interlocutors are actors, activists, poets, anthropologists, critics, newscasters, musicians, journalists, *performeros*, and literati. They're unified by a series of ongoing concerns: the demands of democracy on its citizenry, the struggle against racism and xenophobia, the odyssey of self-expression, the tension between religion and secularism, the passion for gestures and words, and my lifelong obsession with language. All the *conversateurs* are Hispanics in the broadest sense of the term, that is, participants in Hispanic civilization north and south of the Rio Grande. None of the conversations is designed as an exposé, which makes me refrain from exclamation marks.

I thank Joseph Tovares for the invitation to engage my guests on camera. I also want to express my appreciation to each and every one of the interviewees for their generosity of time and energy. The logistical help provided by Margaret Carsley, Patricia Alvarado, and Arturo Steinberg of PBS-WGBH was immense. These discussions owe much to them. *Gracias* to my students Aaron Britt and Daniela Hernández for their research and to Bobbie Helinski for secretarial work. I also want to express my gratitude to Walter Cummins in New Jersey, Jules Chametzky in Massachusetts, Laurence Goldstein in Michigan, Steve Moore in Illinois, as well as Marilyn and the late Tom Auer in Colorado for their editorial support. John Mulvihill carefully copyedited the manuscript. Patti Hartmann at the University of Arizona Press encouraged this compilation from the start. With enviable patience and conviction, she chaperoned it through the editorial channel. I have a deep appreciation for her.

Unless identified otherwise, all translations of interviews conducted in Spanish (or in both Spanish and English) are by myself.

Conversations with Ilan Stavans

Books and Quilts

Marjorie Agosín

Marjorie Agosín (Chile, b. 1955) is a professor of Spanish at Wellesley College. She is responsible for, among other books, Scraps of Life *(1987),* Circle of Madness: Mothers of the Plaza de Mayo *(1991),* Dear Anne Frank *(1992),* A Cross and a Star: Memoirs of a Jewish Girl in Chile *(1995),* A Dream of Light and Shadow *(1995),* The Alphabet in My Hands *(2000), and* The Angel of Memory *(2001). This interview relates to Agosín's increasing emphasis on* lo judío, *that is, things Jewish, in her oeuvre. Conducted in Spanish, it took place in Amherst, Massachusetts, April 1995.*

IS: How did you come to terms with your Jewish identity?

MA: In Santiago, Chile, where I was raised, I went to Jewish school, the Instituto Hebreo. It is still one of the best in the country. I had a Jewish upbringing, although nonreligious. I perceived my Judaism as did my parents: as a cultural legacy. Since my father was first professor and then dean at a Chilean university, the environment at home was intellectually stimulating but also secular, nonobservant. My school's orientation was Bundist—that is, the majority of teachers who taught there, those from Israel, were socialists. With the passing of time I have struggled to unite my political views and my Jewish heritage. Mine is indeed a curious biography. My sister and I were born in Bethesda, Maryland. My parents were in the United States because my father was working for the National Institutes of Health. He had emigrated from Marseilles to Valparaiso when he was three months old, and I also returned to Chile when I was three months old and my sister was two and a half. This, I think, shows the extent to which ours is a family of exiles, wanderers in the never-ending Jewish diaspora. Then, when I was around fourteen or fifteen, we returned to the U.S., this time for political reasons: A dictatorship prevailed and persecution was frequent. My father was attacked on various fronts: the right-wing rulers disliked him for his left-wing political views, and since he had grants from the Rockefeller Foundation, the National Institutes of Health, and other organizations, the communist press accused him of having sold his soul to the devil—

that is, Yankee imperialism. I have a vivid memory of late one night when he received phone calls attacking him for being a dirty capitalist, or accusing him of being a Jewish socialist. I was mortified—for him and for the rest of the family.

IS: Around 1976 you started working for human rights and the Catholic Church . . .

MA: I did it while already in the United States. As I see it, it was at once a natural and a naive move. I make the connection between collective and personal suffering, on the one hand, and my Judaism on the other. And it is as a result of my involvement that my Jewish identity became strong. Now that I'm about to turn forty, I feel I'm part of a long chain of generations and that I have a responsibility to continue what others did before me and what my successors will do after I die. Nowadays I want to read everything about Judaism, to know it all. Why do I feel this way? Perhaps because I feel we are the last generation to hear firsthand personal accounts emerging from the Holocaust. And that, you see, is where politics and tradition come together. As Elie Wiesel puts it, the terrible suffering of those victims is for us to safeguard, for us to let the world know about. We are their witnesses, we are their voice. Add to it the fact that in my eyes, the experience of Holocaust survivors shares immensely with that of the Madres de la Plaza de Mayo and other victims of Latin America's repressive dictatorships. These mothers are old, and we have to carry on their voice, their message. For me, the principles of human rights can be found in the Talmud, which, as you know, claims that he who saves a single human life saves the world entire.

IS: To save: to save lives, to save a message, to save memory. To be a Jew is to be an activist—to react to suffering. You build a bridge between Judaism and politics.

MA: Indeed. We have been pointed at as a different, unique minority, and that makes us siblings of the Latin American *desaparecidos*. Fifteen percent of the desaparecidos during the *guerra sucia*, the Dirty War, were Jewish. The link is strong and clear.

I guess my attitude can be explained through my growing up in a household where social justice was an imperative. We heard about freedom and equality every day. Those were topics we often discussed at the dining room table. They were embedded in our education, in the way we perceived the universe. In my socialist family, we were encouraged not to have a hierarchical way of understanding those around us. We related to all people in the same way. My poetry from early on has made bridges between the Holocaust and repression in Chile. In my poem "Naked in the Barbed Wire Forests of Germany," for example, American and European women in concentration camps are equivalent. The Jewish community in Argentina, during World War II and in Chile under Pinochet, become one. I always wrote to denounce, to give voice to the oppressed, to pay respect to those who died, to rescue memory from oblivion.

All this is highlighted by a major event that took place in my life in 1976, while I was at Indiana University. At the time, the Chilean writer Antonio Skármeta, ten years my elder and part of the same literary generation as Ariel Dorfman, came to give a lecture. He had been living in exile for a few years, and, as part of his talk, he showed us an *arpillera,* a quilt made of scraps of cloth created by Chilean women under Augusto Pinochet's dictatorship in which they expressed their outrage against repression and crime. Through these quilts, the mothers, wives, and sisters of desaparecidos told their relatives' tragic story. They wanted the world to know. They wanted others to acknowledge their suffering. I was instantly overwhelmed by Skármeta's material.

Although I knew little at that time about semiotics, the arpillera was the type of folklore that spoke to me deeply. I became fascinated by how Chilean women could reconstruct their suffering through materials so close to their feminine world, and then inject a political, essentially male, dimension in their message. It is popular culture at its best. And what was their message? To me, they seemed to be saying that there's no great separation between art and the quotidian. Furthermore, often arpillera makers would make their quilts with pieces of clothing belonging to the dead—their own assassinated husbands and children. Soon I began meditating and writing about the phenomenon and have made contributions to their understanding and dissemination. First, I established contact with these women, which, needless to say, was extremely dangerous. Their children were guerrilla fighters and participated in freedom movements. But I didn't care: I went to Chile to look for their traces. I realized they were associated with the Catholic Church. I spent time at their workshops. I interviewed them time and time again. And I ended up writing a book, *Scraps of Life,* the only one available on the subject. The *New York Times* wrote a few articles on the arpilleras, a documentary was done in Canada, and people began sending money to Chile. My relationship with these women, who are between seventy and eighty years old today, has solidified since then: I have read to them my Anne Frank poems, which they have turned into songs. Even though they know almost nothing about Judaism, they sympathized with and understood me well, much like I sympathized with them. Of course now that democracy is back, the arpilleras are becoming a thing of the past. But I'm sure the art will flourish again the day darkness settles in again on the human heart.

IS: So what makes you Jewish?

MA: Having in my unconscious a 4,000-year-long history of persecution. That, precisely, makes me understand the world around me. No doubt I owe a lot to my parents because, thanks to the education I received, I'm able to have a tête-à-tête with an Algerian or a Palestinian without any condescending subterfuges. And so I wonder what I am: a Latin American writer in exile? A United States writer? A Jewish writer who is part of the never-ending diaspora? This is a question of one's own identity, of course. I know I'm certainly not an American writer. I'm not a U.S.-Hispanic writer either, like Julia Alvarez or Sandra Cisneros, even if I'm as American as they are. You see, I'm convinced that a writer *is* his or her own language, and I'm a Latin American writer because my mother tongue is Spanish. I feel close to Neruda, María Luisa Bombal, Nicanor Parra, and José Donoso. They are part of me . . . they *are* me. In Chile I'm perceived as a curiosity. While I've been physically absent from Chile, I'm still close. And I remain loyal to my Spanish language. I'm concerned that I have a presence there—that I'm known and recognized. I want to be there. When a review of one of my books appears in *El Mercurio,* it matters much more than one in the *New York Times.* And I'm opening a new window in Chilean letters, a country known for its pro-Germanic roots, its racism and anti-Semitism.

IS: Why, then, don't you return to Chile?

MA: I wouldn't have anything to do in Chile. No academic jobs. Besides, it's a complex country without memory, with lots of envy and resentment toward those who left. I wouldn't have a space. But hey, I also don't have a space in the United States—or should I say, I do and I don't.

IS: An imaginary diaspora . . .

MA: In some way this type of transient existence is marvelous: After all, Jews are from nowhere.

IS: The native language is generally addressed as "the mother tongue," whereas the acquired, second language is the father tongue—or better, the spousal tongue. You said your first loyalty was to Spanish. What then is the role of English in your life? Is it merely a utilitarian, functional language?

MA: I don't have an important relationship with the English language. Perhaps the reason is that I'm primarily a poet. Poets have a primitive way of approaching language. They perceive it as a magical, religious, instinctive vehicle of communication. I sometimes communicate with my husband and children in English. I do so in order for them to understand me. But I would never acknowledge it as my own tongue. Every single text that creates in me a fiesta of emotions is in Spanish.

Against Oblivion

Felipe Alfau

Felipe Alfau (Spain, 1902–1999) is the author of Old Tales from Spain *(1928),* Locos: A Comedy of Gestures *(1936),* Chromos *(1990), and* Sentimental Songs/La poesía cursi *(1992). Alfau was a famous recluse whose early work appeared in English when he was in his twenties and thirties. He then disappeared from the cultural radar until 1988, when* Locos *was reprinted by the small experimental publishing house Dalkey Archive Press, in Normal, Illinois. Conducted in Spanish, this interview is excerpted from ten hours of taped conversations that took place in a geriatric home in Queens, New York, in the early 1990s. Alfau never published anything more.*

IS: Why did you become a writer?

FA: I'm not a professional writer. Only by necessity have I ever received payment for my work. Dalkey Archive Press offered money for my two novels, but I refused to accept it. For my poems I received $500 because I needed to pay the monthly bill here, in the retirement home. The truth is, I was never interested in writing, nor did I ever dream of making a living at my craft. I hate full-time authors. I hate intellectuals that make a living from abstractions and evasions. The art of writing has turned into an excess. Today, literature is a waste. It should be abolished, at least in the form we know: as a moneymaking endeavor.

IS: How do you think writers should support themselves?

FA: I'm not sure, but certainly not by selling their books like jewelry.

IS: Yet I know you first submitted *Locos* to a New York publisher for financial reasons. You wrote it in English because you needed money.

FA: Who doesn't? And when I got a job, a stable job, I took the manuscript back. It was scheduled for publication under the title *Madrileños*. I changed my mind and asked the editor to return the text.

IS: Had it been accepted?

FA: Yes. It was already in galley form.

IS: And you took it back?

FA: I didn't need the money anymore. I had a wife and a daughter, and enough to support them.

IS: You come from a family of journalists, translators, and fiction writers. Your father was involved with several newspapers, at least on this side of the Atlantic. Your sister Monserrat, married to Felipe Teixidor, was close to the publishing house Editorial Porrúa, S.A., in Mexico City. She did translations.

FA: There was a possibility of her translating *Locos*.

IS: What happened?

FA: I don't think the publisher at Porrúa liked the book. I don't blame him . . .

IS: One of your other sisters, Jesusa Alfau de Solalinde, who married a professor and lived in Wisconsin, wrote a well-received novel, *Los débiles*, before she turned twenty.

FA: Jesusa and her husband, the philologist Antonio Solalinde, did like my first novel. I remember that a magazine in Wisconsin published an article about it, a scholarly one, back in the forties. But all that is now lost. Jesusa and the others were all very serious about their work . . . I wasn't. That's why they were far better writers than I am.

IS: I see a contradiction here. Were the members of your family "professional writers" in your eyes?

FA: No, they were journalists, translators, and people devoted to their art. They didn't write to make money. On the contrary, they wrote and if money came, it was welcome. The world has changed for the worse, there's no question about that.

IS: Even in the early thirties, your style, your views of literature weren't commercial. Sorry to put it this way, but how could you ever dream of getting some money, even a little, from the sale of a manuscript?

FA: I got $250 for *Locos*. But you are right. In fact, I don't see how anybody could like my books or could even understand them. They are unreadable.

IS: Are you being modest?

FA: I'm always surprised when I see positive reactions to my two novels. My editor is obstinate. He sends me only those reviews that celebrate my work. I have repeatedly asked him to send me the negative ones, but he silently refuses. Those are the ones that interest me, the negative reviews. As the author, I'm a supporter of my work, or at least I have to take responsibility for the product, don't you think? What I need to know is what I did wrong. And that can only come from negative comments.

IS: Do you have any friends in this retirement home?

FA: No, everybody here is a little crazy. Like me, they have lived too long. They say things that don't make sense and act suspiciously.

IS: What do you do all day?

FA: I wait. I read the paper or watch TV. I just wait.

IS: Does your family ever come to visit you?

FA: No, they all live far away. My daughter lives in California.

IS: So you are on your own all day?

FA: Yes. Once in a while I talk to someone about politics, but the result is always predictable. People are stupid.

IS: As you know, I have been interviewing friends you had a long time ago because I'm contemplating the idea of writing your biography.

FA: A waste of time. My life doesn't have anything out of the ordinary.

IS: I will find that out for myself. Besides, you gave me your permission and Dalkey Archive Press wants to publish the biography as soon as possible.

FA: They will lose money. They have already lost a lot with my books.

IS: You're wrong. One of the editors told me that when *Locos* was published, the company was in serious financial trouble. *Locos* helped them recover.

FA: Impossible.

IS: You were born in Barcelona 1902.

FA: Ninety years ago . . . too long ago. I'm more than ready to leave this boring, repetitive universe. I swear I can't wait to depart.

IS: But you wouldn't commit suicide, would you?

FA: No, my Catholic education prohibits taking the laws of nature into your own hands.

IS: Do you believe in God? Because if you don't—and I suspect you're a skeptic—why then rely on Catholic values? Why not commit suicide?

FA: Would you? You are Jewish . . . You share with me similar values. Will you commit suicide if you reach my age and turn out to be as bored as I am?

IS: I would, notwithstanding the offense I would inflict on my beloved ones. If and when the day comes, I only hope to be brave enough. To me it's all a matter of courage.

FA: As for me, I'm a skeptic, as you said. I cannot but have doubts regarding the afterlife. What if there's a God? What if all our uncertainties are a children's game? What if we are punished for our sins?

IS: Well, if we are, I won't be aware of it since I'll be already dead.

FA: I wish I was sure it was all a joke.

IS: You have lived more than seventy years of your life in the United States. Do you still feel Iberian, a citizen from Spain? Or are you now an American like everybody else around here?

FA: Neither one nor the other. I guess I'm a frontier man that belongs to a world that is no more. I'm a traditionalist stubbornly loyal to what some would think are outmoded principles.

IS: Like monarchy?

FA: Certainly. Democracy is a disgrace. Machiavelli was absolutely right: The difference between tyranny and democracy is that in tyranny you need to serve only one master, whereas in a pluralistic society you have to obey the many. I always thought Generalissimo Francisco Franco was a trustworthy ruler of Spain, and thus supported him. Since his death, the Iberian Peninsula is in complete chaos. In fact, at the time of the Spanish civil war, I championed Franco's cause in this country as much as I could.

IS: You wrote the poems included in *Sentimental Songs* in Spanish, but everything else you wrote in English. Did you ever write any prose in Spanish?

FA: Never. In fact, I'm wrong. When I was a young man, between eighteen and twenty-five, I wrote music criticism for *La Prensa*, a newspaper in Spanish in New York City. Thank God, all that rubbish is now forgotten. The poems I wrote in my mother tongue because poetry is too close to the heart, whereas fiction is a mental activity, an invention, something foreign, distant.

IS: The fact that you switched from Spanish to English is puzzling to me. I can think of only a handful of other writers who have mastered a second language and used it to write their oeuvre: Joseph Conrad, Vladimir Nabokov, Joseph Brodsky, and Jerzy Kosinski. Was it hard to switch from one language to another?

FA: It took a while. I never studied English in school. My parents, after a life of wandering in the Philippines, the Caribbean, and several cities on the Iberian Peninsula, immigrated to the United States. I arrived when I was fourteen, in 1916. A child picks up a new language rather easily. An adolescent has a harder time, and an adult may never accomplish the task of mastering a second language. I took some courses in philosophy at Columbia University, but by and large, I was a self-educated man. I always wanted to be an orchestra conductor. That interest led me to the study of music. I was also in love with mathematics and with physics. As you can see, my novels are evidence of those life-long passions.

IS: Did the fact that you spoke and wrote in a language other than your mother tongue ever give you a feeling of being in exile? Of living in a universe that wasn't yours.

FA: No. By mere chance we are born in a specific geography and time. I always wished to travel through time, to champion a life beyond my individual boundaries. Unfortunately, I never succeeded.

IS: You have a daughter from your first marriage, Chiquita.

FA: I left her when she was little. We hardly lived together. She gave birth to twins.

IS: Does she speak Spanish? Do her kids speak it?

FA: No. A few words perhaps.

IS: You didn't care to perpetuate your linguistic lineage within your family?

FA: No, I didn't. And the explanation is simple: Man is alone on this planet. Our projects, our goals regarding the children we bear, are often transformed by unforeseen circumstances, by forces beyond our control. The only thing we are accountable for is our own self.

IS: Gustavo Pérez-Firmat, a Cuban poet who teaches at Duke University, once wrote a poem. I remember its opening stanza: "The fact that I write in English, and not in Spanish, already falsifies what I wanted to say."

FA: Untrue . . .

IS: In a conversation with Joseph Brodsky, he told me Pérez-Firmat is mistaken. Language is only a vehicle through which we verbalize thoughts. Thus, words don't falsify, only the speaker does.

FA: When I read the lousy Spanish translation, made in Barcelona, of *Chromos*, I thought my message had been deformed, my intentions inverted. The translator often misunderstands a sentence. Unfortunately, the mistakes are not rare. The art of translation is difficult, to say the least. One cannot substitute one word in a language with its equivalent in another. The task is to make two cultures find a common path, a bridge. Translators must be anthropologists if they want to succeed in their profession.

IS: The first paragraph of *Chromos* is symptomatic of the dilemmas a non-native English speaker must deal with when living in the United States. Here it is: "The moment one learns English, complications set in. Try as one may, one cannot elude this conclusion, one must invariably come back to it. This applies to all persons, including those born to the language and, at times, even more so to Latins, including Spaniards. It manifests itself in an awareness of implications and intricacies to which one had never given a thought; it afflicts one with that officiousness of philosophy which, having no business of its own, gets in everybody's way and, in the case of Latins, they lose that racial characteristic of taking things for granted and leaving them to their own devices without inquiring into causes, motives or ends, to meddle indiscreetly into reasons which are none of one's affair and to become not only self-conscious, but conscious of other things which never gave a damn for one's existence."

FA: My English is Iberian—an acquisition. It's half English and half my own creation, the result of an immigrant experience.

IS: One could conclude that in a country like the United States, made of immigrants, the English language is a hybrid.

FA: It is. Every generation, every ethnic group, creates its own deformations.

IS: Like your characters, those dreamers in *Chromos* that live in Manhattan without anybody noticing them, speaking a language very much their own.

FA: Yes, like them.

IS: Farrar and Reinhart published *Locos* in 1936.

FA: It was only sold to subscribers, as part of one of those failed projects attempting to sell books. Almost nobody read it then.

IS: Are you surprised by the recent discovery of your work? Are you amazed by the attention you are receiving?

FA: All this has come too late. Truly, I don't care anymore.

IS: An anticlimax, perhaps?

FA: No . . .

IS: Are you bitter? Did the world betray you? In other words, is all this attention well deserved but badly timed?

FA: That is for others to judge.

IS: What is?

FA: If my work has some value.

IS: Do you think it does? Does it deserve to be read in the future?

FA: I have forgotten what I wrote more than fifty years ago. Besides, my novels were written in an unprofessional way, especially *Chromos*.

IS: What do you mean?

FA: I was a translator for Morgan Bank in Manhattan for many, many years. In the office, between one document and another, I would write a paragraph or two. I then pasted together the whole book, as in a collage.

IS: Did you ever attempt to translate your own work?

FA: Never. Why would I?

IS: Were you ever a good reader?

FA: No. I only read about mathematics, physics, and music. I told you I'm a failed musician. Today, I do read the *New York Times* every day, from the first to the last page. In fact, that is the one I read first. I like to find out at what age people died and the cause. If they are younger (and they are, more often than not), I try to remember what I was doing at the age when death took these people's breath away.

IS: Do you do the crossword puzzle?

FA: No. Occasionally.

IS: In *Sentimental Songs* there's one poem entitled "Afro-Ideal Evocation," which some critics find racist, antiblack.

FA: As a child, when I first came to this country, I thought blacks were dirty people that didn't wash themselves enough. I have learned to live in this society, but I do believe the United States has degenerated in the last three decades because of the influx of citizens from the Caribbean and Hispanic America.

IS: Do you think whites are superior?

FA: I trust Western civilizations to be built upon the wisdom of the Greek and Roman empires. Purity is fundamental if continuity is to be achieved. Take New York City as an example. In the fifties this was a safe place to live, but now so many immigrants have invaded its streets and neighborhoods, making it a violent jungle.

IS: But you were also an immigrant . . .

FA: Yes. Others must have felt suspicious of me, even if I'm European.

IS: Aren't you old-fashioned?

FA: Obviously. My ideas are wrong in today's cultural climate, but they are mine.

IS: A couple of friends of yours, among them Chandler Brossard, say you are also an anti-Semite.

FA: I'm not. In Spain, Jews have been seen as Christ-killers by the Church. Yet to me, they are wise and educated. I had many Jewish friends: Daniel and Toby Talbot, for instance . . . You know Chandler Brossard was always an eccentric. He says outrageous things.

IS: So you are not an anti-Semite?

FA: I was taught to keep a distance from Jews, but I didn't. Brossard may as well tell you I'm anticommunist.

IS: Are you?

FA: It's irrelevant, especially in today's world.

IS: Are you capable of hatred?

FA: What do you mean?

IS: Could you hate somebody enough to drive that person to death?

FA: Of course not. I'm not a man of action. I'm a voyeur. I observe and meditate.

IS: Tell me, are you acquainted with Jorge Luis Borges, Pirandello, or Nabokov? Some, including me, have compared you to them.

FA: I have heard the names, but I don't know what those men did.

IS: Never read a story or a play by them?

FA: I didn't know they wrote stories and plays.

IS: At times, when I talk to you, I get the impression you are a Robinson Crusoe of sorts, or a Kaspar Hauser—a man isolated from society, yet knowledgeable of the essence of things. Why do you think your novels took so long to get attention and incite interest?

FA: Perhaps because they didn't belong to the cultural climate of the past, but they fit into the present.

IS: Why?

FA: I don't know. That's a question for critics to answer.

IS: Don't you have some sort of explanation?

FA: No.

IS: Do you see yourself as a time traveler, a man with a vision?

FA: I see myself as an old man ready for death, ready for rest. I already told you that, didn't I? I repeat myself: I have been repeating myself for a long time.

IS: But you did it anonymously . . . until somebody decided to listen.

FA: It was better when nobody cared. Some people think I'm a celebrity, but I don't even understand what that means. Better to be all alone, alone and silent.

Beginnings

Isabel Allende

Isabel Allende (Peru, b. 1942) is the Chilean author of The House of the Spirits *(1985),* The Stories of Eva Luna *(1991),* Aphrodite *(1998), and* Daughter of Fortune *(1999). This interview took place in Manhattan in April 1988 after Allende lectured at Barnard College. Her daughter Paula was already ill. Her terrible agony was chronicled in a successful memoir released in 1995.*

IS: When did you get your start in journalism?

IA: At seventeen I left school. I started to work as a secretary at the United Nations in the Department of Information, as an assistant to good journalists, to important people. Sometimes I had to do their work because they weren't there or were sick. I wrote press releases and that type of thing.

IS: Political themes?

IA: They were about the worldwide campaign against hunger, FAOS, programs, agriculture, etc.

IS: How long were they?

IA: Pretty short. The press wasn't interested in what we wrote, so the shorter, the better. We prepared the notes and delivered them to the journalists with the hope that they would be published. I was part of public relations at the United Nations.

IS: Do you have copies?

IA: I don't. I'm forty-five years old now. Those pieces were written a long time ago. In the FAO campaign against world hunger, we were offered a TV program. Channel 13 of the Catholic University, the country's first channel, offered us a quarter of an hour a week to explain what the campaign was about. The day of the first broadcast my boss got sick. He called on the telephone to ask me to apologize on his behalf. I went and the director said to me, "I'm sorry but someone must go on the air, say something, fill fifteen minutes of TV time." I was frightened and inexperienced and must have appeared audacious. But I jumped right in and talked about whatever crossed my mind.

IS: Did you have something prepared?

IA: Very little. I had gone to give my boss's apology at 11 A.M. The program aired at 3 P.M. I gathered pictures, formulated a script quickly, edited video, found music . . . I did everything in three hours. It must not have turned out so badly, considering the quality of Chilean TV at the time. As a reward, they offered me a weekly show. I accepted.

IS: Did you write *and* appear on TV?

IA: I did everything: I wrote, I was in front of the TV cameras, I made the films, I edited manuscripts . . . Except for making publicity ads, I did everything.

IS: Did you have any form of training?

IA: None, but no one in Chile had it. Whatever junk I produced was more or less acceptable because no one knew anything. We were experimenting . . . As a discipline journalism was being born in Santiago. People educated themselves as a journalist through years of experience.

IS: How long were you on the show?

IA: Quite a while. It was so fascinating to me that I got a scholarship in Belgium for a year and left with my husband and daughter. By that time I had already married. Let's recap. It was at eighteen or nineteen years of age when I worked for the United Nations Department of Information. Soon after I started working on TV. I got married at nineteen, my daughter was born, and we left for Belgium 1962 or 1963. My husband, who also had a scholarship, studied engineering and I studied TV and radio. I studied with a group of thirty people from Africa, all men of course. Those were my sole formal studies.

IS: And how long were you in Belgium?

IA: Eight or nine months: a total of two semesters. It allowed me to see the world and polish my French. It wasn't the first time I had left Chile, as my parents were diplomats, but it was a unique experience because it was the first time I had studied something formally. Had I had some college education, the course would have been more helpful. But because I knew nothing about technology, I didn't make use of it. We later moved to Switzerland, where my parents were ambassadors, and we spent two months with them while I was pregnant with my second child. We then returned to Santiago. By that time I was sick, as a result of which I didn't begin work immediately. I stayed at home doing translations. Around that time, someone that was forming a vanguard feminist magazine read a letter of mine that I had written to my mother.

She was a friend of mine. She wanted me to collaborate with her. All my professional training I gained through experience on that magazine. It was a private enterprise that functioned as a business. We discussed fashion; women bought it because it had many interesting essays. It still exists, but its direction has changed from vanguard—quite important in Chile—to a publication comparable to *Cosmopolitan.*

IS: What types of articles did you write?

IA: I began writing humorous articles, later interviews and later still outrageous reports, anything spectacular. For example, interviewing prostitutes, dressing up as a chorister to gain access to the stage of a frivolous cabaret and see a striptease, drugs——I got involved in every aspect of society.

IS: Have you reread those articles?

IA: They seem sanctimonious. If I had to rewrite them today, I would do it with another perspective, using different language.

IS: Were they printed with your name?

IA: Almost all of them, save the love letters. I had for years . . .

IS: "Doctora Corazón."

IA: Indeed, Ilan. I had a false name: Francisca Román. I did it so both columns would be taken seriously.

IS: Did you get paid?

IA: A fixed salary. It was good enough to help my husband support our family. At the time I worked at another TV show, where I got paid more or less the same. With both salaries I could have supported my two children, but badly. That's the rule: In Chile journalists were paid badly.

IS: What did you do on TV?

IA: Comedies once a week. I had a fifteen to twenty minute spot.

IS: On a private or on a state channel?

IA: First on the university's and then on the government's. But if truth be told, I went through all the channels. They hired me because I was one of the few people who did comedy. Plus I was a woman . . .

IS: What type of comedy?

IA: Feminist humor. For instance, it wanted to demonstrate that men are easy targets—they are easily deceived. We placed a hidden camera in a store downtown, and a friend of mine, an actress, would walk around in blue jeans, her hair down, without makeup. Men didn't look at her.

We dressed her up to be stereotypically sexy: fishnets, fake eyelashes, and a purse. She was the same woman, only dressed differently. She walked around the same place, and we would film the men's faces as they turned around to look at her. We filmed what they said with our candid camera.

IS: Did you have any problems because of the type of material you used?

IA: No, because the press had total and absolute freedom in Chile. People liked it; everybody—or almost everybody—knew me. I had the sense of belonging to a community, of walking through my country as if it were my house. I was part of the collective. I never felt alone. Plus, I was an eternal teenager. I didn't mature until the military takeover. I lived happily, like an irresponsible child.

IS: Did you write any stories during that period?

IA: Concurrent with all the other jobs I had, I began to produce a children's magazine. We had a section for stories, and once I published one of my own, without my name. They were awful stories, which didn't stand the test of time. And I also wrote plays.

IS: What was bad about the stories?

IA: They were careless. The language was not serious. I didn't know how to write then . . . Yes, I was ignorant.

IS: When did you learn to write with care?

IA: With *The House of the Spirits.*

IS: Did it bother you at the time that you wrote carelessly?

IA: No, I didn't know any better.

IS: But by the time you wrote *The House of the Spirits* you had taken notice . . .

IA: Years of silence had gone by. I had suffered a great deal; I had grown over a period of ten years. I was not the same person. Before, what had interested me was impact, to scandalize, to astonish, to make people laugh. I was interested in the effect, not durability, quality. I was interested in reaching many people and in shaking them.

IS: Why write without your name?

IA: I was embarrassed. I felt incapable of writing anything of importance. I had low self-esteem: much laughter and humor so long as I didn't take myself seriously. When I tried to do so, I flinched. This problem with identity is characteristic of my generation: there were two possible attitudes—being aggressive, assertive, combative, or being timid. I was on the borderline. At some level I was audacious and daring, disrespectful and irreverent, but with others I felt embarrassed. One of the facets that made me feel the most embarrassed was literature.

IS: What did you read?

IA: I read everything. I have always been an anarchic reader. I would read long novels, especially feminist ones, which I loved then and still love today. But my curiosity was far-ranging. I read mostly Latin American literature. Each and every book by important Latin American authors that was released paraded in front of my eyes. I also read French authors, such as Marguerite Yourcenar and Marguerite Duras, and several female authors from the United States . . .

IS: Did you read plays?

IA: No, I have never been interested in the theater. But I had the opportunity to write three plays for Tomás Vidiella's company, who staged my plays very professionally. The junk that I wrote, he staged and enriched. The first one, *The Ambassador,* written in 1970, was the story of a guerrilla group that kidnaps an ambassador and who has to interact with him for a year in a basement. In the interim, they get to know each other and love each other. It had a dramatic ending. It was not too successful, despite its great direction. The second play, *La balada de medio pelo,* in 1972, was successful. It was medley of music and sketches, portraying the day-to-day life of the middle class. *The Seven Mirrors* in 1973, the third play, was a musical, which I wrote before the takeover. It was the most successful of the three, touring the country for over a year.

IS: Did you make any money from them?

IA: Quite little. I couldn't have lived off of it . . .

IS: What attracted you to the theater?

IA: I loved to dress up. I loved the dramatic aspects of life; I love the theater: rehearsals, costumes, props, curtains . . .

IS: Have you written any more plays in the last few years?

IA: Not recently, I haven't.

IS: Did you ever act?

IA: Only among friends. A little while ago, at a conference in Houston, a group of Chilean actors let me act in a musical: I played the role of a fruit vendor in the first act and that of a prostitute in the second . . . I have always had stage fright. On TV, there isn't an audience, only the camera. While I worked for television, I never thought of the many people who watched me. But on the stage, you have your audience before you.

IS: What about movies . . . ?

IA: Yes, I did a couple of stints for movies. There was a company that formed in Chile to make shorts, previews that played before the feature presentations at the theaters. We made one or two editorials, with vivid journalistic sections. I loved the work and the experimentation of the genre. The first thing I did was make a mistake: a new contraceptive called Pelet had just been brought to Chile, which was injected underneath the skin in the arm and secreted hormones for a year. The woman need not worry about getting pregnant for quite a while. Just as soon as Pelet was being distributed in hospitals and maternity clinics, I went to film a documentary. It was a simple, painless procedure, but I filmed it close up in Technicolor, and when people saw it on the screen it looked like a bullet the size of a canon. No one got Pelet in Chile; it was a total failure. Not only was my objective not accomplished, but it had a completely opposite impact from what I had intended.

IS: How many movies or documentaries did you make?

IA: Three or four . . . They were called *Ellas,* and they ended with the military takeover.

IS: During your three years in TV, did appearing before the camera cause any problems within your family?

IA: I have always been weird. It wasn't only the fact that I appeared on TV, but I also had a car painted with flowers and naked angels; I dressed in long dresses and hats, and walked around with a dog. I was edgy, offbeat, antiestablishment. For my kids, I was a bit of an embarrassment, a source of shame and of fascination. They didn't want me to go look for them at school because all their classmates would come out to look at my car and to look at their strange mother. My husband, in that sense, was marvelous; he never had any reserve toward me in public. My parents didn't live in Chile. Had they lived in Chile, would they have had a problem as diplomats? My mother's family was very conservative. Perhaps, though, it's obvious that a lot of people criticized me severely. But I didn't care. My mother didn't agree with me then, and she does not agree with me now, on what I have done and still do, but she loves me unconditionally; no one should speak ill of her daughter because she defends me like a samurai. My stepfather also supports me, although with hesitation, advising me to be careful.

IS: Let's talk about the military takeover in Santiago and your departure in 1975. Upon leaving your country, did you work in the theater, TV, or journalism?

IA: I couldn't find work. It is difficult for a foreigner to break through in Venezuelan TV, so much so that all those circles are closed. I also couldn't find work as a correspondent. I made a few educational shows for children, for which they paid me handsomely. None of them aired. I also wrote plays, two of them, although nothing worked out.

IS: Do you own copies of your plays, those you wrote before and after your exile?

IA: I have them filed.

IS: What did you do then?

IA: All kinds of work. All I could do as a journalist was publish some humorous articles in the daily *El Nacional* in Caracas, once a week. They paid me little. They were printed in the Sunday supplement and then on any given day in the C section, in a column called *Los impertinentes* in Chile. Later, that name was lost because three people collaborated on the same column.

IS: This time you had problems because you wrote on inappropriate subjects or themes.

IA: Once, I wrote about the military in Venezuela and they almost threw me out of the country, but the director of the newspaper intervened himself.

IS: What happened to your creativity then?

IA: I was so badly off I don't remember. Those were years of poverty. My husband worked outside of Caracas, far away. Because we lived in the capital, I rarely saw him, once a month or every two months. We made a superhuman effort to provide for our family. We desperately missed the life we had before. Our economic situation changed when my husband, from whom I'm now divorced, had better luck at work. We returned to Caracas. I started to work at school in double shifts, since we needed money: morning and evening.

IS: As a teacher?

IA: No, as an administrator. Although our finances improved, my personal condition worsened noticeably. I wanted to dress like a person, but I couldn't wear a hat or walk with a dog. I couldn't have a painted car. All that had ended. I had to begin acting like a respectable woman. I was in charge of the money at the Colegio Marroco: I charged tuition, paid the teachers. Imagine how difficult it must have been for me, since I don't know how to add or subtract. I got the job through Maria Elena Marroco . . . a friend. She had faith in me; she wanted us to be partners. She founded the school and I helped her. The school was called Instituto de Orientación en Arte y Ciencia, but it was a horrible name. I thought the name should consist of a single word. I thought it best that the school be named after its founder, Marroco, because that way she would be a presence in education in the country. I insisted that she call it Colegio Marroco. The school still exists today; it is well respected and well known.

IS: Did the school have anything to do with Chilean funds, students, or activities?

IA: Not at all.

IS: How long did you work there?

IA: Four and a half years . . . From 1979 to 1982, when *The House of the Spirits* was published, and I was already writing *Of Love and of Shadow*.

IS: Did you do any work with children or youth that was creative? Theater, writing . . .

IA: I didn't write anything, except for the humorous articles for *El Nacional*. I locked myself in from time to time when I had anxiety attacks, and I would write things.

IS: What types of things?

IA: Diaries, stories, ideas for stories, ideas for soap operas.

IS: Did you send them anywhere?

IA: Nowhere. I wrote them with the idea that they were erasing something. I have the impression, now looking back, that I was preparing myself for something greater: *The House of the Spirits* was gestating within me like a child, and I didn't know I had it in me. The moment I sat down to write the novel, it came out as if someone were dictating it to me.

IS: What did you read between 1979 and 1982?

IA: More or less the same. There was little time to read because I worked twelve hours, from 7 A.M. to 7 P.M., without a lunch break. I worked that way at the school because I was part of elite society together with María Elena Marroco. When I left, I had a few shares; I sold them, and I was able to live for a year, until profits from book sales started coming in.

IS: When did you stop writing the column in *El Nacional*—when *The House of the Spirits* was released?

IA: It was published until 1985. I stopped writing it because it required time and I didn't have it. Besides, humor depends on situations with which the readers can identify, when they believe that what they read can happen to them. As elaborate or weird as it may be, what makes people laugh is always a defense mechanism against identifying oneself. By then, I didn't frequent the streets too much, I didn't work in the school, I didn't have the contact I had before with children or with the people from whom I got my ideas. The articles became more and more intellectual. Each time they had a more rhetorical humor, less colloquial . . . they were less humorous.

IS: Did you write *The House of the Spirits* in 1982?

IA: I would wake up at 6 A.M. I would work all day long, but the routine didn't require much concentration. My head took flight in other spheres. When I got home, I showered and ate with the kids. Then I would lock myself in and write. Let's say I began at 9:00 and I worked until I was too tired, say 11 P.M. or 12 P.M.; about three or four hours. They were very productive hours. I wrote about six or seven pages a day. Although I was physically exhausted, I was excited at the prospect of creating.

IS: In terms of mechanics, what structure did you follow when writing the novel?

IA: I didn't limit myself to structure at first. I didn't have a scheme I mind. Halfway through, I realized that there were some characters that didn't age, whom time had not followed, that upon reappearing were the same age they were at the beginning. I had used a historical fact as a reference point, but I didn't calculate the sequence well. So I opened up a file for each principal character and wrote up each of their lives independently. Later, I interwove them, like someone who embroiders. In Caracas, I still have the names of the characters in a synopsis, with dates. There are no dates in *The House of the Spirits,* but as an author, I knew in which year each event occurred and how old the characters would be.

IS: Did you write the novel by hand, on a typewriter, or on a word processor?

IA: On a typewriter. *Of Love and of Shadow* I wrote on an electronic typewriter, with an incorporated corrector, and *Eva Luna* with a word processor. I wrote more versions of *Of Love and of Shadow* than of any other novel because it is a testimonial novel and the border between fiction and reality was one I often forgot.

IS: How did you correct *The House of the Spirits*?

IA: I wrote and corrected it until I felt each page turned out well. I rewrote the book many times. My typewriter didn't have correcting tape: I had to correct it with Typex; therefore there were some pages that were corrected so much that they looked like cardboard. Dumb things happened to me, which today, with a word processor, seem ridiculous. I wanted to change the name of the conte de Satini: at first it was conte de Bilber. Upon reading the manuscript, my mother told me my father had a second last name, the name Bilber, and that I should not use that name because the character was perverse. On a conscious level, I was not aware that that was my father; I must have heard it when I was little. Thus, I had to find a name with the same number of letters, so I could type it in within the space of "Bilber." I erased each page—how absurd! Or, for example, I made a lot of spelling errors. I've always been a bad speller, now less so than before, because I've been schooled. I made horrific errors: throughout the whole book I wrote "Esteban Trueba" with an accent. "Esteban" doesn't have an accent, and I had to erase them with Typex, the whole manuscript.

IS: How many versions did you write?

IA: About four . . . There were chapters that I rewrote many times. There were parts that caused me a lot of problems, like the monologue in which Esteban Trueba asks the prostitute to save his niece. It was impossible to put myself in the place of a man who was so stubborn, so proud and powerful. I couldn't resolve it: I tried to tell it from the prostitute's point of view or with an omniscient narrator.

IS: Do you have copies of every version?

IA: I tore up many . . . I was tired of so much paper. Sometimes, I confused versions. I didn't know what I had written first and last. I destroyed what I considered superfluous. Later, I realized that I had destroyed things that could have helped me or that were written better in previous versions.

IS: Did anyone read them?

IA: The only person that read my book before publication was my mother. She's the only one who reads my manuscripts.

IS: Does her opinion matter a lot to you?

IA: I only trust her to critique a book. I changed many things because of her.

IS: Did you seek her advice while you were writing?

IA: With no one. I gave her what I considered finished, but after her revision I rewrote the entire book. The only ones I asked were the children, and only about my mood. I told them I was happy because I had written something well. Or that I was upset and frustrated because my material was good for nothing. They knew I was writing something that was important to me, but they didn't know what.

IS: How long did it take you to write *The House of the Spirits*?

IA: A year, from January 8, 1981, until January 8, 1982.

IS: Is there some sort of mystical meaning to January 8—someone's birthday?

IA: No. That's the date on which I began, and it went so well, that that was the date I set as the magic date. Since then, I always start a book on January 8.

IS: What happens if you finish it before?

IA: I wait . . . Sometimes I cheat, to be honest.

IS: Were you pressured to finish it?

IA: I promised myself I would finish it in a year. While I was writing, I was so fascinated; I understood I could continue eternally. So I set a final date at random. I had to find some sort of discipline to do so. I finished it on January 8 and gave it to my mother.

IS: When was the final version ready?

IA: Around March 1982, and it was published in October. I sent it to Latin American publishers; nobody wanted it. I sent it to Carmen Balcells; she took a month to write me back telling me she wanted to be my agent and that she wanted to promote my book. Carmen was honest with me. She told me: "Isabel, you have written a magnificent book, but this does not mean you are a writer. Only time will tell who you are. Perhaps you have missed the target and you have a while to go."

Salsa and Soul

Rubén Blades

Rubén Blades (Panama City, b. 1948) is the salsa artist responsible for "Pedro Navaja," among other classics. His albums include Buscando América *and* Caminando. *His film credits include* The Milagro Beanfield War *(1988) and* The Cradle Will Rock *(1999), in which he played Diego Rivera. This interview took place in Boston, September 2002, and relates to the release of Blades's album* Mundo.

IS: *Mundo,* your last album, seems to me more reflective, more mature than any other you've done in your prolific musical career. It's an album about world: world music as a system of interconnected influences, from Ireland to Brazil, from Islamic rhythms to flamenco and salsa.

RB: It's the result of an accumulation of experiences. I was born and grew up in Panama. We have coasts on both sides; we have access to the Pacific Ocean, to the Atlantic Ocean. Panama was always a place where all kinds of sounds and people kept coming and going. I grew up listening to all kinds of music. Recently all the discoveries related to genetics brought me back to the realization that we all come from the same source. Our shared background is the same.

IS: I'm especially struck by the Muslim influence in the record. Islam played a huge role in the shaping of Hispanic civilization.

RB: Many times in New York, I'll go to a store to buy cigarettes or water or milk, and I will see the clerk and I will talk to him in Spanish and he'll look at me and not understand me and say "Um, I don't understand Spanish." I say: "Well, where are you from?" "Egypt, Lebanon . . ." It isn't only that we look the same, a lot of the people who originally came to America from Spain had been under Moor domination for six hundred years. Culturally speaking the background these people had when they came here was a background that was as much Arabic as it was Spanish. The flamenco is a Moorish chant . . . In one way or another, we have been in contact with these sounds. We just haven't pinpointed where they came from.

IS: *Mundo* displays the two sides of Rubén Blades that enchant me: Blades the storyteller and Blades the political activist, always conscious of his view of the world and how things are in constant change. Let me start first with the storytelling aspect. How did this act of telling stories come to you, and why did you look to disseminate it through music?

RB: It came about because of the culture in Panama itself. It's a young country, so there's a lot of storytelling. We are developing, and oral traditions are still alive. Particularly in my case I have my grandmother, who spent a lot of time with me.

IS: Your grandmother on your father's side.

RB: Yes: an exceptional woman, educated with a fiercely independent free spirit. At the beginning, she was the one who first started to read to me. We went from *The Three Bears* to *The Three Musketeers* to *The Iliad*. The idea of stories, the pleasure it provided me to hear these stories and later to read them myself, just gave me this whole new horizon. Not only did I feel good about how I felt, I also wanted to continue doing this for other people as well. It became my medium.

IS: Since the medium is music, it might reach an almost illiterate population—or at least, a public not accustomed to reading. One song on *Mundo*, called "Sebastián," about a neighborhood lunatic, captured my imagination.

RB: I've known many "Sebastiáns." "En cada barrio, hay por lo menos un loco . . ."—in each neighborhood there's at least one crazy person. And that's true for family, too. You always have someone in the family that's a little off. The song was inspired by a friend of mine, Horacio Valdés, who plays in a Panamanian acoustic rock group called Sans Miserables. When I heard the story as told by Horacio, I immediately said: "Horacio, I would like to rewrite this." Horacio had composed a piece, but I thought it needed more exploration: the girlfriend he invented waiting for him to return after he goes to fetch the star that she asked him for and drowns, the spaceship that he was building to go with her to build stars, to get stars . . . all of that stuff deserved to be explored.

In *Mundo* there are three love stories: "Sebastián" was one of them, where I address the topic of alienation; then there's the man in "Ella," who is loved by a woman and cannot understand why she loves him in a different way; and the third is about a captain and a mermaid, doomed to love each other without ever finding a place to live together.

IS: Arguably the most famous song you've written is "Pedro Navaja." How did the song materialize? By the way, *blades* is the plural of the Spanish word *navaja*.

RB: Pedro hasn't knifed me yet, thank God . . . He came as a direct result of my curiosity with Bobby Darin's "Mack the Knife." Originally, when I was in Panama, I loved rock 'n' roll. Then I started singing doo-wop in English. Everybody had doo-wop roots. Frankie Lymon and the Teenagers were popular in Panama. And it was something that you could do. All you needed to get is the right echo and the right building and you sounded like you were on the radio or you had your own record. And it was easy. We didn't need instruments. We just vocalized . . . So, in the midst of this rock 'n' roll craze, which I lived from its inception, I remember listening to Elvis Presley's "Heartbreak Hotel." I heard it in Panama two months after it had been released in the United States. The North Americans were there in the Canal Zone, so there was access to all that was happening, musically speaking. But we loved doo-wop. And then we heard Bobby Darin and Bill Haley and the Comets and all those groups, and I loved "Mack the Knife." It stayed with me: the melody was haunting. When I started to grow up, I started to incorporate into my feeling a lot of things that I observed. There was a gang called The Black Sneakers, that is, Las Zapatillas Negras. There was another gang called The Gold Tooth, that is, Los Dientes de Oro. You pick out the sneakers, the tooth . . . I got to New York in 1969 for the first time and returned in 1974 after I graduated from law school in Panama. It was then that I saw the pimps in the Forty-second Street area: they wore the coats, the big hats with the wide rim . . . These items started coalescing and then, all of a sudden, boom, "Pedro Navaja" came.

IS: Have you ever done the song in English or in any—it's in Spanish, it's so stuck in Spanish. Could it be in anything other than Spanish?

RB: Tony Touch, a New York rapper.

IS: A rap version . . . ?

RB: It can be done. If you can translate a book into a different language from its original, you can do it with music. Sometimes though, it's funny because I find if you translate Kafka into English, it doesn't have the same intensity as Kafka into Spanish.

IS: Which probably would lose something.

RB: Absolutely.

IS: On the other hand, it would reach a different audience.

RB: Yes. What I like to do is put translations in the albums when it's so cheap.

IS: We were talking about storytelling in your music, and I wanted to talk also about politics. You have been an intensely political figure, both as a musician and as an activist in a variety of realms and fields. You ran for office in Panama in 1994, and you came in third out of seven.

RB: Seven candidates, twenty-seven parties.

IS: What did you learn from that, and why would you do it?

RB: For me the political act has always . . . I've always interpreted it as a self-defensive act. I feel attacked by corruption.

IS: Attacked—you mean accosted?

RB: I feel personally attacked by these people, these candidates that are supposedly in charge of the administration of our future, our hopes, you know. And all of a sudden they are not only mediocre by a tremendous percentage, but also they look to serve themselves, not the country. And they get into that position because we allow them to get there. And the media in general tends to support certain positions, and so, I found that as a singer I had the liberty to write a song and interpret it, not just in my view. I have to also make it clear that I never wrote politically. I wrote from a humane point of view, a social point of view, not ideologically; that's why the songs have sustained themselves through the years. It was an act of self-defense. And when I ran for office . . .

IS: For the office of president.

RB: For president in Panama. I told people in Panama and in Latin America that we aren't condemned to this situation of two political parties—we can create a third party.

IS: Where does corruption come from? Can it be cleaned by a single politician or a celebrity that comes into politics?

RB: One can't eliminate corruption. The Church has been telling us the value of virtue for over two thousand years, and there could be an argument over how good or bad it's been. You can limit the opportunity for corruption and with that drastically better the general conditions of a society. I don't know how feasible this would be in countries with a tremendous amount of population.

IS: Such as Mexico or Brazil.

RB: Mexico, I don't know. . . And maybe not in Brazil, either.

IS: But is it possible in Panama?

RB: In places like Panama . . .

IS: Which has about 3 million people.

RB: Less than 3 million. I'm totally convinced it can be done. I'm totally convinced it can be done.

IS: And how could it be done? Why would people trust you? A person who has spent more than thirty years outside to clean a mess that is five hundred years old.

RB: I don't think that they necessarily felt that I was capable of doing it on my own. And they were right about that. No one can do it on his own. People voted for me in 1994 as an anti-vote. They said, "You know, we're not going to vote for the problem; we're going to vote for our hope that we can get out of this choice of what do we want: a heart attack or cancer? We're going to go and vote for this opportunity. We are not sure what this is going to be, but we suspect it's going to be better than what we're getting." In the future, I'm not going to run again in 2004 because I don't deserve to run. Since I haven't been in Panama, I'm just going to support a candidate.

IS: And who's he?

RB: Martín Torrijos . . .

IS: The dictator's son.

RB: Yes, Omar Torrijos's son. Martín Torrijos has the civilian will. He respects the democratic process. He has the will. That's all I was looking for, the will to change whatever measure—the inefficiency, the mediocrity that we have in terms of public administration.

IS: And we know of course that will is never enough in politics . . . but that's another story. Let me ask you, what do you mean by support? If he becomes president of Panama and he wants to name you a secretary of education or secretary of culture, would you take a job like that?

RB: I would take it.

IS: Would you sacrifice your career as a musician or as an actor: two successful careers that are thirty, forty years old?

RB: Absolutely . . . My country is more important than making a record or film. He has a chance to win an election in Panama. And one thing that happens all the time—too often—they have so many people who were critical: "Oh, we don't like this." How many people are willing to go and work and be responsible and assume a public responsibility for what they say they believe in? I have to do this. Now if you ask me, would you rather not have that feeling? Sometimes, yes. But I do! And it's a reaffirmation, a validation of everything I said. I wrote about this, but now, it's not about songs. "That's nice, the songs you wrote, very nice, but now, go and work, if you have the opportunity to change people's lives—not to sing about it."

IS: You have been in the United States for longer than you've been in your own native country Panama.

RB: I came in 1974, so it's twenty-nine years—you're right, Ilan.

IS: Are you an American citizen?

RB: I'm a Panamanian citizen with a green card.

IS: With a green card.

RB: Which now are blue . . .

IS: Which enables you to move freely and speak freely north of the Rio Grande. Why not become an American and run for public office in the U.S., where there is a large percentage of Latinos underrepresented in the public sphere that would need a figure that could change the way things are?

RB: There're many talented people here. Panama needs me more than the United States. We are a smaller country. Few of us have gone out abroad and achieved success. I think it's important that the reflection of the success does not annul the affection and the recognition of your character, which was formed there. It's important that successful people abroad return to their country and try to help and explain whatever is not understood in these areas, and utilize that public perception to try to better conditions—especially now when people don't trust the establishment anymore.

IS: Do you feel American even though you have a green or a blue card?

RB: I've always been an American in the broader sense of the term.

IS: America the continent.

RB: Absolutely. The level of experiences that I've achieved, in New York in particular, made me the person that I am . . . That's why I love it so much, and I mean from my gut. It formed me as a person. In the contacts I made in the city, in the country in general, I found excellent examples of behavior, as much as I've also found big disappointments in politics, in the domestic and international policies of the country. But in the general sense of the country, the way that the country is built around the idea of people coming in and supporting a constitution—that's something that is to be commended.

IS: You've talked about success, and in the media you've been described as probably the most successful Panamanian outside of Panama.

RB: That depends on who you talk to.

IS: Does your success have to do with your white skin? Would your pattern have been different if you were, as a substantial number of people in Panama are, of African descent?

RB: Absolutely. It would have been difficult in some areas, because of racial prejudice, which eliminates opportunities. However, maybe not in the field of music . . .

IS: Why not?

RB: Music is identified in many ways with people who are black or people who are of color or people who are mixes like I am. I laugh, because in Latin America whenever I see white people I say, "You know, you are a suspicious white, you know, because of the background." Especially in the Caribbean, where there are all kinds of mixes. Just as one drop of white in coffee doesn't make the coffee white, the whole notion of drops of blood is silly . . . Racism is a social problem, a cultural problem. But I agree with you: it's more difficult, but perhaps because I went into music and not into business, I would have been tolerated no matter what color.

IS: In Latin America, success brings terrible consequences. It creates envy, and there's nothing worse than to be successful. There's resentment because you live abroad, and that was reflected in the 1994 political campaign. There's resentment because you have been successful in the United States. I'm less interested in why people are resentful than how you handle your own success and how you use it, if you use it in any particular way.

RB: Whenever one talks about societies that have been crushed by the lack of opportunity, I feel sometimes like the guy who survived a war. Why me, I ask, and why the rest didn't make it? But I didn't build my happiness on someone else's unhappiness. If you have a problem with my success, that's your problem and not mine. I understand it—spiritually, logically, I understand it, but I'm not going to make that problem my own. However, I do understand in areas where failure is sort of like the national *contraseña.* The word means "password": if you do well by yourself, then there's an assumption that you think you're better than the rest. People tend to tell you to go to hell before you do anything, because in their minds they're not prepared for someone who's been successful and will be gracious about it and not rub it in their faces, which often happens in our original countries. Yes, a lot of people don't know how to deal with success, and I think that all has to do with how we were raised. Basically, it's your family . . . Again, people say that money corrupts, power corrupts. I disagree: it unmasks you.

IS: Let me return to *Mundo.* It has three elements you've reflected upon: the portrait of our present musical landscape as a polyrhythmic labyrinth; the quest of a mature Rubén Blades for a more genuine, un-adulterated voice; and the sense of satisfaction in your own accomplishments. Where do you go from now on?

RB: When I go back to Panama, I know I'll do good. It's not just a romantic dream: I believe Panamanians can improve their condition, and I'm looking forward to having a role in the shaping of a better future. I'm also going to get into writing books.

IS: Really? I'm glad to hear about it.

RB: Yes, I don't have your discipline, Ilan, but . . .

IS: But you have the admirable discipline of the musician and the actor.

RB: At times I've had my finger in too many pies . . . But now I'm going to go to Panama and have time to look into other aspects of life. I want to better my personal relations, rekindle them: with my father, for instance, who'll be eighty soon, with my brothers and sister, with my friends.

Identity and Archaeology

David Carrasco

David Carrasco (USA, b. 1944) is a professor of archaeology at Harvard University. He is best known for his book City of Sacrifice: The Aztec Empire and the Role of Violence in Civilization *(1999). Carrasco is also the editor of the* Oxford Encyclopedia of Mesoamerican Cultures *(2001). This interview took place in Boston, in April 2001, a year after Carrasco began teaching at Harvard. It relates to his more public recognition as a Chicano scholar.*

IS: How did you come to the study of the pre-Columbian past in Mesoamerica and how did you recognize yourself as a historian of religion?

DC: My study began as a teenager when I had a powerful experience during my first visit to the Museo de Antropología in Mexico City. My tía Milena, who lives in Mexico City, took me to the museum, the old museum near the Zócalo. As I witnessed, for the first time, the virile Aztec sculptures, the delicate featherwork, the exquisite Maya jades and painted ritual pottery, as well as the ephemeral jewelry which pre-Colombian peoples had made, I had a very complex emotional experience. I was fourteen years old and began to feel a kind of spiritual dizziness. Afterwards I remember going outside into the grand Zócalo where a series of ambivalent sensations worked their way through my mind and feelings. As I sized up this disorientation, I began to recognize feelings of both shame and respect. In the face of these cultural and artistic masterpieces I remembered that I had been taught in schools, films, and television in the United States to feel ashamed of my Mexican roots, ancestors, and the cruelty of the Aztecs. I carried to the museum that day a sense of shame and inferiority. But at the same time, scraping against those internalized lessons was the awareness that Mexico had marvelous civilizations at its roots, peoples who knew beauty, developed philosophy, sculpted gods and humans from stones and trees, turned time into closely watched calendars. The teachings of the inferiority and the negativity about ancient Mexican civilization had been a lie. It wasn't just the Greeks, Romans, and Egyptians who achieved complex levels of social order and art. These Mexicans peoples and their. cultures demanded our respect and invited our inquiry. I realized then and there that deep and fascinating human stories as well as significant cultural issues could be found and studied in Mexico City. I decided I would somehow focus on understanding this great civilization.

IS: Mexico City at one point was called Tenochtitlán, before the Spaniards arrived. Today Mexico City has some 22 million people. If one were allowed to revisit Tenochtitlán, how would it look to us?

DC: We're fortunate to have both Spanish eyewitness accounts of Tenochtitlán at the height of its powers as well as symbolic statements by the Aztecs telling us what the city meant to them. An Aztec singer called the city "the foundation of heaven," and Bernal Díaz del Castillo, a soldier in Cortés's troops, wrote in his memoirs that the city reminded him of a living legend. By "foundation of heaven" the Aztecs meant that Tenochtitlán was both the center of the universe and a cosmic city; it rooted the gods in heaven to the struggles and creativity of everyday life in the Aztec world. By "cosmic city" I mean something like Italo Calvino's notion of some cities rising to the prestige of being "the sum of all wonders." The city was structured into four great quarters, each with a major ceremonial center housing powerful deities who were cared for and worshiped by the people who carried on their lives as parents and children, carpenters and musicians, farmers and craftsmen, warriors and merchants. In the center of the city was the greatest ceremonial precinct of the empire, where over eighty ceremonial buildings served as temples, schools, palaces, skull racks, sweat baths, and more. Many of these structures were painted and decorated with religious symbols and deity images. The most prestigious building was the Great Aztec Temple that rose majestically above the city and housed two major deities, Tlaloc, the rain god, and Huitzilopochtli, the god of war.

We know of these structures and places from archaeology, pictorial manuscripts that have survived, but also from the eyewitness accounts of Díaz del Castillo, Hernando Cortés, and a few others. Díaz del Castillo has a marvelous series of passages of what the city looked like on the day they arrived. He describes the order and beauty of the monumental architecture, the gardens, the zoo, and the palaces. This impressed the Spaniard to no end as he witnessed not only the large pyramid structures but also palaces, ball courts, large passageways both on land and on water. Díaz del Castillo compares this city to some of the great cities that he had experienced and heard about in Europe, including Venice and Salamanca. His sense of awe in the midst of the Aztec city is expressed in this passage which I recall: "we were amazed and said that it was like the enchantments they tell of in the legend of Amadis, on account of the great towers and buildings rising from the water, and all built of masonry. And some of the soldiers even asked whether the things that we saw were not a dream." Finally, one of the most impressive things, both to the Spaniards and to us looking back, was the huge, bustling marketplace in the precinct of Tlatelolco. The marketplace had over sixty thousand merchants and traders involved in bartering and exchanging all manner of goods, animals, cloths, foodstuffs, all under the watchful eyes of local judges who settled disputes and managed the fair exchanges between the people. One of the places that the Spaniards compared it to was the great markets of Salamanca. So you have not only this tremendous religious architecture but also economic structures combined together to make this foundation of heaven.

IS: Who were the Aztecs?

DC: It is more correct to refer to the people who settled the two central cities of Tenochtitlán and Tlatelolco with the term "Mexica." These are the ethnic groups who claimed to have come from a legendary place of origin called "Aztlán," which is where the term "Aztec" comes from. The erroneous designation of Aztec for these and other peoples who settled what became the Triple Alliance empire of central Mexico and beyond comes from the nineteenth-century German naturalist Alexander von Humboldt and was picked up and made popular by William Prescott in his best-selling, still today, *History of the Conquest of Mexico and Peru*. We are forced by habit and popular usage to keep the term "Aztec" and intermix it with "Mexica" or "Tenochca," which is what they sometimes called themselves. In fact, there was significant diversity among the peoples who formed the Mexica, or Aztec, world. The migratory ethnic groups who came into the valley of Mexico in the fourteenth century brought developed farming and fighting skills, and they served as mercenaries and farmers in the established communities and especially Culhuacan and Azcapotzalco. One of their major problems was the lack of political recognition and legitimacy, which resided in the hands of the descendants of the Toltecs. So the Mexicas sought access to these royal families through intermarriage and eventually acquired connections to the royal dynasties. Through their own political astuteness, farming techniques, and military prowess, they begin to integrate a political unit in the valley of Mexico, in the city of Tenochtitlán. While there were a number of languages spoken by various groups, their Nahuatl language becomes the lingua franca of the area. This tension between ethnic diversity and the Mexica struggle for unity through their imperial policies of tribute, sacrifice, and warfare is very important. It's not only very important in the history of the city; it comes to play a very big role in the collapse of the city under the force of the Spanish invasion.

IS: When a society lives by and through diversity, the issue of tolerance is crucial. Was tolerance an important concept for the Aztecs?

DC: The Aztecs were not tolerant in the way we think of it, but there was as a result of this diversity a certain strategy that the Aztecs developed in order to integrate their empire. And one of the things that they did, for instance, was to allow different communities to still keep their local gods as long as representations of those local gods also came to the Aztec capital and were kept in an all-inclusive temple where the gods of all the communities were. But the people in those communities were allowed to speak their languages, carry on many of their own rituals and traditions. The way that they were not tolerant was in terms of the tributary payments that had to be made to the capital by the four hundred cities and towns in this tremendous empire. This was absolutely a requirement to pay the different types of tribute, which could be foodstuffs, animal skins, feathers, crafted costumes, and all kinds of goods that supported this remarkable capital and empire.

IS: What was the concept of violence for the Aztecs?

DC: In my study of the history of cities, I've come to see that urban traditions are founded *in part*, on violence, on institutionalized violence. Walter Burkert is correct when he wrote in his book *Homo Necans* that "all orders and forms of authority in human society are founded on institutionalized violence." What he means is that especially in socially stratified societies, social, religious, and economic authorities are constructed vertically with inequalities of access. These fundamental differentiations of access and use of knowledge, technology, and social status are protected by both persuasive *and* coercive institutions. What becomes fundamental in urban hierarchies such as the Aztecs is that there privilege and official violence are supported by sacred stories, religious claims, and ties which the rulers claim to have with the gods. Notice how the Aztecs, Romans, even the North Americans have violent upheavals as part of their sacred foundations. These powerful violent episodes at the foundation become a kind of charter about triumph over an evil enemy or a renegade outsider or a bad sibling, someone close to home who has gone bad. This original violence becomes institutionalized in the story of the nation, in the raising of children, in the training of the populace to deal with threats. For the Aztecs, their foundation myth told the story of military conflict at the sacred mountain of origins in which a male sibling, filled with righteous rage, utterly destroyed his female counterpart and the scores of outsiders who came from other lands to attack. When the Aztecs wanted to take over another territory and its riches and met any resistance, they often rejuvenated this story and brought enemy warriors to the center of their city where their temple, a replica of the sacred mountain of origins, became the scene for a repetition of the original violent victory. That's institutionalized violence. And we find a version of this founding violence in many if not every one of the great urban traditions. Now one of the things that's so important about Mesoamerican urban history is that it's one of the seven areas of what we call primary urban generation.

IS: Explain to me . . .

DC: There are only seven areas in the history of the world where cities were invented sui generis, uniquely and independent of other urban influences. And those are northern China, Mesopotamia, Egypt, the Indus Valley, southwestern Nigeria, Peru, and central Mexico. How strange that they are often referred to as the third world. These are the places where people invented cities without any stimulation from other cities. The urban history of the earth spread out from those seven areas. In all seven of these areas there are founding myths of violence which supported the kings and usually the warrior kings in their achievement of authority through violence rooted in sacred myths and expressed through a military elite. The Mexicas, the Aztecs, inherited a much older Mesoamerican history of violence and mythic violence. The Aztecs come into the valley of Mexico in around the twelfth century. But urban life, that is, socially stratified society manifested in monumental architecture, pyramidal social structures, and the development of luxuries in

Mesoamerica, starts around 1500 B.C. in several different locations and spreads out to incorporate larger geographies. Priest-rulers who are often elite warriors are supported by a trained military subculture who are served by ranks of assistants, fed by farmers, armed by craftsmen, and entertained by artists and musicians—all breathing a series of myths and sacred stories that organize their thinking and social interaction. We have found in the archaeological and written record of Mesoamerica complex cosmological stories and art which often say that the world, the sun, the universe or planets, and groups of people come into being as a result of some kind of sacrifice, rupture, and loss. One sacrificial pattern in Mesoamerica pits one group of gods against another group of gods—sort of Cain and Abel on a grand scale. The conflict is resolved through killing, warfare, the dismemberment of a group or individual. For instance, one of the royal myths that the Aztecs inherited has to do with the creation of the Fifth Sun. The Aztecs believed that the universe had gone through four previous solar systems, or what they called "Suns." In the cosmic darkness at the end of the fourth era, the gods gathered to find a way to bring up a new sun in Teotihuacán, the place we call today "the pyramids" in Mexico. Two gods vied for the honor of which would be the first to throw himself into the cosmic fire in hopes of giving energy to the sun. One god, the Pimply Faced One, built up his courage to face the pain and cast himself into the fire, out of which soon flew a spotted eagle. The other god follows with his self-sacrifice and a ocelot jumped from the fire. Interestingly, the eagle and the ocelot were the emblems for the two top military units in Aztec society who were committed to throwing themselves into the fire of war. Soon, the rosy dawn began to appear, but when the sun rose above the horizon it stopped and, according to one text, "wobbled from side to side." The universe was not stable or really in motion. And then, as a way of getting the sun to move across the heavens, one god was chosen to go and dispatch the other gods with the sacrificial knife. It was only when all of these gods were sacrificed and gave their own blood that the sun began to move in an orderly fashion in the universe and civilization was created. This is how one urban tradition legitimated its own violent practices, giving the cult of warriors the place of honor and authority.

IS: Were children and women sacrificed?

DC: What is crucial to understand is that what we are calling sacrifice, which means to set something apart in order to make it holy, the Aztecs called a "debt-payment." In the surviving texts describing these rites, they are usually referred to as a debt-payment, a sacred *exchange* with the gods. Everyone owed the gods—everyone at all levels of society owed those gods in Teotihuacán for giving up their own lives to create the sun and its rejuvenating powers that entered into corn, animals, human bodies, and gave light to the earth. Humans, in this worldview, were constantly in debt to the deities, the creative forces, and their most precious gift was their own blood, which had been infused into humans as a result of the cosmogonic sacrifices. So, for instance, children's ears were pierced at an early age to give small amounts of blood, young priests were taught to bleed their thighs, more advanced priests their tongues, and so forth. These were auto-sacrifices, self-sacrifices. Or better, debt-payments. And auto-sacrifice was the primary mode of sacrifice, not killing others but giving your own blood often in small rituals where you would puncture your earlobe or a finger or some other body part, and you would provide back to the gods who were in agricultural form, in the form of corn or other plants, you would give back to them some blood that they had given to you so that humankind could be created and fed. This practice takes on new dimensions within the geopolitical world of the Aztecs and their conflicts with other communities. Human sacrifice, mainly but not only of warriors, came to be one of the constant ways in which they communicated their own imperial position. Who was sacrificed? Well, the majority of the sacrificial victims were warriors from other communities. Remembering the notion of the debt-payment once more, it's crucial to understand that before an enemy warrior was ritually killed, they were *always* changed in a fundamental, ontological way. That is, their *mode of being* was changed into a deity. They were put through intensive rituals which functioned to empty out their human identities and fill them up with the divine fire of deities who had previously died in mythic times in order to give their lives to humans, plants, and the earth. This practice is not unlike the Christian idea of *imitatio Dei*, or imitating Jesus even to the point of dying in order to expiate the sins or debts in the world. But a close reading of the surviving data teaches me that women were also sacrificed in at least four of the eighteen months of the Aztec calendar, and occasionally children were also sacrificed. It's important to emphasize that these sacrifices were always put within a ritual setting in which the sacrificial victim was transformed, that is, emptied of their human identity and filled with the identity of a deity who had lived back in the cosmic period so that that original creation could be repeated.

IS: The concept of sacrifice—sacrificing our own children, spouses, even our enemies—is terribly shocking to us. In the past, you've gone out of the way to say, to explain, to what extent the previous anthropologists and historians of religion and sociologists have not talked about sacrifice because it's a topic that can alienate readers. What was the reaction of the Spaniards to this, and why can't we digest such an essential aspect of Aztec culture?

DC: In the study of religion, by both anthropologists and certainly by theologians and historians of religions, the rough, the destructive side of religion has often been avoided. People still want to see religion as the theologies of hope, something that enhances our lives, which it certainly does. Religion does provide types of . . .

IS: Spiritual . . .

DC: Yes, spiritual uplift. But the history of religions teaches us that religions also have this violent dimension to them. Martyrdoms appear in many religions, including the so-called major religions. Human suffering is often seen as having a religious meaning, and sometimes religious practitioners increase their pain and the suffering of others out of the belief that it has some redemptive power for themselves, their deity, or the world. Ritual killing of animals and humans appears in many different religious traditions. And for some reason historians of religions and anthropologists have shied away from looking at this dimension of religion and the celebration of the painful death. I've tried to address this larger problem and pattern somewhat in this book, *City of Sacrifice.*

When the Spaniards arrived, they at first were horrified by this type of visual, public bloodletting. They tried in their own way to stop this type of practice. And the Aztecs saw that these Spaniards were upset with this and sometimes they would use certain tricks to horrify the Spaniards, to make them feel repulsed so they would stay away from the Aztecs. But the record is very clear that when the Spaniards came, they brought another type of sacrifice that was religiously justified. I believe the Spaniards tortured, raped, and killed and murdered many more indigenous peoples in the first five years of the Spanish occupation than the Aztecs sacrificed in decades. One scholar calls the Spaniards the "mass sacrifice society" and the "massacre society." And in another manifestation the Spaniards brought vivid images of ritual violence and sacrifice with them, in the image of the pathetic, bleeding Jesus on the cross, and told the Mexicas that this was a noble destiny for them. Ritual violence among the Spaniards was so visible to the Aztecs because they always came with Jesus on the cross in front of them who was bleeding, who was suffering, who's been beaten . . .

IS: And tortured . . .

DC: Yes, and tortured. So from the Aztec perception it was the Spaniards who brought the ritual of sacrifice with them and placed it in all their important buildings. I think that one of the things that is tough about the Aztec record is just how public and pervasive this bloodletting and debt-payment in the form of blood as a creative and destructive force was. And it's crucial to realize that the real challenge of understanding the Aztecs is their dual face. Here was a people who conceived of the uniquely marvelous Calendar Stone, and developed accurate calendar systems, accomplished so much in sculpture, featherwork, astronomy, poetry, and craft industries, who *also* became committed to cosmic regeneration through the thrust of the ceremonial knife. These were the people about whom one Franciscan priest observed that after traveling in the Mediterranean world and in the Caribbean he had never witnessed families who loved their children as much as the Mexicas.

IS: It's ironic the way history handles the encounter between Spaniards and pre-Columbian cultures, particularly Aztec culture. In Latin America, among the Latino population in the United States, the Spaniards are perceived as the violent ones, the ones that perpetrated the killings, the decimators. Pre-Columbian culture is perceived as bucolic, pure, almost naive. But the description that you're offering is quite different: the Spaniards might have been violent, but they certainly didn't encounter a pacifist culture.

DC: To understand this shared capacity for aggression and violence, I return to my understanding of the nature of cities. You see the Spaniards come from an urbanized culture that also is founded upon certain structures of authority, male violence, institutionalized violence. Not only the Catholic image of the violence against Jesus and also the tradition of Catholic martyrs which comes with them, but also the Spanish monarchy itself had recently been involved in such powerful violent ejections and the killings of Jews and Muslims in their territories. When they came to encounter the Indians, they already had a mindset, a kind of hyper-masculine mindset that told them that the spread of Spanish culture it-self was tied up with violent activities that were religiously justified. Of courses, there are many tender, peaceful, and nurturing dimensions in Spanish culture as well. But those values and practices were simply not emphasized during what you referred to as the "encounter," the *encuentro* between Europe and the Aztecs. However, we also find an urbanized culture in the Americas. And here you have some of the same types of aggressive, violent institutions with local versions of hypermasculinity in service to the elites. In Anahuac as well as in Spain it was the elites who have direct access to the gods and the goods. One way, often el-egantly as in the Nahuatl forms of speech, they defend their privileged access to the gods and the goods is through persuasion. But if persua-sion doesn't work, then it's through coercion. And it's very important for Chicanos, Latinos, to understand that what they are inheriting here is the full range of urban genius and urban conflicts in the Mesoamerican tradition, not just a wonderful peaceful, nature-loving indigenous people, but people who are fully human in this world.

IS: Complex.

DC: That's right: complex and fully human . . .

IS: In Western society people are more or less comfortable with bibli-cal knowledge, Greek and Roman knowledge, and knowledge of other civilizations. Bu at least at the public level, we are unfamiliar with pre-Columbian civilization. That goes particularly for Latinos and Latin Americans.

DC: In part, it's a certain type of racism. In the sense that people in the United States are much more comfortable remembering and talking with their children about the Greeks, the Romans, and even the Egyptians who are far away in space and time and therefore safer to confront. From Harvard to Stanford and many places in between, there is a desire to claim some sort of descent from these *superior, sophisticated* cultures. So-phisticated, yes, but superior, not really. We in the U.S. benefit psycho-logically from a sense of inheritance of the rational sides of these cul-tures while ignoring the violence, the brutality, the complexity. More to the point, the U.S. doesn't have a history of violating these cultures or their descendants, which is not the case with Latin America. In order to deal with the Maya and the Aztec and the Toltecs and the Apache, Anglos have to face up to the fact that the United States was founded, geographically, economically, and even psychologically on programs of land-grabbing, colonizing, and violating indigenous peoples in the Americas as well as devaluing cultural mixtures that are fundamental to our history. Fundamental like the decimation of indigenous peoples. Therefore, to face them, to learn about them, in a sense, is to face U.S. history much more head-on and with its own complexities and its own shameful episodes as well as its glorious episodes.

IS: Mexico has managed to incorporate its past, architecturally, historically, socially, into the present. Where is Tenochtitlán, the empire capital, in today's Mexico? Is it to be found? Can you sense it? Can you taste it?

DC: Carlos Fuentes has a phrase about Mexico City: "the true image of gigantic heaven." What he means in part is that the layers of history and culture that make up Mexico City *permeate one another.* As I mentioned earlier, the pre-Columbian city was laid out in a very orderly fashion as a cosmic image on earth. And this replica of the heaven on earth is still visible in some ways in Mexico City today. For instance, the Great Aztec Temple is located and is being excavated still right next to the National Cathedral in the Zócalo, in what was the heart of Mexico City. The more and more that Mexico City modernizes and renews itself, it barely has to scrape the earth to build a subway or fix some plumbing and it runs into the pre-Columbian city, because it's right there right below the surface. And each time this happens, both the indigenous memory and the story of the encounter between Moctezuma and Cortés are brought to the surface of our minds and into the substance of our drams. *Renovación* means "nostalgia" in Mexico. Every time some new renovation project is undertaken, they find some Aztec monument, Aztec burial, some remarkable piece of architecture or stone. And it constantly brings back to Mexicans the fact that they are also indigenous as well as Spanish and mestizo.

Driven

Junot Díaz

Junot Díaz (USA, b. 1967) is the author of the volume of interrelated stories Drown *(1996). This interview took place in Boston, in April 2003, as Díaz was preparing to become a faculty member at the Massachusetts Institute of Technology.*

IS: How does a story comes to be?

JD: I tend to start with silence. And it's usually a silence around an issue, a silence around a time in my life, a silence about certain kinds of relationships, certain kinds of things boys do. Silence is wrapped around them, whether it's a societal silence or a more personal individual one. When I detect one of those in myself, that's when I have the makings of a story. I like to put my hand through forbidden spaces. Once I've identified the silence, I lock myself up in a bare room with no music and no light, just sitting down and trying to bang out a story.

IS: And it may take you how long?

JD: Damn long . . . My friends will call me up and say, "How are you doing?" "Oh I'm still working on that story," a story that I've been working on for three years. They gleefully hang up, because they know no matter how badly they do, they can't do worse than this. Yes, it takes me a long time.

IS: Do you rewrite the story many times?

JD: Even though I'll set out a plan for myself, in the end there's some sort of nexus of emotions and experience that I can call my instincts which guides me more than anything. I'll write a story the first time but something won't be right about it. I'll keep revisiting it till something inside of me says that it's right. I'll do about thirty drafts, and this is me lying to you. It's usually more . . . The women whom I've dated will attest to it: there's always, like, seventy drafts hanging out in a pile. I'm slow. I don't want to say I'm a perfectionist because it leaves you to think that the finished work is perfection. Anyway, I'm kind of restless.

IS: Between the first and final one, be that the thirtieth or the seventieth, are you surprised by how it has changed?

JD: Definitely. In fact, it's a great way of characterizing it. When you're writing, you're tapping areas of yourselves that are not normally under scrutiny in your consciousness. Those areas often ambush me halfway through a story or surprise me. One of the greatest joys is finding these areas and finding these reactions and these voices and characters inside of me. They don't speak to my individual subjectivity as much as they speak to the people who put all these things into me. It's a Whitmanesque idea of multitudes. Even when I'm alone, all the people that ever had a impact on me, good or bad, they're still with me.

IS: Describe the sensation seeing the story printed. Do you regret it has finally reached the stage in which you have no longer any control?

JD: I'm not that finicky about it. Writing is a compromise—I recognize that from the moment I have an abstract idea to the instant I begin to translate it on the page. Franz Wright said: "Art is the death mask of its conception." By the time it's on paper, it's already a corrupt form of what you've imagined. I'm so used to it—it's part of the process, so much so that it doesn't bother me to see the page printed. Actually, it's just nice, because for my friends, who live in different places, at that point it's easier to get it.

IS: There's a quality in your prose of being crisp even after a second reading.

JD: It's thanks to my mother, simply because of where she came from, an arid, southern region of the Dominican Republic. People there are known for their *poca palabra*. My mother's terseness, her single-mindedness, her stoic attitude, had a strong impact on me. My sense of what language can do, how much you could communicate with few words, I owe it to her. And of course, there are other people. In my formative years, I adored Edward Rivera, Toni Morrison, Edward P. Jones. But I was also impacted a lot by other kinds of fiction, Stephen King for example, and a lot of other white people.

IS: Silence . . . What role does silence play in our daily life?

JD: In the Dominican Republic silence is the essential part of life. Not that they are quiet, not at all. But there are aspects of life you simply don't talk about, at all.

IS: Forbidden anecdotes.

JD: Vast. My mother's experience under a dictatorship made you pretend that what you saw wasn't real. You couldn't say to people "Yo, that's a death house. Everyone's getting killed and tortured and kidnapped in it." Even though you saw it around you, it was silence you opted for. You couldn't say, "Hey, the Tainos, did you see all their petroglyphs? Can you see all the names of the cities and towns? And some of their words?" Nobody would dare say, "Hey, we've exterminated them, haven't you noticed?" The same goes for slavery, Negrophobia, etc. It's hilarious how it takes certain events to shake up the silence. For example, the U.S. invasion of the Dominican Republic in 1965, which demolished the nation's democratic aspirations and embraced a puppet regime of Joaquín Balaguer devoted to torture. No one in the community where I grew up would ever talk about it. But then came 9/11 and people suddenly began to talk. Say well, you know, 9/11 was terrible, but the military government in the Dominican Republic was worse. It destroyed people's dreams without a second thought.

IS: So the writer breaks the silence. Or better, he makes the silence tangible. Are there Dominican writers that had an impact on your upbringing or in the shaping of your world that ultimately allowed you into the literary room? Any writers that you read as a young man from the Dominican Republic?

JD: No. Mine is the kind of background where the distance between me and the literary elites in Santo Domingo was huge. It was almost interstellar. Afterward, as I was exposed to the work of authors, I became hungry. Viriato Sención, who wrote *They Forged the Signature of God*—he tangled with the legacies of Trujillo directly and explored the nightmare brought about by Joaquín Balaguer's regime. Sención is phenomenally important. And, of course, the poet Pedro Mir. But they came so much later in my development as a writer, it makes me sad.

IS: You were born in Santo Domingo and came as a boy to the United States and were raised in New Jersey. You see yourself as a part of the Dominican diaspora and other diasporas as well, so that you have become a confluence for many of them. What is the connection between you and the Dominican Republic—from where you are, from New York City, from Syracuse University where you teach, from wherever you find yourself? Is it one of center and periphery? Is it one of nostalgia?

JD: I'm too directly involved for it to be nostalgic. In a sense I go back to Santo Domingo too much, and I've got family on the island. I stay in our family home and see things too clearly to be nostalgic. The center/

periphery equation becomes ridiculous when you're in Santo Domingo, where I might find myself sitting across from a cousin of mine who's wearing a pair of Levis, has a pair of Doc Martens on, has a Gap shirt and a Yankees cap, and he says to me, "Junot, you're not Dominican." There's something hilarious about that moment—it brings it all right down to its core. Those in the diaspora haven't only changed as a result of their departure; they changed fundamentally the place they departed from.

IS: You're an integral part of a trend of Latino writers that have entered the academic environment. Is literature threatened by the academic environment, its freshness pushed to become a "subject of analysis"?

JD: Nothing is more familiar than being torn out from where you once belonged, being thrown somewhere new. This is a Caribbean feeling: this sense of cannibalism, the sense of creolization. There's nothing the academic community could do to me, in all its febrile imagination, that I couldn't in turn devour and incorporate. Being in academia has just given me another language to play with. And I mean play in the most sacred form. In no way I'm giving it hierarchy, though—I refuse to. It's too boring to be given hierarchy. But it certainly is useful. I love teaching young people. It's important just to be involved with them. It's an honor also. But at the same time, look, I'm not going to lie: I spend as little time at my university setting as I can. I leave . . . I go back to my neighborhood, there in upper Manhattan, and hang out with people who would bring a lot of flavor if we could hold committee meetings on the corner of 142nd Street.

IS: In *Drown,* the stories of course are intertwined and linked by a series of characters. And these are two brothers that appear that allow you to explore issues of masculinity and the male, the role of men in Dominican society, in New Jersey, in Latino society, in American society, in African society. I understand that's the topic you're exploring in your novel. I wonder about it: about how Latinos, the writer, the Latino writer explores those issues and what you're trying to do.

JD: A good question. You have to understand, Ilan: I began to write during the debates between Stanley Crouch and Toni Morrison, and between Alice Walker and Ishmael Reed. It was in the late eighties. Those two black men were attacking these women for being writers of pathology, for maligning the African American male. I was at Rutgers at the

time, which has a strong women's studies program, with a solid feminist tradition. I remember the debates so clearly because we were all
having them. Our community organization would invite different speakers. What killed me as a person who likes these kind of things, likes
seeing where people are shutting their mouths and holding back, was
that from my sense of it, I agreed with the women. I grew up in a community where the men I knew—sure we had a lot of crap on us—but for
the most part the stuff that I saw from the men was taking advantage
and being abusive of women. I thought women like Toni Morrison and
Alice Walker let the dudes that I had grown up with off easy. Part of my
project was to think about masculinity and think about writing it, but
also doing it kind of from an inside/informer perspective. I don't think
men can be feminists. We might have a profeminist project, but our male
privilege prevents us from being real feminists. I surely wanted to have
a profeminist project. For me creating these stories about masculinity
and exploring masculinity from an inside perspective was fun. *Drown* is
read against the immigrant tradition. So there's certain trajectories and
arcs, narrative arcs in the immigrant tradition, that push you toward an
aesthetic like the one in *The Rise of Michael Levinsky* . . . Is that the name of
the novel?

IS: You mean *David Levinsky*?

JD: Yeah. In it the protagonist makes it. In a way, because readers look
at the tradition, they fail to see that the arc in *Drown* is about the creation
of a New Jersey immigrant Dominican male subjectivity. The book is a
"how to" guide to how boys are assembled—one specific boy, at least.
Yunior is a nice, young kid. He feels powerfully towards his mother,
dreams powerfully about his missing father, and looks up to his older
brother who's in place of the father, teaching him how to be a boy. But
then, as he meets his father, he comes to realize that the man is abusive
to his mother. And his brother also gets into abusive relationships with
girls. Yunior thinks, "I don't want that in my life." He's conflicted, but
by the time he's a late teenager, he becomes exactly the male he didn't
want to be. He himself can't imagine how it happened. It simply did.

IS: Art is a death mask.

Life in Translation

Ariel Dorfman

Ariel Dorfman (Chile, b. 1942) is the author of, among other books, How to Read Donald Duck *(1975),* Widows *(1984),* The Last Song of Manuel Sendero *(1987),* Death and the Maiden *(1992),* Konfidenz *(1995),* The Nanny and the Iceberg *(1999), and* Blake's Therapy *(2001). Conducted in both Spanish and English, this interview took place in Durham, North Carolina, November 1999.*

IS: Would you please map for me your transition from Spanish to English—what each of these languages means to you?

AD: I have spent my entire life switching languages. The book I'm presently starting to write, a memoir, deals with this phenomenon. It is an attempt at a self-portrait that would also be a portrait of the world I have been crossing or traversing since I was very little. I was born in Buenos Aires, Argentina, but at two and a half years of age I moved with my family to New York, where I had a traumatic experience. I contracted pneumonia. I entered the hospital speaking Spanish, but when I came out I didn't speak a word of it and I wouldn't do so for another ten years. My first language was Spanish, but I erased it in relation to speaking it, although I could still understand. I understood everything my parents would say to me, but I would answer them in English. Then, for complicated reasons, when I was twelve we went back to Latin America—more specifically to Chile, where I had to relearn Spanish. Soon I became enraptured with it, until 1968, when I went to Berkeley. At that point I was entirely bilingual. I had kept writing in English while in Chile, but I had also begun writing essays in Spanish. By then I had already produced a book or two. At Berkeley I was a research scholar, and it was there I realized that everything I was writing about in fiction concerned my Latin American experience—the experience of the marginal, of the underdeveloped. Around that time I made a commitment to myself never again to write in English—a foolish proposal, no doubt. I then returned to Chile (it was the early seventies, an explosive revolutionary time in Latin America, when Salvador Allende had just come to power), and I swore that henceforth I would write only in Spanish. As I saw it, I had readopted, or had been readopted by, the Spanish language. But the gods of the twentieth century decided to play the cards differently. I went into exile at the end of 1973 and continued to write most of my fiction in Spanish, in exile, far from Chile. I spent some years in Paris and in Holland, and in 1980 my family and I came to the United States, supposedly for a very short period. We got stranded here, and the stranding meant that I had to make a living writing in English. I had to support my kids; I had to begin a new life. As time went by, very gradually—this is where I find myself at the moment—I began to accept the fact of my bicultural, bilingual, split life—and the split of languages that I inhabit, or that inhabit me. I ceased to be at odds with my binary identity. I ceased to fight. I'm currently finishing a BBC project, a screenplay in English, I'm working on a play in Spanish, and I have the memoir I was telling you about, which will probably be in both tongues. I'm also thinking of a novel that will have one chapter in Spanish and one in English.

IS: Talk to me a bit more about that novel. By writing it in both languages, you must necessarily be visualizing a bilingual reader, one as fluent in them as you are. But is there such an audience out there, one big enough for the publisher to be ready to embark on a risky project like this? Or are you only writing it in that way and the alternative chapters will then be translated into the other language?

AD: An intriguing question. I'm only writing it that way in order to express myself the way I want to. *Máscara*, published in 1988, is the first of my novels that I wrote in Spanish, then rewrote in English, only to then use what I had redone in English to change the Spanish version. I had an editor at Viking who would work on the English text, and then I would change the Spanish accordingly. I did that because, as you, Ilan, know very well, there are very few editors in Latin America: your book undergoes little change between the time you submit it and the finished text. Once again, in this new novel I will do the translation myself. It will probably be a monolingual text written by a bilingual writer. But the issue of an audience ad hoc to my needs concerns me deeply. For me the perfect audience would be one made of some 40 to 60 million people like I am. I honestly think that if I had that audience, I would write in an entirely different way. I would write the way I live: switching languages, going in and out, like the Nuyoricans and Chicanos. When you come to our house, you realize that first we say things in Spanish and then switch to English; we mix everything up. But when I'm in the world, a world organized categorically in a Kantian fashion, a world in which languages organize societies and create wars, one must acquire or perhaps call on a different self. Although I have never written a book with a specific market in mind, I do take into account whether somebody is going to read my text or not, whether someone is going to understand it or not. By the way, in my new novel I may create a landscape in which I have an entirely bilingual country.

IS: Henry James once tried to describe the difference between the first, original tongue, and its counterpart, the second, acquired one. He called the first the mother tongue and the second the wife or mistress tongue. It was a logical approach: James happened to be addressing someone who had English as a second tongue, and he said, memorably, that English behaves as a mistress—it will be loyal to you if you take care of her, but it will betray you, be angry and offensive, if you misbehave. Taking that as a starting point, could you describe what Spanish means to you and likewise English? How do they behave toward you and you toward them? Which one would you rather have in an intimate moment? Which is the language of fury and which the language of dreams?

AD: Gosh, I wish I knew the answer. The fact that Henry James would talk about mistresses and wives is already a very gender-conscious approach to the issue. Personally I'm not surprised that he would put it in those terms. In my own case, I don't know which one came first, which one is nearest to me. One is the mother tongue in the sense that it's the language my mother spoke to me when I was a baby. But I have no memories of it. The language of my childhood is English. Spanish very slowly became the language of my maturation; it also became the language of love because it's the tongue in which I fell in love with Angélica, my wife. (Coincidentally, she was an English teacher when I met her.) In a way, I think I'm married to both languages, but marriage implies divorce and separation. Perhaps I have two mothers: two origins, two beginnings. Or is it two mother-wives? This does not preclude the fact that oftentimes I feel as if I don't have a language at all—a sort of aphasia. I can stumble, lose my sense of what language I am using, and not find a word in either tongue; I can search for the word, but the word is not there. Probably the deepest side of myself inhabits that language geography. When I'm writing, if the voice, the inner voice, comes to me in one language, I will follow through; I let the language choose me. By the way, languages in my life have never been neutral or apolitical. They often put me in awkward positions. During the seventies and early eighties, I would find myself enjoying English, and I felt closest to it, even when English was the language of empire, the language of aggression and oppression. In spite of the fact that the language of Shakespeare, Jane Austen, and Humphrey Bogart was a gringo tongue (even if I spoke it better than the gringos), was often understood as an enemy language, I felt close to it. This makes me think of Rubén Darío's admonition: "Vamos a rezar en inglés"—we will pray in English.

IS: Did that create guilt?

AD: I think so, for a large part of my life. Remember that I was born into a very well to do family by Chilean standards, and I would try to hide that fact. I kept on saying to myself: I should be writing in Spanish, because Spanish is the language of identity, the language of community shared by millions of people with whom I'm creating a New World, I'm dreaming the revolution, and I'm dreaming the return to democracy. Once settled in the United States, I told myself: you are using English to help others understand Latin America, to analyze the many contradictions of the region, to explore the vicissitudes of Latin American intellectuals. But then I began to recognize that, deep inside myself, I always felt a bit of a stranger in Spanish. That does not embarrass me anymore. Nowadays I don't try to hide my social background: I'm who I am, and it is because of who I am that I can write the way I write. I don't see my bilingualism as a curse anymore. I've lived outside Chile for over two decades already and am accustomed to the linguistic dilemmas we've been talking about—they aren't new for me.

IS: Incidentally, I once talked to Oscar Hijuelos about the same topic. He isn't fully bilingual: his Spanish language is in his unconscious background. He told me that the disappearance of his Spanish tongue took place at a very early age, when he entered a hospital for a few months to recover from a very serious sickness. The hospital was in New York, and he soon discovered that unless he requested whatever he needed in English, the nurse practitioner wasn't going to do the things his way. Just like you, he entered speaking Spanish and left speaking English. What is curious, I think, is that both of you lost, or found, a tongue in a hospital. A hospital, a sickness, and a recovery—these were the ingredients.

AD: Extraordinary. As for me, I can't remember a single thing that happened in that hospital—not a single thing. Everything has been erased from memory.

IS: I have in front of me two versions of *Konfidenz*, in Spanish and English. As you know, often when a text is translated from Spanish to English, the resulting text is much smaller in size—in pages. But in your book there's only one page difference, 175 and 176, which seems to me incredible. As writers we often need to further explain, or substantially delete, segments of the text for a translation to be successful. We are addressing a different audience, with different cultural needs. But if length is any indication, you have achieved a perfect balance. Balance of syntax and grammar. Balance of content. Balance of cultures. You add and take in the same proportion.

AD: I began to try solving the problems of exile by writing simultaneously for an audience back home and for one abroad. By doing so, I was hoping that words would become the meeting ground of what was within and without, outside and inside. The text was the in-between, a fusion, an amalgamation, signifying one way and another depending on who was reading. Likewise, my characters have a tendency, though grounded in certain reality, to become ghosts—to signify other realities. *Death and the Maiden* takes place in a country that could be Chile (it's probably Chile), but that can be any place in Africa, in the Middle East, in Eastern Europe, under the same circumstances. The same with *Konfidenz*, which makes the reader think it is about Latin America, although in fact it is about Nazis, Jews, and the resistance during World War II. I started doing this with *Widows*, which, although it is about the *desaparecidos* in Argentina, is set in Greece, and to do so I created a pseudonymous Danish author, who is supposedly the one writing the whole story. A very Latin American idea, I should add, harking back to Borges, Julio Cortázar, Alejo Carpentier, and even Pablo Neruda: we are all echoes, shadows of something original—hand-me-downs, residuals, anticipations of something utopian still to appear.

IS: Was *Death and the Maiden* written in Spanish?

AD: Yes, and then I almost immediately and very feverishly translated it into English.

IS: Spinoza wrote *Ethics* in Latin but thought it in Hebrew. And one could say something similar about Kafka's German, if not about Nabokov's English and French. Could you describe your Spanish to me? Soon after I left Mexico, my editors back home begin to complain that the columns and stories I would send from New York were written in Spanish but thought out in English. And my Spanish today, well . . . it's bookish, abstract, alien, foreign, anything but regional.

AD: Likewise with me: my Spanish is haunted by English, and vice versa. People in Latin America react toward my Spanish by saying, "We don't know where you fit." Consequently, and like you, I'm drawn to bilingual writers, certainly the ones you mentioned or those that sound bilingual. I used to feel uncomfortable because I didn't belong, but now I'm happy to be loyal to my calling.

IS: Yours, then, is written English with a Spanish accent?

AD: Yes. For instance, when I write for the *New York Times* an editor may suggest changing an adjective to make the sentence correct. But I fight with my life against it. I want to write for the gringo with a sense of familiarity. After all, I'm also a gringo. I was brought up in this country, and I know what it means and feels to be a U.S. citizen. But I also want to convey in my writing a sense of alienation, distance, and discomfort. I will fight against stubborn editors to retain my own syntax, my own voice. Maybe I am trying to be true *and* translated simultaneously.

IS: Bilingual writers, writers fully active in two or more languages, might have an internalized translator. It makes it easier for editors to come directly to us, since at least one intermediary—the translator—is unneeded. You are your own translator. So in the old saying, *traduttore traditore,* the only one guilty here is oneself. On the other hand, translators are the closest to a perfect reader one can ever dream of having. They know the dirty tricks, the subterfuges, the many masks a writer has. A translator can bring out the best in a writer and also the worst. As I think you will agree, often a translation improves the original—the second reader, the perfect reader, elevates the text to a higher standard. But by being your own translator (and here I also talk of myself), we are miserably deprived of that gift. We are deprived of the dialogue one can have with one's best possible reader.

AD: I couldn't agree with you more. It's a wonderful observation. You do miss a step. One of the problems one has as a writer is that you tend to fall in love with your own language, with your own words. When you yourself translate them, I think you tend to be literal and, thus, you miss that step: in a sense, what you miss is to be betrayed. But there's a positive and a negative aspect to betrayal. On the one hand, it can be the worst possible fate for a work of art, and not capriciously did Dante place traitors at the heart of hell. I myself think loyalty is the most important of all human qualities. On the other hand, as I've experienced life, I realize that there are moments of, let's call it, "good betrayal": moments when you have to leave yourself, the past, and certain people behind in order to grow. You have to cross a border at a certain point and turn back on a few things. Pure loyalty also comes at a loss of self. You give yourself entirely to someone else, so you may not know who you are. I don't know if I have a translator inside: the two inhabiting me are contiguous, as if there's a customs office between them. I go back and forth—as if I had simultaneously two faces, which I could switch on and off.

IS: You come from a Jewish family. I wonder if there were other tongues aside from English and Spanish, French, or Yiddish, perhaps. Also, I wonder if the environment in which you grew up championed polyglotism. You already told me how you would talk to your parents in English and they would respond in Spanish.

AD: I began thinking about all these things only recently. For instance, I have realized, while writing my memoir, that both of my parents were bilingual. That is, I knew it all along, but in the past few months the fact has acquired new importance. My father was born in Russia, and Russian was his first language. He still speaks it perfectly. He is trilingual: English, Spanish, and Russian. Both he and my mother also speak a little bit of French. And my mother was brought up with Yiddish—her first language—because she was born in Romania, and at three months old she left for Buenos Aires. She still speaks some Yiddish and understands some German. Obviously my maternal grandparents spoke Yiddish, and my paternal ones spoke Russian. Thus, my two parents had the experience of acquiring a second language. All this is to say that, you're right, Ilan, my childhood milieu was multilingual, but also, as I told you before, having two languages at times felt like having a birthmark on my childhood face—an invisible, yet painful birthmark. Now I realize that it was also exhilarating.

IS: We've been talking about translation and polyglotism, about memory, suffering, and justice. Would you consider yourself, now more than before, a Jewish writer? Of course a Jewish writer is a person that is Jewish that writes. But I would like to go further. You have discussed Kafka's influence on you, and betrayal of a certain past and a certain pattern as a strategy to move onward with life. Every Jewish writer is a hybrid: a transnational, transgenerational, transcultural, and translingual entity, one that goes places but has no specific address, and has influences that come from far beyond his immediate milieu, and often his work cannot find an echo in that milieu. Considering your own present ambivalence toward Chile—when I saw you last, you told me you couldn't live in Chile any longer—I wonder how you feel about the "Jewish question."

AD: I have changed in this regard. For most of my life I thought I was Jewish merely by accident, that I was Latin American by choice, and that it had befallen me to be an English-speaking person. Let me stress it once more: my identity was centrally that of Latin America, which I defined as a resistant Latin America and a revolutionary Latin America. I perceived the region as eternally hopeful, in a permanent journey toward a better future, toward a promised land. But as the years go by, I feel that I belong but also that I don't belong. No matter how much I drink of Latin America, I'm never full; I'm always missing something in my relationship toward the continent, both as I see it and as the region sees me or avoids seeing me. Consequently, already for some time I have begun defining myself as a Latin American who is everywhere and nowhere. I feel at home in many places, and, to be perfectly honest, I like and feel comfortable with my wandering condition. Often I'm struck by nostalgia and sadness, by the realization that I will always be globetrotting, that I will never call a piece of land my own. I think that is my destiny, a preview of a new breed of humanity, a cross-national breed. When I begin to define myself in these abstract terms, I realize that by definition I'm as old as my ancestors—that is, I am Jewish. If for decades I thought of Jews simply as being the observers of a series of religious habits and I observe none of these (my mother was brought up in a Zionist household, and my father was an agnostic who rejected the very idea of Judaism and fought for world revolution), now I have discovered I might be Jewish in the deepest sense. After all, I am messianic, profoundly (perhaps perversely) ethical; like a Talmudist I discover multiple readings in every text. Recently I went to the Jewish Museum in New York and was mesmerized by photos and images of the shtetl, which I felt were looking at me, not only the other way around. Some eyes in those photos were my eyes, calling to me from inside my past. So there you find me, Ilan: while I used to answer that I would be Jewish until the day when there was no more anti-Semitism, today I am more conscious of my background. Jewish characters have appeared in my work: in *The Last Song of Manuel Sendero,* for instance, David, one of the protagonists (which happens to have been the name of both my grand-fathers), is an eternal wanderer; and Judaism and Nazism are at the center of *Konfidenz.* I must add to all this that I never experienced an excessive amount of anti-Semitism in Chile, not from the Left and not even under Pinochet. Unlike dictators in Argentina, like Perón and the tyrants of the Dirty War, Augusto Pinochet was not an anti-Semite.

IS: Why was *Death and the Maiden* so successful in Israel?

AD: I have heard that it was a magnificent production. But its success may also be due to its literary structure. The play is deliberately written to allow different audiences to read into it their own dilemmas, allegorically speaking. It is something of a deformed mirror, and, as you remember, a mirror appears at the very end. If the public, collectively speaking, is worried about the problems on stage (justice, evil, memory, how one tells one's own tragic story so that it's confirmed by others, and what happens if one suddenly ceases to be marginal and acquires enormous power, which can be exercised against a former enemy), then it will be attracted to my characters and their questions. As you know, the play was very successful on Broadway, but it was successful in monetary and artistic terms, not in engaging the community to ask questions about itself. It had fine actors and was sold out for six months. But as with the movie adaptation directed by Roman Polanski, no one wrote an opinion piece saying, "Here is a set of questions affecting us deeply, which we should address." People saw it as one more play or motion picture. It was different in Israel, Belgrade, Belfast, Brazil, and Kenya. Audiences were able to read their own experiences into the text. In Israel in particular, what people saw on stage was not the Latin American but the Jewish and the Israel experience. As a people, Jews have been about as deeply hurt as one can possibly be in this world—in relation to the persecution, damage, and destruction brought upon us. I believe that anybody who is Jewish has to ask himself whether to pardon those who committed atrocities against us, especially today, as anti-Semitism, ethnic violence, and chauvinism rear their heads again. Also, the three characters in *Death and the Maiden* could be Palestinian, and that was an issue I discussed with the Israeli director when the play was in rehearsal. Israel, then, probably used Chile as a mirror, and so did Germany, which, by the way, is where my play has been most successful—sixty-four different productions at this point, I think. Perhaps Germans are also exploring their guilt—their multiple pasts.

My Sax Life

Paquito D'Rivera

Paquito D'Rivera (Cuba, b. 1948) is a jazz artist whose numerous albums in-
clude Return to Ipanema *(1989),* Havana Cafe *(1992),* Island Stories *(1997),*
Historia del soldado *(2002), and* The Best of Paquito D'Rivera *(2002). In*
1997 he received a Grammy for best Latin jazz performance. This interview
took place in Boston, Massachusetts, September 2002. It reviews his life and
oeuvre. After the interview, D'Rivera went on tour with Yo-Yo Ma to promote
the album Obligado Brazil.

IS: Comparatively speaking, what is your relationship to the saxophone and the clarinet—physically and musically?

PD'R: The saxophone is a direct descendant of the clarinet. The way
one approaches each of them is totally different, though. The clarinet is
a hard instrument. It's easy to make a horrible sound. It can sound beautiful, but it's a challenge. And in order to do it right, you have to concentrate all your time.

IS: And the saxophone?

PD'R: The saxophone is the most beautiful instrument ever invented.
It's a forgiving instrument, *un instrumento agradecido,* you know? Leave
the saxophone for two, three weeks. When you pick it up, it sounds fine.
But with the clarinet, you put it down, pick up again and arghhhhh.
Maybe the clarinet is a female instrument: you just never know what's
wrong with her.

IS: Your father played saxophone.

PD'R: My father was a classical saxophone player. He imported the
style of the French school to Havana in the early forties.

IS: You have played the *saxo* since the age of five. And by six you were
already playing in public.

PD'R: Yes.

IS: So when did you discover the clarinet?

PD'R: Oh, much later. My father wanted me to be an alto player. But I
was too small to play the alto, so he ordered a small soprano saxophone
for me. Later on, when I picked up the alto, my father told me that alto

players have to play clarinet too. His dream, he confessed, was for me to be a classical clarinet player in the symphony. I did that for a little while, but I never liked it too much.

IS: You are famous for bringing together all sorts of rhythms and movements into your own style—the classical and the Caribbean music. In the seventies, you were part of the group Irakere, known for juxtaposing rock, classical, and salsa. How does this collusion come alive in you?

PD'R: It's my father's fault, too.

IS: Always blaming the father.

PD'R: Tito was my father's name. He was an Ellingtonian person, in that the great Duke Ellington said that there are only two kinds of music: good and bad. My father always listened to the phonograph. Later on the high fidelity LPs and all that came along, but when I was little it was the phonograph. He would play Benny Goodman at Carnegie Hall—playing swing, for example. Next, he played the Mozart concerto for clarinet, played by Benny Goodman, too. For me, classical music and jazz are all music. That's the environment I grew up in. I didn't discover the difference between Dámaso Pérez Prado and Igor Stravinsky until I was twelve or thirteen. But then again, they sounded the same to me.

IS: Much of the music you heard in Havana came from the United States.

PD'R: I remember when Nat King Cole was there with his wonderful trio. I wasn't allowed to be in the audience because it was a cabaret, the Tropicana. But I was in the orchestra pit with the Armando Romeo Orchestra. Watching Nat King Cole singing and playing that beautiful piano, I felt mesmerized . . . It made me dream of traveling to New York, which is Benny Goodman's fault.

IS: Not your father's fault in this case.

PD'R: Well, my father played the record for me: Benny Goodman in 1938, the famous concert in Carnegie Hall, the first time a jazz band played in the place—a gorgeous live recording with Benny Goodman, Teddy Wilson, Harry James, Gene Krupa, and Lionel Hampton. I asked my father, "What is that?" He said, "This music is called swing, and it's played at Carnegie Hall." I said, "Carne y frijol?" He replied, "No, no, no: Carnegie Hall, a theater in New York City." He talked to me about New York City, where all the fine music came from, and ever since then

I had this dream of being a musician in the jungle of New York.

IS: But prior to 1980, when you finally moved to *la jungla,* the early period of your career was spent in Cuba, particularly under Fidel Castro's revolution. How should we compare those two periods?

PD'R: It's too sad. The country had actually managed to get rid of a dictator . . .

IS: Fulgencio Batista.

PD'R: Cuba slowly deteriorated . . . Liberties were taken away. I decided I wanted to leave, but in order to do so I had to abandon my wife and son. In the end, I had to wait a total of eight years to see them again. And I didn't see my mother for nine years because she left in 1968. I didn't see her until 1977, when I saw her in Canada.

IS: It was an international campaign to bring your son out of Cuba.

PD'R: Yes. It was a high price to pay, but everything in life has a price, and I'm happy I paid it. Now my son is a clarinet player and writer.

IS: The New York of your dreams as a little boy and as an adolescent—did it clash with the reality of New York when you finally arrived?

PD'R: Not at all.

IS: What did you find in New York when you arrived?

PD'R: Latin people from all extractions, people from all different types of backgrounds.

IS: At that point your relationship with Dizzy Gillespie intensified.

PD'R: I had met Dizzy Gillespie in Havana. It was curious. I went to my house and I found a paper bag that said, "Paquito, we have been looking for you. Where are you? Dizzy Gillespie." Nobody knew Gillespie the trumpet player was on the island because they don't announce anything in the newspaper, just repeat trivialities about Fidel Castro. So I went to the corner bodega, showed the bag, and said, "What type of joke is this?" The bodega owner answered: "No, Dizzy Gillespie himself wrote it." Then I said, "¡Ay, Jesús!" The owner said, "Yeah, there was a strange character looking for you." "Strange character—what's that?" And he said, "It's a black guy dressed like Sherlock Holmes." And I said, "Oh, that's Dizzy, man." Later on I met him in the Havana Libre Hotel. He had a jam session and Stan Getz was there also, as well as David Damran, Earl "Fatha" Hines. We all played a concert that night at the Teatro Mellá.

IS: Were you close?

PD'R: Very close . . . Dizzy was a generous man. He helped me a lot. I was never a part of his orchestra. I always worked with him as a guest artist and on special projects, because he said, "You have to pursue your own career as a bandleader." I said, "You know, Dizzy, I want to play with you." And he said, "Yeah, but I don't want you to play with me. You go and do your own thing." That was nice of him.

IS: How should one define jazz?

PD'R: I always quote Herbie Hancock on that. Years ago in *Downbeat* magazine, Herbie Hancock said, "Jazz is something impossible to define and easy to recognize." Jazz is the music of the United States of America. It is the music of the immigrants. All of us that come make a contribution to the music. And if it keeps the spirit, you know, the energy of that music, you can call it jazz. You know, it's an art and it's subjective.

IS: And Latin jazz?

PD'R: From the beginning Jelly Roll Morton was talking about the Latin "tinge" in American music. He called it the "Spanish tinge" in American music, but you know what he meant by that. The Spanish tinge in American music . . . Ever since the contribution of people like Alberto Socarras, the Cuban flautist who played the first jazz flute solo in the history of jazz. Then Mario Bauza, Chano Pozo, Chico O'Farrill, Antonio Carlos Jobim, Jorge Dalto, Michel Camilo, and so many of them. Thousands of us around making a contribution. Juan Tizol wrote some of the most important pieces in the book of Duke Ellington—for example, "Caravan" and "Perdido." Everybody thinks that Ellington wrote that. Ellington didn't write that. Juan Tizol, the Puerto Rican valve trombonist, did.

IS: To return to an earlier idea, one of the admirable aspects of your oeuvre is the fearlessness with which you tackle the classics: Stravinsky, Bach, Mozart . . . Talk about the difference between using somebody else's piece and doing your own composing starting from scratch.

PD'R: Everyone uses the same twelve notes. Mozart or Machito, we all use the same twelve notes. All you have to do is to interpret that thing. When you are creating something, half of the battle is won because what you are doing is part of you. Now, when you have to understand the music of other people—you have to do that understanding. You have to pay respect to what that person had been devoting his time to writing. I analyze first what he was trying to do. If he's alive, I will call him.

IS: And talk directly . . . ?

PD'R: Oh, yeah. "Will you come home and have some black beans and rice?" That is the best way you can go to some piece of music.

IS: Do you feel constrained when you are using somebody else's piece by the piece itself?

PD'R: There's not any system for that. For example, when I recorded that CD you have, there's the first Spanish version of Stravinsky's *Soldier's Tale.* That is the most difficult piece I've ever played, but difficulty is not a milestone in art. Some pieces are difficult and sound horrible. But this piece is difficult and the result is absolutely beautiful. It's one of the most beautiful pieces ever written. Seven instruments. Well, Stravinsky was a genius. It's a pleasure to work on that.

IS: It's a pleasure and a pressure . . .

PD'R: And it's worth it.

IS: Can one teach jazz?

PD'R: No.

IS: Why not?

PD'R: My father was a natural teacher. Some people are born with that. My bass player, Oscar Stagnaro, I've learned so much from him. I learn all the time from him because he knows how to explain things. For me it's hard to explain things. What do I do? I love to do clinics where I play and then people ask questions and I say, "You know something? I don't know, let's find out." It's important to say "I don't know." It's most important to be honest with your students. You come here to study with me; okay, let's find out how I do this because I don't know how . . . I'm a natural musician, so I do certain things, but I don't know how I do them. They make me find out how I did this or why I cannot do that.

IS: The students also help you understand the process of making music.

PD'R: Of course. My father always said, "We should pay the students to study with us because we learn more." When you teach, you learn . . .

IS: By the way, we've talked about your father. How about your mother?

PD'R: Oh, my mother was my lawyer. She defended me even if I did something wrong. She always defended me. And she is a creative person—a fashion designer. Now she's retired.

IS: Does she live with you?

PD'R: She lives around the same neighborhood and she cooks for me all the time.

IS: She does?

PD'R: Yes, and travels with me and loves to drive. She's in good shape.

IS: One of the things I've noticed recently in your career is that you have begun writing. Recently, not too long ago, you published a book that is billed as an autobiography—it's filled with anecdotes: *Mi Vida Saxual.*

PD'R: *My Sax Life.*

IS: It's in the process of being translated into English, and I understand also that you have finished, or are almost finishing, a novel.

PD'R: Yes, this is not recent. I have been writing ever since I was a little kid in school. I won several prizes for my compositions, about my teacher or about the cute girl in the class—especially that.

IS: Those got good grades, I guess.

PD'R: And about a great composer that I admired: for example, Mozart. I wrote some compositions about Mozart.

IS: What's the difference between composing music and writing an essay or writing a novel in terms of creation?

PD'R: I will tell you something . . . another journalist asked me that question and I never formulated that question to myself, but now I know how I did it. I write the same way I compose or the same way I improvise: in a improvisational way, and in a jazzy way. Sometimes even my writing looks a little disorganized, in the sense that I go back and forth. That's the way I improvise. That's the way I play.

IS: You leave it to random, to accident, to spontaneity?

PD'R: Yeah.

IS: Is that the way you deal with your life in general?

PD'R: No, I have to have structure. I like to improvise, but I have to know what's on top of what I'm going to improvise. Every improvising has some type of foundation, like a building, you know? You must know where you're going first. Then how you go there. Well, let's take this way, this other way, this path which is beautiful with trees and all. Then go to the lake, so you can improvise how you get there. But you should know where you're going.

IS: In *Soldier's Tale,* you collaborated with the Argentinean performer Nacha Guevara, and I understand also you're doing a collaboration with her based on the life or the work of José Martí, who influenced you quite a bit.

PD'R: Oh yes. Martí is my god. He's a person I admire and this is the proof . . . [D'Rivera shows a necklace.] Here you go, José Martí.

IS: It's his image.

PD'R: This is a 1916 gold coin with the image of José Martí.

IS: Why is he so important to you?

PD'R: Martí was a genius, an individual with so much knowledge, but especially with so much desire to learn. He was a person who analyzed others and who paid respect to others. When he wrote about José White, for example, a fantastic Cuban, an Afro-Cuban violinist who was a son of slaves. He was born to a slave parent and he became the director of the Paris Conservatory. He wrote beautiful pieces about his playing and his approach to music and all that. Martí is a special character. He is known mostly for being a patriot, and a person who died young by defending his country and all that. But he was also a great poet, great writer. And I'm delighted to do this with Nacha Guevara.

IS: And like you, Martí was displaced, in exile. Exile has been good to you.

PD'R: No, exile is good for nobody. But I'm a happy man.

Poetry and Politics

Martín Espada

Martín Espada (Puerto Rico, b. 1957) is the author of, among other books, The Immigrant Iceboy's Bolero *(1984),* City of Coughing and Dead Radiators *(1993), and* A Mayan Astronomer in Hell's Kitchen *(2002). This interview took place in Boston, Massachusetts, April 2002. After the interview, Espada released* Alabanza: New and Selected Poems, 1982–2002 *(2003).*

IS: Poetry and politics, in you and your work, the two converge. What does a poem do?

ME: A professor of mine, Herbert Hill, used to say that ideas have consequences, and I believe that. And of course poems communicate ideas in a variety of ways, and one never knows of course what kind of impact the poem is going to have, who it's going to reach, what change it might engender, and I don't put too many expectations on an individual poem. Eduardo Galliano has contributed the idea that when we are looking at change, social and political, it's an act of madness, of foolishness to think that a work of art by itself can accomplish it. He says it would be equally foolish to think that it couldn't contribute to making that change. Personally, I see what I do as a small contribution to that change. The crossroads of poetry and politics is a place where craft encounters commitment, where the spirit of dissent encounters the imagination, where we labor to create a culture of conscience. There the dynamic of oppression and resistance distills itself through the image, the senses. It is essential that we see and hear, taste and touch and smell in the world of the political poem. It is essential for the political poem to be crowded with exact, human details. We must work to give history a human face, eyes, nose, mouth. If we do otherwise, then we risk all the familiar perils of political poetry. The complacency you refer to is indeed widespread among poets, and often begins with the rationalization that good political poetry is impossible. Aside from the huge body of evidence to the contrary, this argument strikes me as utterly arbitrary. We can write about anything, in theory—but not things political. This is akin to saying that we should never write any poems with trees in them.

(Parenthetically, if we're going to write political poems, we should know our trees; we must draw our metaphors from the world around us, and our metaphors have to be accurate.) True, there's a great deal of bad political poetry out there, filled with rhetoric, but this does not prove the impossibility of the political poem. There's a great deal of bad love poetry or bad nature poetry in circulation, yet no one seriously argues that love poems or nature poems are impossible. The argument that political poetry is a contradiction in terms is advanced by complacent poets who defend their lethargy with impressive fury. They justify their apathy with passion. If only these poets devoted the same energies to writing poems that mattered to other human beings. I want to see poems pinned on the refrigerator, carried in wallets until they crumble, read aloud on the phone at 3 A.M. I want to see poems that are political in the broad sense of urgent engagement with the human condition, poems that defend human dignity.

IS: How did you discover poetry? Or better, when did you first see yourself as a poet?

ME: I discovered poetry when I was fifteen years old. At that age, I was a terrible student. In fact, I failed English one semester in the eighth grade. By the tenth grade, I was more interested in the exploration of mood-altering substances in the parking lot than in the mysteries of poetry. And yet those mysteries found me. A tenth-grade teacher confronted a group of us young thugs in the back row of his classroom and gave us an assignment: We had to produce our own issue of the *New Yorker* magazine. We had never seen the *New Yorker* magazine. We were all New Yorkers, but that was a different New York. Nevertheless, the magazine was passed from hand to hand, down the hierarchy of thuggery, until it came at last to me. All that was left, at the back of the magazine, was a poem. I was rather agitated. However, I didn't want to fail English again, so I went to the window, sat down, and wrote a poem. It was raining that day. I wrote a poem about rain. I don't have the poem anymore, of course, and I don't remember it, except for one line—"tiny silver hammers pounding the earth"—to describe rain. I had just invented my first metaphor. I didn't know what a metaphor was. I found out a week later and went strutting down the hallway. But I discovered something else that day. I discovered that I loved words. I loved slamming words into each other and watching them spin around the room. I soon

discovered too that I had something to say with all those words. Virtu-
ally from the start, I have written about the idea of justice, in practical,
philosophical, and political terms.

IS: Let's talk more about the tension between Puerto Rico as an island
and the Puerto Rican diaspora. Do you feel a connection with island
literature today, and with its poetry in particular?

ME: There's a definite tension between Puerto Rico and the Puerto
Ricans of the diaspora. The island and the diaspora represent opposite
poles of identity in constant reaction to each other. We are a colonized
people, by definition divided. We will remain powerless as long as we
are engaged in distracted squabbles over authenticity, ethnic purity, our
own brand of "blood quantum." In spite of all this, Puerto Rico is poetry
to me. The impact on my senses, and on my sense of history, is over-
whelming. Moreover, I feel a strong connection with two poets of the
island: Clemente Soto Vélez and Juan Antonio Corretjer. These were
major nationalist poets imprisoned in the 1930s and '40s for their pro-
independence ideas and activities. I met and read with Corretjer, but my
deepest influence came from Soto Vélez, who became a close friend and
mentor in the last decade of his life (he died in 1994). Soto provided a
political and ethical example for me to follow. His poems were powerfully surreal, yet totally engaged with the fate of humankind. Again,
inspiration does not necessarily equal imitation; yet, to the extent that
my poems ever leap into surreal and fantastic places, I owe it to him.

IS: There's a lack of interest of U.S. newspapers and magazines in Puerto
Rican poetry, which is hardly reviewed in any significant fashion.

ME: Let's look at simple demographics. There are precious few Puerto
Rican editors employed by newspapers and magazines and publishing
houses in this country. Puerto Rican writers and especially readers are
widely regarded as nonexistent. Puerto Rican literature is received by
Anglos as Puerto Rican food is received, in the words of our friend Earl
Shorris: "dinner with the doorman, a janitor's repast, the flavor of failure." That won't sell. No Puerto Rican writer has ever received a major
book award in the U.S. On the other hand, I would prefer that we be left
alone rather than be manipulated and twisted into knots by the mainstream media. I was recently interviewed for a *New York Times* article
about Nuyorican poetry, and I was appalled at the results. My words
were grossly distorted so that a false debate was created between me

and some of the Nuyorican poets in the article. I was quoted as opposing the creation of a film about Miguel Piñero, an early influence of mine. I said no such thing. Instead, I warned the reporter that I had never seen the film. I also said that many more films should be made about Puerto Rican writers like Clemente Soto Vélez. Other writers interviewed for the piece were furious as well. One young poet was supposedly "energized" by the Piñero film—in contrast to me—but she hadn't seen the film either. In other words, writers who had not seen this movie were asked about the movie, and then pitted against each other in a phony, manufactured argument about this movie they hadn't seen. In the *New York Times, por favor.*

IS: Since World War II poets have been "bought" by academic institutions to teach in English departments and in creative writing programs. You are part of this trend. Can you reflect on the tension between literature and the university at the level of language, pedagogy, politics, etc.?

ME: Certainly, the academy has been perfecting its stronghold over poetry since the days of Pound and Eliot. Though I receive a paycheck from the English department at the University of Massachusetts, Amherst, they haven't "bought" me. I haven't mutilated my ideas, or censored the expression of my ideas, to suit the academy—and no one has asked me to do so. On the other hand, I'm critical of MFA programs as a rule. They do a terrible job recruiting poets of color; they rely on reading lists that are often relentlessly white; they turn out poets who mimic their masters in a pose of detached, hip cynicism; they train their students in the arts of social climbing and professional ambition above the arts of poetry; they hand out countless degrees as credentials for teaching jobs that don't exist; they are run autocratically; they are extremely resistant to change, especially political change, and exercise a chilling effect on real academic freedom. Bulletin: No one needs an MFA to be a good poet. There are decent MFA programs, but not many. I work outside the MFA system, and I am glad for it.

IS: Your Puerto Ricanness is at the core of your identity and of the poetry that you've been writing since 1981 or '82 when your first book was published. And yet, you were not born in Puerto Rico; you were born in Brooklyn. How did the Puerto Ricanness come to you: from the neighborhood, from the family, when you were a child?

ME: Well, first of all, New York is the largest Puerto Rican city in the world. More Puerto Ricans in New York than San Juan. I was surrounded by that from the beginning. My father, Frank Espada, was an activist, a leader in the Puerto Rican community of New York in the 1960s, and so his role in the community was reflected everywhere around me. Later on he made a transition and worked as a documentary photographer, recording the life of the Puerto Rican community, and again that had a big impact on me. It was quite natural to develop and to nurture that identity, even though I was born in Brooklyn and not in San Juan.

IS: When did words become in you a tool to begin exploring your own universe and to begin communicating the ideas that were in your mind?

ME: I can remember early on the influence of my father and his use of language. But I can recall a political use of language in particular. Again, this was natural. This was endemic to the environment. When I was about seven years old, my father participated in a demonstration at the New York World's Fair. He was protesting, with other members of the Congress of Racial Equality (core), discriminatory hiring practices on the part of the Shaeffer Brewing Company. And there were many, many arrests at that world's fair, and one of the people arrested was my father, who disappeared for at least a week, and no one explained this to me at the age of seven. I simply assumed that my father was dead, and I would sit holding a picture of him and crying, and that's the way it was up until the moment he walked through the door. And I looked at him and said, I thought you were dead. He thought that was funny and he started laughing. And then he realized on another level that he had to begin explaining all of this to me, that the time had come. He sat down and he began to explain it to me, at the age of seven. Over the years I would follow him to various kinds of events, demonstrations, what have you, rallies. He had a storefront in Brooklyn, East New York, on Blake Avenue, called East New York Action, and I would go visit there. Now my first art, if you will, was visual. I drew, constantly. And I would draw demonstrations, depictions of these demonstrations on the back of flyers announcing the demonstrations. You know, it was just part of my environment. There's a blank piece of paper. It happens to announce a demonstration, but I flip it over and I draw on it. I remember this being part of the whole ethos. And I was raised with an ethos of resistance all around me.

IS: When did you eventually or finally make it to Puerto Rico, and what was the experience of having been born in the so-called diaspora, on the mainland, and being exposed to the island culture? You have poems that deal with this. I'd like you to reflect a little bit.

ME: Yes. I first went to the island at the age of ten; so this was around 1967. And for me it was first and foremost an explosion of the senses. I came from Brooklyn. I came from that urban environment, that industrialized city, and I found myself in Puerto Rico. It was absolutely remarkable to see the trees. To for the first time in my life actually hold a real coconut in my hand, not the hairy shriveled-up thing we see in the supermarket, but a big green shell, and miraculously if you cut the top of that shell off, you could drink right out of the damn thing. It was a revelation. It was miraculous. I was surrounded by miracles. The island revealed itself to me in that way, as an explosion of the senses. And being that little fat kid, I ate and drank my way across the island like Pac Man. For me, Puerto Rico is a constant learning experience. The island is, I believe, only 111 miles long, and yet to me it is enormous, and so deep and so rich, and I'm always going to be mining something from the experience of being there.

IS: The poetics of compassion . . . And yet, somewhere in your past you were a bouncer at a bar and also an amateur boxer, I've read somewhere.

ME: I wasn't an amateur boxer. I simply did that on an informal basis, you know, in various and sundry situations. I was a bouncer in a bar in Madison, Wisconsin, of all places. And the physical was definitely there. Now mind you, being a bouncer can be a compassionate business because most of the time you're not punching people in the face; you are helping people who have had too much to drink find the way out the door and eventually home. And that was what I did most of the time. If someone blacked out—and I could stand there and watch someone drink seven, eight, nine hours and slowly killing themselves. But once that person indeed had blacked out, it was my job to find the coat, to find the hat, to find the books, to call a cab, and to carry that person and all of their worldly possessions down the stairs, get that person and the stuff into the cab, and make sure that that person got home.

IS: Today aside from being a poet, which is I would assume the essence of your, of who you are, you're also a professor, but you have been a lawyer, and a lawyer involved in a variety of different areas of law. Tell me about that and tell me how that informs yet again your condition of poetry.

ME: Well, both as a poet and a lawyer, I was engaged in the business of advocacy, speaking on behalf of those without an opportunity to be heard. It made perfect sense. It was perfectly congruent. Sometimes people would ask me, How could you be a poet and a lawyer? They are two totally contrary ways of using the brain. But for me it was perfectly congruent. I was an advocate both as a poet and a lawyer, speaking on behalf of people without an opportunity to be heard in the Latino community, immigrants, the poor, and so on. I went to Northeastern University Law School in Boston, graduated from there, and pursued the practice of law in the Boston area. I did bilingual education law with an organization called META. And later and primarily worked as a supervisor of a program called Su Clínica Legal, which is a legal services program for low-income Spanish-speaking tenants in Chelsea, which is a city right outside of Boston, representing immigrants from Puerto Rico, the Dominican Republic, Guatemala, El Salvador, and occasionally even from Vietnam and Cambodia when necessary. And we did the things that tenant lawyers do: eviction defense, no-heat cases, rats and roaches, crazy landlords. And I wrote about those things; I wrote lawyer poems. And to this day once in a while, I read one and I still get this familiar kind of chill.

IS: In your poetry I see obvious influences from Whitman and Neruda. The elasticity that Whitman brought to American literature in many ways opened the door for somebody like you. The passion and the pathos of somebody like the Chilean poet Pablo Neruda is also there. When did you discover the early poems and poets that influenced you, and how did they influence you?

ME: I began writing poetry before I knew what it was. I started using poetic devices before I knew that these devices had names, that these tools had actually been used before and came from somebody else's toolbox, so to speak. I began writing poetry when I was fifteen years old, and there were no books of poetry in my house. That was not part of our experience, per se. My parents read. My father in particular would read books about politics and history, but I didn't read poetry and they didn't read poetry as a rule. I just began writing it and later on I would discover that there was a place for me. There was a history and a tradition from which I emerged that I only dimly perceived at first, and discovered perhaps in a strange kind of attempt to find out who I was, both as a person and a poet. I didn't start at the beginning. I didn't start with Whitman and move forward. I moved backwards to Whitman, and I was greatly influenced by Allen Ginsberg. I was influenced by Langston Hughes, by Carl Sandburg, by Neruda. And only later did I realize that they were all descended from Walt Whitman. And then once I discovered Whitman, that was like going to the source, that was the fountain from which the waters sprang. And I actually carried *Leaves of Grass* under my arm—as he instructed me to do, by the way; I mean, it's in the book—and would open it periodically and realize I had discovered a kind of bible. And what strikes me even now as I read Whitman, as with his disciples like Neruda, is the profound empathy, a kind of poetics of compassion, which guides everything that Whitman does. Whitman is about this ultimate empathy, this deep fellow feeling.

IS: How do you perceive his influence on the beat generation?

ME: Williams of course wrote the famous introduction to Ginsberg's *Howl:* "Hold back the edges of your gowns, Ladies, we are going through hell." Again, I would say that Williams was a presence but not a major influence for the beats. Whitman was their guru. (Mine, too.)

IS: In between Whitman and Ginsberg is, of course, William Carlos Williams . . .

ME: Williams was a wonderful poet. Like most of his readers, I had no idea he was Puerto Rican when I first encountered him. Even without this knowledge, I loved his precise, jeweled images of urban life, the green bottle in the trash, the fire engine. He is not a major influence on my work, but he is certainly present.

IS: There appears to be a few degrees of separation between your work and the Nuyorican tradition. It all comes down, I guess, to what one perceives as street poetry. Pietri, Algarín, Piñero, Estevez . . . there's an urgency in their voice, urgency and roughness. Your style, in contrast, is more lyrical.

ME: I've various links to the Nuyorican tradition: I'm culturally Nuyorican—that is, a Puerto Rican born and raised in New York City. I'm writing from the same general experience and perspective as the poets of the Nuyorican school. In my twenties, I was inspired and influenced by several major Nuyorican works: *Puerto Rican Obituary*, by Pedro Pietri; *Down These Mean Streets*, by Piri Thomas; and *Short Eyes* by Miguel Piñero. Now, to be inspired by a writer is not to say that I must imitate that writer. To be influenced by a writer is not to say that I must emulate that writer. Hopefully, our inspirations and influences lead us to discover our own unique voices. Though I was born and raised in New York, I evolved as a poet elsewhere, particularly in Boston, where I practiced tenant law in the Latino community. My use of language is indeed different from most poets of the Nuyorican tradition. I don't want to sound like anyone else. Moreover, why should we invent and repeat our own clichés? The language, though "lyrical," is hopefully accessible, available to the community that provoked these poems in the first place. When I gave a reading just the other day at the local jail, the Puerto Rican inmates responded strongly. The experience, the point of view of the community, is still reflected in the poems. I'm ultimately more interested in what unites the Puerto Rican community, and its writers, than in what divides us.

IS: There's often among Latino writers a perceived sense of burden. As a so-called ethnic writer, one is destined to become the spokesperson for your people; you're destined to use political tools and infuse your work with that. You don't share this concept of burden. It is for you something altogether different. It comes naturally. It comes also from the tradition in Latin America of the writer that represents the voiceless. Do you feel a constraint for Latino writers forced to represent, forced to speak out for, others? What does that create in you?

ME: I don't feel that this is a burden. I don't feel that it's something I'm forced to do. It's a privilege. It's a responsibility, but also an honor. I have a subject. I have something to say. For me one of the great dilemmas of contemporary poetry in this country is that most poets don't have anything to say and they're writing poems instead of putting down new tile in the bathroom or horseback riding or tending the garden or something else that could have been done just as easily. I feel blessed with a certain kind of gift, which is the gift of a tale to tell. That's a gift. It's not a burden at all.

IS: Tell me how the story comes to you and how it gets formed. How is the poem born and how does it mature? How does it become an entity? And once published, does it keep on evolving or does it stop evolving?

ME: Well, many of my poems are narrative poems; so it does begin quite literally with a story. Over the years I've developed the same eye for a story that a journalist might develop, let's say. There are certain kinds of instincts. You watch events unfold before you or someone tells you the tale and you find yourself translating it into poetry. There's a reflex action which takes over. I think of it sometimes as a kind of internal tuning fork and I hear it high pitched. I sometimes think that sound, that *tingggggggg* that I'm hearing, it's a sound that can only be heard by poets and dogs. You know . . . a very high-pitched sound. There's instincts cultivated over many years of experience because that's the combination. It's a combination of instinct plus experience, plus practice, practice, practice. All of that creates the impulse towards a poem. There are situations where I'll sit up in bed at three o'clock in the morning and realize that something that happened to me when I was sixteen years old is a poem.

IS: And how long does it take to become a fully developed poem? How long do you work and rework?

ME: The poems are idiosyncratic. Some of them come quickly. In fact, some of the poems that have gained the most circulation for me are the ones that came most quickly and most easily.

IS: As if they were dictated to you?

ME: As if dictated, and it almost feels like cheating. Right? I didn't work hard enough on that one; why do you want that one? I wrote a poem about a janitor called "Jorge the Church Janitor Finally Quits," which is in the voice of a janitor friend of mine I knew that worked at church, in fact in Harvard Square in Cambridge years ago. And one night he had enough and he walked off the job, and when I found out that he had done this I was so angry about it that I sat down and wrote the poem on the back of a napkin in about ten minutes.

IS: And that was it?

ME: That was it. I remember another occasion when I wrote a poem in my head while I was sitting with my wife watching a production of the *Nutcracker* in Boston (her idea, not mine.) And I was so bored, and after staring at the exit sign for a good long time, I began to develop a poem about a totally unrelated scenario. After we got out of the theater, I said we've got to get some place fast. We went to a nearby restaurant, and I said I need something to write on. And she gave me a paper bag, that's all she had in her purse. And said I need something to write with. She found a magic marker. I tore the bag open lengthwise so I would have enough space to write on. And I wrote this poem with a magic marker.

IS: But others take longer.

ME: Others take much longer. I scratch and chip away at anything that doesn't look like a poem. And that could take years. And if I don't feel like it's ready, I'll hold it back. I won't send it out or I won't include it in a book until I feel that it is in its least objectionable form.

IS: You speak Spanish and English, or better, English and Spanish. These are two universes, these are two ways of life, these are two languages. And as far as I know, you mostly or only write in English, although your poems are infused with Spanish. What's your relationship with English and Spanish?

ME: I have the entire range of emotions you describe with respect to both languages. I love both languages and I struggle with both languages, and English is my first language and Spanish my second language, but they blend into each other. They influence each other. And I find more and more with my poetry that that is the case. And the relationship between the two languages has taken various forms over the years. There are poems I've written in English which have been translated into Spanish where I serve as the cotranslator. There are other situations where I will blend the two languages and bounce them off of one another. I recently did a poem called "En la calle San Sebastián," about a famous street in Old San Juan, Puerto Rico, which is famous in particular for its music. I alternate one line of Spanish with one line of English throughout the poem. The alternating line in Spanish is "En la calle San Sebastián," and I'm trying to evoke the sound of the music through doing that because of course Spanish has that great power, that great musicality.

IS: And when you do that as you do in that poem, are you conscious or even perhaps paralyzed by the fact that someone in the audience might not speak Spanish and that there might be a line in that case or a few words sprinkled in other cases that might pass by that person's understanding? Do you feel compelled to explain everything that is in the other language?

ME: I try to be accessible. I'm trying to communicate. That accessibility when it comes to the use of Spanish in the body of an English language poem can be achieved in a variety of ways. I think of it in terms of the "three C's": context, cognates, and crossover words. I'll try to employ some of those devices in the process of putting a bilingual poem out into the world. And oftentimes that seems to be enough. On the other hand, I don't feel obligated to explain all the time. I don't feel obligated to translate all the time. There's a point at which I think the reader must do some of the work. And hopefully the poet can motivate the reader to do that work. If I get the reader engaged, then the reader will want to know what certain words mean. If I use a word like *alabanza* in a poem, and I repeat that word over and over again, emphasizing its importance, hopefully the poem conveys what that word means, but if readers in English don't know that it means praise, they will go to the dictionary and look it up.

Onto the Diaspora

Isaac Goldemberg

Isaac Goldemberg (Chepén, Peru, b. 1945) is the author of, among other books,
The Fragmented Life of Don Jacobo Lerner *(1976),* Play by Play *(1985),*
and El gran libro de América judía *(1998). Conducted in Spanish, and trans-*
lated into English by Daniela Hernández, this interview took place in Manhat-
tan, April 1986. After the encounter, Goldemberg became part of the faculty of
Hostos Community College in New York. He wrote a play, Hotel Amerikka,
and also released a revised version of The Fragmented Life of Don Jacobo
Lerner.

IS: Although not altogether new, in the past twenty years there has
emerged a fresh Jewish faction in Latin American literature. Obviously,
your novels and poems are part of this new faction. What is the cause of
this recent emergence?

IG: It's true that the spearheaders of this Jewish faction, as you call it,
are not new. Its ancestry is substantial, especially in Argentina where
the Jews have submerged themselves in the national artistic and intellectual spheres more so than in other countries. This implies that the
phenomenon is neither new nor sporadic. I would call it generational: it
recurs every twenty years approximately, with names sometimes of importance and others totally unknown, but not nonexistent. Each of these
generations describes its own reality according to circumstances during
their lifetime. The generation of Alberto Gerchunoff, which moved from
a shtetl-like environment to the city, had an exclusive perspective, different from that of the 1940s and '50s. Its mission to homogenize the
immigrant farmer's life with that of the gaucho of the pampa was clear.
Rozenmacher, Szichman, and others followed him. Each of them responded first to the needs of their own country and then to those of the
continent. Because I don't doubt—and this needs to be stated—that all
Latin American countries will primordially unite under one flag: Margo
Glantz or Esther Seligson do their own job in Mexico, Gerchunoff in
Argentina, myself in Peru. The phenomenon isn't monolithic. We need
first to investigate how a specific author is connected to his national

literature, and secondly the relationship he has with the rest of the continent. There are always parallels and similar circumstances, of course: in our case Judaism unites us, as does emigration to these indigenous lands, exotic and multicolored. But the differences stand out: my artistic training associates me with Salazar Bondy, with Alfredo Bryce Echenique, and with the Gerchunoff tradition. In the same way, Rulfo is Mexican, Argüedas Peruvian, Cortázar Argentinean—and only later are they Latin American.

IS: Talk about your relationship with the rest of Peru's literary circle: Ciro Alegría, José María Argüedas, and in particular Mario Vargas Llosa, whom critics recognize as your legitimate teacher and predecessor.

IG: My relationship with Vargas Llosa is not a personal relationship. We are not friends, and we see each other only in passing. By some strange coincidence his biography is similar to mine. Although he is some ten or eleven years older than me, we are both provincials. He arrived in Lima at an early age, around ten years of age; I was eight. For him, city life came as a surprise, as it did for me. We were both students of Leoncio Prado. We were both part of almost identical bourgeois society in Lima. There are even some similar family occurrences: his father reached back to him, as did mine. The severities of the reader are, as usual, pronounced: readers think that I bow down and copy *The Time of the Hero* in writing about my experiences in the Leoncio Prado Military School. They perceive an imitation. In *Play by Play,* a number of characters, all students of this institution, are being interviewed by an invisible being. The interlocutor at one moment refers to this novel by Vargas Llosa. They defend themselves against the scorn they have suffered in it, knowing that inside the college they have lived a life of horror, but they pretend to forget it and defend their environment that way. It's ironic, because generally in novels other novels are not mentioned, as if it were forbidden that one fantasy combine with another. A curious phenomenon takes place in Peru: narration abounds, especially of stories—of characters young and old. As if both were ghostly ages. In that sense, I'm a recognized contemporary of Vargas Llosa, Argüedas, and Bryce Echenique. That way of unraveling these important stages, not dealt with in the social sciences, has become part of literature. The writer, perhaps, has a self-imposed responsibility to shape these realities through fiction.

IS: This faction to whom I've referred has definite singular connotations, which distinguish it from the rest of the literature of the continent. Above all, it comes from a minority responding to the needs of a small group of citizens—their migratory and adaptive adventures and vicissitudes; their ethnic and religious anomalies. On the other hand, literature and politics in Latin America are inseparable. Its ideology and theory are essential material, an incessant fountain of viewpoints or concerns that every narrator, sooner or later, recognizes as his own. In your opinion, what ideological or political project should this new Jewish faction undertake? How to see Jews? Integration on a national level or distinction as a minority?

IG: An interesting question . . . A previous generation lived innocently with the anxiety of betrayal. They preferred not to discuss the Hebrew theme for fear of seeming too foreign to their historic reality. As if their countries could not accept a pluralistic society, as if they had to sacrifice their culture for integration. There's no conflict between being a political writer and not being one: each routine act, each minutia is a political act, a political standpoint and perspective. There's no division between life and ideology. Inherent to the relationship one maintains with Judaism, one must also have a political stance. That is to say, one must consciously assume that posture which would otherwise remain latent. Between a political stance and an attitude there are only intellectual differences. Or Judaism should be viewed as a vision of regression or as a vision of collective advancement. The Jew who is ideologically reactionary will side with the former: he will isolate himself in his ghetto and ignore his nation's future. On the other hand, the progressive will find that his religious and ethnic background will inflict change and aspire to the transformation of society. It's my call to hold a progressive stance, what for many signifies a step toward socialism.

IS: Can you be more specific? What entails the progress you describe for new Jewish communities in our countries?

IG: It entails living in liberty . . .

IS: By being a minority?

IG: Not as a minority but as unrestricted bearers of their religious heritage. Here is where categories of political power come into play. Power as such is attainable for any human being. Upon gaining it, that person ceases to be in the minority. The 6 million Indians in Peru are a minority even though numerically they are the majority. Their status as a minority is a result of their lack of power. The Jewish voice will be equal to that of the rest of the pluralities once they have equal power. I'm not referring, I must say, to financial power. I'm referring to the power to speak and to vote, of participating in the development of the nation.

IS: As citizens of the 1980s, we know well that there are various models of socialism. What relation does yours have with your experience in Cuba and Nicaragua?

IG: American citizens believe that capitalism and democracy are synonymous. They have been victims of brainwashing that confuses terms because of ideological ends. I propose a democratic socialism of a humanist line. A system that is not only economic but political and has multiple parties. There's no single formula by which all countries should arrive at socialism. Each country has its own uniqueness, and as a result its political system must conform to those distinctions. I would like to think that the best way to arrive at this change is through elections. But the example that eventually refutes that possibility is Chile, where democratic triumph failed due to an American intervention. Be that as it may, I believe that a democratic and egalitarian world is best.

IS: Why does this political posture not appear in your works? Do you hide it?

IG: I haven't done it yet because it hasn't presented itself. I'm currently working on a new text where that posture is more evident.

IS: Should literature by Jews, then, be a means of reflecting circumstances or a means of affecting and transforming them?

IG: I think it should transform them. Due to the peculiar position in which we find ourselves, we should see our respective countries from a more beneficial angle. If the Jewish writer questions himself on what it means to be Argentinean, he does it from a totally different perspective than a non-Jew uses to question himself. If we could unite these two perspectives, we surely would have a more holistic vision. That will be our contribution, as it will be that of blacks, the Chinese, Japanese, etc.

IS: The reader who looks for the Latin American Jewish writer is then crucial in that platform you describe. Your novel *Play by Play* has an epigraph, a paragraph by Macedonio Fernández, that conjures up a Joycean reader or another model reader. Who is the reader to which you direct your prose? Is it a general audience? The members of other national minorities? Or is it the Jew, your coreligionist, exclusively?

IG: I would like to think that readers for whom one writes are part of all sectors of society and are not part of sects. That question, however, cannot have such a simple answer. There's an intrinsic desire in every Jewish author to self-define himself, and that desire frequently meets obstacles unusual for other novelists. For any Colombian or Uruguayan, it's enough to define himself as a citizen of his country in order to be accepted. By defining himself as Peruvian, the Jew immediately faces scrutiny. Why are you Peruvian? people ask him. Your parents weren't born here; you are first generation, second at most. What right do you have to call yourself a citizen of a country to which you are a stranger? However, my case is different: I'm free from that scrutiny because my father is a Jew and my mother an Indian: half and half. In the end, Jewish qualities and customs will always have peculiarities because we are impatient to define ourselves. It is part of our nature to keep narrating, come wind or high water, what we are and what we love each instant. What is ours, what makes up this faction is a type of new Talmud: we are constructing a lay Talmud that is legitimately ours. Our odyssey is not accidental. Eventually it will be evident that it is also not exclusive. There are, as I've told you, two differences: one, the zeal to recount emigration. And two, that obsession with identity.

IS: Tell me about the bridge between this new Jewish faction in Latin America and the legendary tradition of Yiddish authors. I'm referring to Sholem Aleichem, I. L. Peretz, Mendele Mocher Sforim, Isaac Bashevis Singer, and the rest.

IG: That bridge cannot be generalized because it pertains to personal experience. The "boom" is a decadent tradition; Sholem Aleichem is a force that was but that has lost some of its impact. It depends on the relationship one has maintained with them: if one has read their works, if one has learned about them through the family's oral tradition. It also depends on what wants to be told. If someone wants to recreate the impact of immigration, surely he will have to turn to the literary fountain. If he wants to investigate the humor, parody, or the irony that runs through his veins, Sholem Aleichem is the place to find it, no doubt. One is not born with that humor, but rather one learns it through literature or through education.

IS: What is your point of contact with them?

IG: I had a lot of contact with them. My father didn't tell me about all of them because he wasn't schooled. Nevertheless, he told me time and time again about the experience in the shtetl. In a certain way, that was our point of unity. Reading allowed me to discover Sholem Aleichem. That village universe of Yiddish literature formed as much a part of me as Ciro Alegría or Argüedas. I began to write when I was twelve. I wrote of my experiences in my native Chepén. Without knowing it, I used elements that Yiddish writers had used. All of a sudden, the scenery of Russia found its way into my fiction. Unconsciously, I made my characters move and function in these settings. All that was pure madness. Chepén is semitropical; all of a sudden my characters were surrounded by snow. Now, all that seems funny to me.

IS: I turn now to your private life and to your everyday journeys. After being born in Peru and emigrating to Israel at age seventeen, why do you now live in New York? Why not in your own country or in Israel? Does that imply some sort of exile?

IG: It implies a sort of exile, of course. It is not a forced exile, but it is not voluntary either. Circumstances made me stay here. In Israel I met a girl from New York. We went to Peru. We planned to live there. When she gave birth, I was looking for work and was planning to study. I was either seventeen or eighteen. Our economic situation was truly catastrophic. I couldn't get any money. She had family here and suggested that we come here together. There were more opportunities here. Nevertheless, it was never in my dreams to live in the United States.

IS: Although you were never against it?

IG: No, not at all. This country, however, has not shaped my literary activity. I've been living here for twenty-one years and I haven't written a single line about New York. I think if I had stayed in Peru, I would have produced more as an author. My work has and always will have my native country and the Hebrew community that lives in it as its central theme. It's been the case that Peruvian critics have focused much more on the facet of the Hebrew question and have ignored that of the Peruvian condition. I think my novels are about Peru, with Jewish characters trying to explain their private experience, but at the same time they do have a Peruvian experience, not a Jewish one. I believe that critics have let themselves get carried away by the exotic, the innovative, without giving what I'm saying about the country the importance it deserves.

IS: I want to return to the theme of language. Above all in *Play by Play,* although also to some extent in *The Fragmented Life of Don Jacobo Lerner,* frequent allusions, as well as semantic and linguistic deformities, occur that juxtapose Spanish and Yiddish. These two languages never reach a bilingual relationship: Spanish predominates, is lord and king, while Yiddish is only a reference. What relationship exists between these two languages?

IG: For my father's generation, Yiddish was a means of returning to the womb. It was a tool used to keep certain messages secret: for example, when they didn't want the servants or a Peruvian to understand them, they used Yiddish. That's the only way they felt free to say it all. Language granted them liberty and protection simultaneously. This duality greatly affected me. My generation has lost most of that. There are scattered words in Yiddish that I'm able to remember. Those words have a magical value, almost esoteric, that sends us back to our ancestral heritage. That phenomenon unfortunately is becoming more and more rare. The old are dying. The youth learned only to understand Yiddish, not to speak it. They only recognize key phrases, pillars of their personal essence that they repeat to each other when the situation merits it. Something else occurs. Children are sent to foreign countries, be it the United States or Israel. They are replaced, those remnants of Yiddish, with the Hebrew they learn in the kibbutz or with English.

IS: How do you feel about this manipulation of language that Jews use as a protective shield?

IG: There's a type of rejection that has its roots in personal motives. In Peru, I never learned Hebrew because I got there late and all my friends had more or less learned it. I couldn't learn English ad hoc because my coworkers had been fluent six or seven years. I arrived fresh from the province without knowing the benefits of those two languages. Something similar happened to me with Yiddish. This situation cornered me, and I felt marginal, exiled from a secret code that I didn't know. I wonder if this tool is uniquely Jewish or if it is used by the indigenous people who come down from the mount and conserve their language to defend themselves from aggression. This manipulation of language is characteristic of every group and I wouldn't rob them of that sense of ownership that is so personal, so intimate. The language used isn't important but rather the purpose with which that tongue is injected, and how it is impacted by the other that comes from our blood.

IS: I imagine that is the reason why in *Play by Play* there are allusions to Quechua. Do you speak it?

IG: My grandmother does. She uses it constantly at home. When I moved to Lima, I lost it completely. For me that has always been an irreparable loss, a tragedy.

IS: Polyglotism is a Jewish trait. Your works have appeared almost simultaneously in English and Spanish, and your book of poetry *Hombre de paso/Just Passing Through* is bilingual. Should bilingualism be an attribute of every modern writer? What is your opinion on that matter?

IG: I'm not a bilingual person. My tongues are part of a tradition and not part of a double language. I've been here many years and have barely managed to learn English. I arrived in the United States with a writer's consciousness, linguistically developed and determined to keep my mother tongue. I arrived thinking that with my name, Isaac Goldemberg, and having arrived at nineteen years of age, that I would assimilate easily to this culture. And that was precisely what I tried to avoid. To conserve my Spanish, I decided to learn English only well enough to communicate, to be able to unveil myself in this society. But never to go further than that.

IS: Again language as a means of protection.

IG: Of course.

IS: How do you see the North American Jewish novel? I'm referring to Philip Roth, to Malamud, to Bellow. Because indubitably they have impacted the history of literature in this country the same way as the new Jewish faction is impacting Latin America.

IG: Neither admiration nor indifference. It's curious: they are far away from my worries. They are narrating an experience that is diametrically opposite from ours. There are similarities of course, points of unity: immigration, the provinces of identical countries, identity. But the assimilation of the Jew in the United States has been mostly toward power, even on the part of writers. Except for Grace Paley, her *Enormous Changes at the Last Minute,* our mentality is completely different from theirs. Reading Roth or Bellow, I get the impression of having before me a writer above all North American who is Jewish only by addition. That cannot happen to me with Gerchunoff, with César Tiempo. It's the fact that we have had the same experience that brings me close to them.

IS: Are you as avid a reader as you are a writer?

IG: As a child, from the time I was eleven until I was sixteen when I left Peru, I was lucky enough to have an incredibly rich library, which I inherited from one of my father's friends. Everything in Spanish translation. There was North American, Russian, German, Yiddish, and French literature. What I read was by authors as diverse as Jules Verne, Tolstoy, Maxim Gorky, Flaubert, Steinbeck, Hemingway. And I read them all without knowing they were famous worldwide. Those were simply books that could have been written by anyone. After leaving Peru, I found out about the reputation of all those names. There was Kafka, Proust, Isaac Babel. All these influences came together within me subconsciously. I didn't refer to Hemingway because someone told me that from him one can learn something. That's the way I developed as a reader, always distant from public opinion. I've seen readers who enter a bookstore and know exactly what book they want to buy: they read the first page, the second. If they like that, they take it; if not, they leave it. I prefer the kind that is not affected by premature judgments, that doesn't consider the writer simply because he is in vogue. But those readers are disappearing. More and more readers have fallen prey to the system.

IS: Would it be possible to create anonymous literature where the Spirit is the generator and not the individual, like Paul Valéry wanted?

IG: I think so.

Shipwrecked

Francisco Goldman

Francisco Goldman (USA, b. 1954) is the author of The Long Night of White Chickens *(1992) and* The Ordinary Seaman *(1997). He is also responsible for a nonfiction account of the Bishop Gerardi murder case in Guatemala. Goldman started his career as a journalist with* Harper's *and* Esquire. *This interview took place in Boston in September 2003, months before the release of Goldman's third book,* The Divine Husband *(2004).*

IS: What drew you to journalism?

FG: I left college after my junior year and moved to New York, hoping to become a fiction writer. But I found it quite difficult to find time to write. I was working in restaurants like people do. I had left school after my junior year, and I remembered that my family in Guatemala had this cottage on the lake at Amatitlán, outside the city, and I thought, I know I can save up a thousand dollars. I can go there and get together the three short stories I need to apply for a writing program. And I went down there and I was so innocent, I had no idea what was going on down there. My uncle said, "Are you crazy? You can't go live in Amatitlán. The police station there was just overrun by guerrillas a week ago." So I spent nine months living in my uncle's house in Guatemala City, working on my short stories. Miraculously when I sent them up to MFA schools, I also sent some up to *Esquire,* and they bought one and then another one. They also said to me, "Would you like to write nonfiction for the magazine?" I said I would very much like to. I'd like to go back to Central America to Guatemala and write about what I'd been seeing there. In fact, I had been absorbing kind of through osmosis, living behind "high walls" in this sort of secure middle-class Central American family and seeing this extraordinary and tragic event beginning to happen.

IS: You were born in Boston. Your father was Jewish, your mother Guatemalan.

FG: My mother is a Catholic mestiza from Guatemala.

IS: Was the Guatemalan side strong in your upbringing?

FG: Extremely . . . My mother was close to the family, and we used to go down there in the summers. I spent so much of my infancy in Central America. I actually spoke Spanish before I spoke English. I've heard tape recordings of myself back then; it's hilarious. That three year old's Spanish accent is much better than mine is now. After that we moved back to Boston but were always traveling down. My grandmother, *abuelita*, was constantly helping to take care of me in Boston; and my cousins were always coming up to school to learn English and staying in our house. The place had Jews, Guatemalans, and New Englanders all the time.

IS: What was your father's role?

FG: My father was in many ways an old-style Boston tough guy, with a pretty scary temper. He was a lot older than my mother, twenty years older practically. My grandfather had come here, as had some of my father's older siblings, before the Russian revolution. My grandfather was a socialist baker and wanted to go back to Russia once the revolution happened. But his kids had become adamantly American; they were baseball and football athletes. I was aware of what Jewish ethnicity meant, but my mother set the intimate domestic tone in that family. I was close to my Guatemalan grandmother and grandfather. My father's mother passed away before I was born, and I have only a few memories of my Russian grandfather.

IS: How did literature come about in your life? What were the early books that you read, the ones that influenced you?

FG: My father was a big reader. I used to be fascinated to come out in the morning and inspect whatever book he'd been reading, and it used to seem to me heroic, monumental, like some great feat of physical strength, that his bookmark could travel something like two hundred pages in one night. I began to pick up the books he was reading. I remember one day finding a copy of James Joyce's *Portrait of the Artist,* which is very readable in its opening chapters. I was probably ten or eleven years old and began to read it. I was completely drawn in. Then it turns into the Joyce that we know, and I couldn't hang on.

IS: Were you a sickly child?

FG: My mother will get mad at me for mentioning this. She will say: "Why do you want people to know you had tuberculosis!?! Are you proud of it!?!" Anyway, while in Guatemala I caught tuberculosis . . . So yes, that's one of the reasons we came back to Boston. New England was alien to us. My world centered on our basement. I lived my life in the basement, hanging around with the young Guatemalan woman, Felita, who was raising me.

IS: You've listed a number of American, British, and Irish authors. Were there also through your mother or through this lady that was helping to raise you some Latin American writers?

FG: I'll never forget the day I stayed home sick—it was in either 1968 or 1969. My mother was reading *A Hundred Years of Solitude* for the first time. She came in and read me part of it. The two of us were utterly transported . . .

IS: Did she read in Spanish?

FG: In Spanish . . . She was reading out loud. She said she loved it and that it was the saddest book in the world. This means she was reading it the way it's supposed to be read. People here often misread that book, thinking, oh, because magical things happen, this must be a fun, magical book. Aren't we having fun reading this book? It's wonderful, of course, but it's also an extraordinary portrait of isolation, solitude, intimate and societal, and a loving but scorching critique. But Macondo, that small village environment, brought memories back to my mother. Strong memories of a kind of Guatemalan solitude, rooted, I think, in the villages of the southern coastal lowlands, where our family originally comes from. Not from the city, but from San Lucía. In any case, it brought all these memories back to her. I've known since then that García Márquez's magic realism was made up of sadness, solitude, isolation, hermetic existences.

IS: I've seen you describe your adolescence as somewhat delinquent . . .

FG: I remember my father, the tears in his eyes saying it couldn't be more difficult, that this was the worst time to raise a kid. He'd probably just come home and found us reeking of pot or one of my friends sitting in the living room with a pint of brown-bagged bourbon on his lap, and politely saying, "Hello Mr. Goldman." In the seventies I was pretty wild. It was after the Vietnam War, or as it was ending. We were the generation whose big brothers went to the war, and that war was a very dark presence. For a lot of reasons I was conflicted. My house was so odd. It looked like an American house on the outside, except that my mother put Spanish grillwork under the windows. The whole house was kitschy, filled with stuff from Latin America. My friends called it La Copacabana. By the time I was an adolescent I mainly wanted to belong, and we were pretty wild. And I had terrible grades. My little sister was the opposite, a violinist, honor roll, and so on. But for a number of reasons, I couldn't settle into myself at all . . .

IS: Even in and through writing?

FG: Writing was probably the only thing I was good at. In fact, I used to actually sell short stories to some of my school friends, and they would pay me sometimes in cash. Many of the teachers were so skeptical of me that sometimes when I handed in a piece of writing, they didn't believe it.

IS: That you had written . . .

FG: I wrote stories for other kids. A few even sent them into the school literary magazine. But when I sent mine, they were rejected.

IS: The editors trusted them but not you.

FG: Yeah.

IS: Bring me back to the Central American war. It doesn't appear to go away . . .

FG: Absolutely . . . What drew me to it was partly literary, though. There was a kind of writer I wanted to be. I knew that to become that kind of writer, I needed to understand these two opposing forces in my life: the United States and Central America.

IS: They were clashing . . .

FG: Right. I understood, too, that the novelists I admired weren't interior, domestic realists but were writers who tried to project these big personal and historical visions, not just Gabriel García Márquez, Mario Vargas Llosa, Günter Grass. Those were the writers that influenced me at that time. The only way for me to follow them, I thought, was to throw myself into this extreme and *total* experience. Yes, I was young and adventurous. I wanted to live through a war. Of course, when I got down to Central America, I fell down a kind of hole it would take me years to find a way out of. Death, violence, injustice, rage, indignation—all those things that will stop your vain creative imaginings cold. It stopped being a learning experience and moved deeper inside me. I had to stop writing fiction because I had no idea how to turn so much pain, sadness, and anger into what is essentially a celebratory art form—as of course such writers as Grass had done.

IS: Reportage—did it have some sort of healing aspect for you?

FG: I don't think of journalism as healing. Just the opposite . . .

IS: Maybe it tears you . . .

FG: It tears you open. It forces you to confront some terrible things, and it's frustrating because I wasn't a particularly good journalist. I got better later on. You feel impotent because you're not really affecting anything. It was a learning experience: you grew as a person, you got out there, you had to overcome your own timidity, overcome your own fear.

IS: You were also the target or the victim of threats and attacks. There is mention of it in the death-squad scene in *The Long Night of White Chickens.*

FG: Where Roger and Moya, the two characters, are out walking one day, and all of a sudden there it is, like the shark fin emerging from the water that you never expected to see, the black Cherokee van pulling up beside you. What happened was I was at that time living in my late grandmother's house in Guatemala City. I was trying to get a novel going but was sharing the house with this extraordinary woman named Jean Marie Simon, who at that point was the main person down there for Amnesty International and America's Watch—very much a targeted woman. She was bringing all kinds of people into the house. Indeed, whatever was left of the urban guerilla structure was coming into the house to speak with her. I was in the role of polite host, asking, "Would you like a cup of coffee or something?" Or maybe like *Hogan's Heroes's* Sergeant Schultz: "I see nothing." Our house was under surveillance and that sort of thing, and one day we came out and there they were. They stopped the black jeep and came out, and they went to pull their weapons out of the car, and like Roger in the book, we . . . , I grabbed her by the arm and we threw ourselves down behind this row of parked ambulances. And then a bus went by, and we got up and we ran using the bus a shield and jumped on the bus, and they immediately got back into the black jeep and went shooting like a rocket through red lights. The thing that always just amazed me, and I put that in the book too, is I had to go to the U.S. embassy to report it, and when I got there the counsul already knew about it. He said to me: "If they had wanted to, they could have splattered you like tomato sauce all over the sidewalk. It was what we call a heavy-handed tail meant to send a message." The message: Get out of the country! At this point Jean Marie moved to a safer place, but I had no money. That's why when you read *The Long Night of White Chickens*, you see those alarms all over the house, where he had milk bottles under every window and he has a rope out the back window in case he has to flee—that was how I was living.

IS: *The Long Night of White Chickens* appeared in 1992. *The Ordinary Seaman* in 1997. *The Divine Husband* in 2004. There is almost a seven-year interval between them.

FG: I come back like a plague.

IS: I'd like to hear your thoughts on the novel as a form and how you embrace and shape a novel. About the time it takes you to put the story together, to intertwine the research.

FG: There's a great Flaubert line, somewhere, where he said the true form of a novel only appears once the illusion of the subject has become an obsession. The form is organic. It only emerges when you utterly believe the world you've created and entered. You don't impose the form on the book; the fiction imposes the form, and it's a search for that form.

IS: Does the form exist previously and is just waiting for you to discover it?

FG: Perhaps, yes. However mystical, you can only get to it through hard work.

IS: To get to it, does one embark on research, permitting the facts and story to coalesce?

FG: You go through writing with your entire being, with your body, with your senses. It's all intuitive: you enter into this world of these characters, a synthetic world you've created. And it's crucial to learn to listen intimately for what comes next. *The Divine Husband*, for example. I came to what I knew would be the last fifth of the book, and I said, Oh my God, you haven't given any thought to how this book is supposed to end! I had a terrible panic. I imagined that after five years of hard work it was all going to fall apart. It was this process of just having to keep writing and thinking and dwelling. And almost like meteors coming out of God knows where into your mind, the solutions started coming, one after another: this leads to this and to this—all of it seeming inevitable. To me this is the most miraculous part of writing a novel: the way so much of what happens really does come from somewhere other than your conscious mind. It comes out of what you've already written in all those preceding pages, but in ways you could never have predicted. So how do you lay the groundwork for that? Sure, research, research, research. *The Divine Husband* took years of research, and I think sometimes that some of the most creative work I did on that book was in the research, much of it long before I began writing. Because it's historical, and involves José Martí.

IS: It's a novel that spans from the late nineteenth century into the twentieth century. Martí, the Cuban writer and revolutionary, plays a role.

FG: He's an important character.

IS: It's also about Guatemala and the United States.

FG: I was drawn to José Martí when I realized that he had spent sixteen decisive months of his life as a very young man in Guatemala City and then goes on to New York City where he spends really the rest of his adulthood—fifteen, sixteen years in New York City. The way the book even began was, at a certain point I almost broke down after *The Long Night of White Chickens*. The war, which had framed my life for so many years, had ended, and so had much else in my life. In a way, I had become that writer who just wanted to play in his basement and live in his little fantasy world. I'd been taken out into this world of hard politics and hard things and something in me retreated. I started just going into the Guatemalan archives, the Guatemala City archives. At one point, I spent a whole month there, every day just reading nineteenth-century newspapers. It was an escape into the past. The library there is so underfunded that in the *hemeroteca*, where they archive newspapers, there weren't even light bulbs; you had to sit by the window to read. It was biblical; it rained twenty-eight straight days. I had never had asthma in my life, but from the fungus on these old newspapers, all of a sudden I got this terrible asthma. Ironically, only by going to live in Mexico City, with its gloriously polluted air, which scours your lungs clean, was I able to recover. Anyway, I immersed myself in that world. What I got from it was, well . . . seemingly useless knowledge. I knew where every brick had been in nineteenth-century Guatemala. But who cares? It could only be good for a novel.

IS: You had to go through a long tunnel in order to finally see the light. So once you've concluded a novel, once all the pieces of the puzzle are in place, what happens? There must be some sense of exhilaration, of freedom . . .

FG: It's different every time. When I finished the first novel, it was like a kind of collapse.

IS: Physical collapse?

FG: So much of my life had ended. A marriage had ended. This war in Central America, which defined my existence for eleven, twelve years ended. This first novel that had consumed me for almost a decade, a real fight against my own limitations, against my inexperience as a writer and so on, had ended. All of a sudden I felt empty and stranded. That is how my second book, *The Ordinary Seaman*, emerged.

IS: Its plot is about a group of shipwrecked sailors.

FG: From Central America, mainly Nicaragua, in a ship stranded in Brooklyn Harbor.

IS: A beautiful image . . .

FG: I myself felt shipwrecked at the time. I put off writing *The Divine Husband*, at least temporarily. By then I was overwhelmed by the amount of research it was going to take.

IS: But you've been designed to do it—a mission.

FG: Yeah. Hopefully the next book will come faster.

IS: The novel has been with us as a cultural expression for over four hundred years. Where are we now with it, and how do you perceive its aging process?

FG: It's such an intimate form of human expression. It will be with us forever.

IS: Can you imagine the world without it?

FG: No, I can't. People write novels with a lot of conviction, partly because we're in a moment of incredible transformation on so many fronts.

IS: Religious?

FG: The way the inner life has changed, for example. Our inner life is changed by the way the world outside is changing, where everything is faster and speeded up, becoming more interconnected or whatever. All those accelerating pressures out there, I think, create a desire, at least in certain types of people who are fiction writers and poets, to interpret it, to answer it, to slow it down, to create something out of that interior space where the cameras can't go.

IS: And so the novel is the form where we can do that . . . ?

FG: The novel is one of the forms and still I think the most vital form for that, that interior journey which connects our most intimate existence and understanding of ourselves to what's going on outside ourselves.

IS: You said we couldn't live without the novel. What would a world without it be like?

FG: Our sense of existence would lack so much eloquence. It would be so superficial; we wouldn't have the idea anymore that we can slow down and spend weeks and weeks and weeks trying to comprehend or imagine this mystery of human life, not just our life but other lives. If there's anything reliably political about the novel, it's that it's an exercise in acknowledging the existence of lives separate from our own. It's really the only thing that can save the world: imagining and acknowledging other people's existences, and understanding that we're all sharing the planet and depend on each other and can't afford to trivialize each other's existence. Fiction can lead us into that journey.

Words and Music

Oscar Hijuelos

Oscar Hijuelos (New York, b. 1951) is the author of Our House in the Last World *(1983),* The Mambo Kings Play Songs of Love *(1989),* The Fourteen Sisters of Emilio Montez O'Brien *(1993),* Mr. Ives' Christmas *(1995),* Empress of the Splendid Season *(1999), and* A Simple Habana Melody *(2002). This interview took place in Manhattan in May 1989, shortly before Hijuelos won the Pulitzer Prize for* The Mambo Kings.

IS: Were you schooled in Spanish?

OH: I spoke in Spanish until I was four years old when I still lived in Holguín, Cuba. It was then that I became ill with nephrosis. I was sick and I was taken to the United States to a hospital in Connecticut. I was hospitalized for a year. I entered the hospital speaking Spanish and left it speaking English. The nurse that took care of me was a strong and strict Protestant. I complained, asked her for medicine, an aspirin. She paid no attention to me. I would scream and cry . . . "Please help me!" When I finally made the same supplication in English, she heeded my request. It was with her that I learned English. That's how I remember my linguistic transition, although truth be told, I doubt that the nurse even existed and that that memory is real. It is possible that my imagination simply went rampant. I do know, though, that from then on I only spoke to my parents in English, and they would answer me in Spanish. I've an older brother who is an artist who speaks a fluent Spanish even though he often makes mistakes. I've lost mine. I can repeat some curse words and romantic lines—nothing more. That year, my family crumbled. It was terrible. Upon returning home, we were all strangers. Even so, I think my parents were still in awe of the fact that I had survived my illness through a simple switch to the American universe. From then on, they saw me as being higher up on the social ladder. It was their understanding that I had the advantages of the civilized world at my feet.

IS: Are your parents artists?

OH: My mother was a housekeeper in Oriente. *Our House in the Last*

World, an autobiographical work, is about her in Cuba, pre-Castro. She is an intelligent and gifted woman who was oppressed and never had the opportunity to apply herself. She is seventy-five years old. She's lived through seventy-five years times five. That's what she says. Did she manifest her creativity in any way? Yes. She wrote poetry, which she never published. In these last couple of months, I've recompiled her poems. I'm editing them with the aim to publish them. She was an extraordinary poet at nineteen, a rare avis who belonged to that naturalist movement, which was dead when she was a little girl. My maternal grandfather was a poet too, as well as a diplomat, a Catalan who traveled to Cuba in 1896 and settled in Oriente. His misfortune was having received an inheritance. He enjoyed himself for three or four years and then he met my mother and started a family. Once they had children, they returned to the island and, disappointed, they came to New York. My father was manic-depressive. His experience with marriage was not good: my mother was fed up and got carried away by spiritualism; he became *abúlico* and reserved. For thirty years, he kept two jobs, and one day, he dropped dead. He drank too much, and he lost all his money. When he died, the family was left with nothing. He died when I was seventeen, and his death greatly impacted me. I had to go out and get a job so that I could support my mother. My brother and I lived in an environment that could have turned us into criminals and drug addicts. I was a servant on 118th Street, in Harlem and the Bronx.

IS: Do you have any feelings toward Cuba?

OH: I often wonder what would have happened to me had I been born fifty years earlier. Would I have been like my father—a good-natured, but tragic, man . . .

IS: Did you read a lot as a child?

OH: Because I was always sick, I spent my days in the house, writing. I only read comic books, the newspaper, or my mother's poetry—she asked me to comment on her poems aloud. I was her editor. And once, having written my commentary, one of the nuns at the local school, who had read what I had written, predicted that I would be a writer. That prophesy, I think, directed my future. She told my mother I had a special talent for "describing nature and human emotions." I didn't start writing seriously until I was twenty-four or twenty-five, that is to say, quite late.

IS: How?

OH: Through the theater. At that time, I was married to an actress and I wanted to write her dramatic scenes. I imitated O'Neill, Tennessee Williams, and Arthur Miller. At the same time, I was in workshops at City College. I was an avid writer; I would shake every time I finished a page. I loved to concoct words. But upon realizing that no one, including my wife, was interested in my work, I decided to abandon the genre and concentrate on the novel and the short story. I learned, during that time, to recognize bad literature. Writing fiction, in contrast with writing for the theater, is a passive act—there are more alternatives for expression and it has a descriptive dimension. Then, I made my living as a musician. Because I never made enough as a writer, until now, I played with jazz and rock bands in bars and cabarets, The Latin Band del Bronx, for example, for seven or eight years. I still do that from time to time. I play the guitar. I have about eight guitars, the majority from Seville. I don't know how to read music . . . I do it by ear.

IS: What can you tell me about Susan Sontag and Donald Barthelme, your teachers in the creative writing program at City College. It was around 1974 and 1975, was it not?

OH: Yes. It was Barthelme who taught me to read. Once, while revising one of my texts, he called me in and said to me, "Read this, this, and this . . ." He gave me some ten novels and books of short stories. I didn't know who he was, nor did I know the authors he suggested. He liked me and I allowed him to mold me. He introduced me to Borges, to García Márquez, to Cortázar—writers in vogue during that insipid decade, or perhaps it was just a bit outmoded. Had I had a teacher less well versed, my progress would have been hindered. The experiences of Hijuelos the reader directly influenced those of Hijuelos the writer. Joseph Heller was also my teacher, but he lacked the charisma and the wisdom of Barthelme. Remember that he and John Barth, with his minimalist art, formed a bridge between my generation in the United States and the literature of Latin America, South Africa, and "marginal" authors like V. S. Naipaul and Czeslaw Milosz.

IS: He had already published *Come Back, Dr. Caligari* and *Unspeakable Practices, Unnatural Acts,* both critically acclaimed. His style and yours, nevertheless, are different. He is a short story writer interested in details; you are a novelist interested in ethnic realism.

OH: In his class I wrote short stories. My mother's spiritualism—*espiritismo*—influenced them. They emerged as imitations of García Márquez, replete with eroticism, exoticism, and magic. I sent them to a university magazine that never published them. I did publish a couple of avant-garde pieces that I now detest. One of them is entitled "Columbus Discovering America": in one of the ships, the crew of the Spanish-Italian admiral mutiny against him. It's 1492, he asks them to calm down, assuring them that soon they will see extraordinary things—the New York Mets, the Empire State Building, etc. Can you imagine? It was "pop art" that destroyed the barriers of logic and reality—an atrocity.

IS: "To become a writer, one must write, and write, and write . . . relentlessly," Barthelme used to say.

OH: I followed his advice to the T. I have piles and piles of manuscripts, some incoherent. I wrote many versions; I had a lot of energy and anxiety.

IS: And Sontag.

OH: With Sontag, I took a course on fiction that as far as I know was the only one offered. She is the most brilliant person, the most intelligent, most critical person that I know. She commented on the errors in my narrations; she pointed out the weaknesses. She liked my texts, which now I think are morbid.

IS: When is it possible to date the emergence of your present style, so terse, dynamic, flexible, imbued with descriptions and intent on giving dimension to emotions?

OH: In *Our House in the Last World.* The first novel I wrote was based on a tour guide in Cuba in 1902, which I found in a library, from which I took portions and parodied them. It ended up being a manuscript of one thousand pages that in an attack of fury I almost threw out. For years, I thought my writings were horrible, that no one wanted to read them. I suffer from immense insecurity, which borders on depression. Before *Our House,* I wrote two novels. I still have one hundred pages of the first one (I remember a single phrase: "There are no mosquitoes"), and the second survives intact, written à la Marguerite Yourcenar. Upon so much effort wasted, I forged my style. Today, I can recognize myself in a single phrase or describe the movement of my words.

IS: Is there something "Cuban" in your style?

OH: The emotional tone, what you call the dimension of emotions.

I've always associated the Cuban with human suffering; from there I base characters who suffer a great deal. Why? Perhaps because I went to public school, lived in public housing, and my first pair of glasses was bought with money from public welfare. I felt like a second-rate citizen, and that is the source of my insecurity. The majority of critics, I was sad to admit, didn't understand *The Mambo Kings*. Of fifty critiques, only two or three actually discuss the book. I have one that opens with "As good as chuchifritos, as tasty as arroz con pollo . . . ," the *New York Times Book Review,* for example. I'm proud of being the first Cuban American to appear on the front page, but the critic didn't understand anything to my liking. He discusses sociology, the novel as "a mosaic of struggle of the immigrants." Little, if at all, of the emotions, of the language. People want stereotypes, which is frustrating because I work my phrases, I polish them . . . who cares? Have you ever heard of Danny Santiago? A writer in Los Angeles who won awards with a novel about Chicanos, and in the end it turned out that his real name was Daniel James, a neurotic evading the CIA and hiding his identity under a Hispanic facade. Santiago thrilled his audience with stereotypes. Can you believe that? What is "Chicano" or "Cuban" is something deeper than that, a secret reality. I'm giving a conference about Santiago at the Smithsonian in 1990. He died a year ago, right? Before writing his "Chicano novel" he wrote movie scripts that can be categorized in the "monster movie" genre. One is called *The Giant Behemoth,* the other *Gorgo.* Can you imagine? He went from writing about monsters to Chicanos. I know that soon the United States will look on Hispanic letters as an aesthetic, well, the same way the Jew was discovered as a writer forty years ago. I also know that this is a country without a soul. Its soul is obviously based on minorities, considered parasites by the majority, that feeling being the only unifying factor.

IS: How much time did you put into *The Mambo Kings Play Songs of Love?*

OH: Six years. After publishing *Our House in the Last World,* I spent some time in Italy where I wrote a little bit. It was the first time I traveled in the Old Continent, and I was in Madrid for my thirty-fourth birthday. I spent it in bars, with women, traveling to Africa, Turkey, all of Europe. After returning to New York, I had serious financial problems. I began to write, but I was never confident in my writing. It took me some five years to accumulate notes, write drafts, and sell the book on the basis of 120 pages. The printing house gave me two months to finish it, publicizing it in their fall 1989 catalog. I'm a quick writer, though disorganized. I had to rely on prior versions, make a collage, create a coherent narrative. From its eccentric fluidity the final draft emerged. The deadlines were a good motivating force; otherwise I would have fallen into depression.

IS: Does that book have an autobiographical element?

OH: Yes. I would have liked to be a Cuban musician in New York in the 1940s. Eugenio, the boy who watches his father and his uncle perform his mambos on *I Love Lucy* with Desi Arnàz and who wishes things would have turned out differently, is Oscar Hijuelos. Furthermore, there's also a dream that inspired me: I suffer, like my father did, from a unique type of skin disease. When I get upset, my arms and my cheeks break out. When I wrote *Our House in the Last World*, I was so upset with myself for my inability to improve certain sections that these miserable eruptions appeared. Then, I had a dream. I dreamt that I saw my father in a river. He had been dead some ten years. He called me and I walked toward him. He told me that the water would cure my infection. It was true. I bathed in the river current, and I was cured. In the novel, Eugenio goes to Desi Arnaz's house wishing to alleviate his symptoms, and the house reminds him of Cuba, bringing him back to his roots . . .

IS: Is there a writer who influenced you in a negative way?

OH: Borges and Barthelme, if any. I think that at times I write like them. Or better, it is they who write through me. There's a section in *The Mambo Kings Play Songs of Love* that is Borgesian—when Néstor is agonizing, I say that "he examined the intricacies of time . . ." It is an homage, and there are others to Barthelme—above all, the drums.

IS: What is your method for writing?

OH: I haven't written in months. These intervals are frequent. I write a lot during six months and then nothing. When I do, I wake up early, excited and full of energy, I eat a light breakfast, and I sit down in front of the typewriter. A manual typewriter, not electric, not a word processor. I never had the money to buy something sophisticated, so I grew accustomed to my old Olivetti. I write until I get tired—eight, nine uninterrupted hours, seven days a week. I prefer to work in the morning. It makes me happy to start at 7:30 or 8:00 A.M. and finish by 6:00 or 6:30

P.M. I don't answer the phone, and I eat whatever I can find in the refrigerator. If I'm getting fed up, I go exercise—running, weights. I walk around the house, look through other books and read good literature to distract myself. By the end, I'm exhausted. Inspiration never comes in hotels, in a stranger's office, or at a university. I need to have my own space. Though, I can make notes in buses or airplanes. I've gone to writing colonies. I like their social atmosphere, but I can never write well; my texts turn out auto-conscious. I never go to cocktail parties. I don't think the writer's life should be glamorous—it's rather a torment, like childbirth.

Critic at Large

Luis Leal

Luis Leal (Linares, Nuevo León, Mexico, b. 1907) is the author of, among other books, Mariano Azuela *(1967),* Breve historia de la literatura hispano-americana *(1971), and* Juan Rulfo *(1983). Leal taught at a number of major U.S. campuses, among them the University of California at Santa Barbara. Conducted in English, this interview took place in Santa Barbara, June 2003. A* Luis Leal Reader *was published in 2005.*

IS: How do you define the role of the critic?

LL: The principal role of the critic should be to analyze and judge literary works; to inform the reading public of the existence of those works, their content, and their values; to formulate theories about that literature; and to establish a canon, that is, lists of readings. However, the Latino critic in the U.S. has some added roles to perform: to recover the literary inheritance of Latinos, and to correct false judgments expressed about that literature. Also, to train future critics.

IS: What is the function of criticism in a democracy?

LL: Without general criticism, democracy could not survive; or rather, without the liberty to criticize, democracy would be impossible. In a dictatorship, of the Right or the Left, the absence of criticism is essential for the dictator to remain in power. Without criticism, progress could not be made in any intellectual fields such as scientific endeavors, higher education, and even the arts and literature. To maintain a democracy, critics must remain free to express their opinions. Censorship is anti-democratic. Literary criticism helps to maintain a free society.

IS: In their history, the Americas have lived through miserable periods of tyranny. Has criticism had any role in those periods? Or better, could it have done anything to prevent human misery?

LL: In the history of Latin America, since the nineteenth century, there have been numerous periods when the nations have lived under tyrannical governments. The most important reason for their existence has been the absence of criticism. Critics had no role during those periods because they have been exiled, and therefore unable to practice any criticism. Some, however, have done it from exile, as was the case during the rule of Porfirio Díaz in Mexico, who was criticized by exiled intellectuals living in the United States.

IS: Is criticism compatible with academia? Doesn't the comfort of the campus and a tenured job undermine the urgency of criticism as such?

LL: I believe that criticism is compatible with academia. If it were not, the centers of higher learning, as we know them today, would not exist. They would be simple institutions dedicated to indoctrinate the students. It is for this reason that academics should not take advantage of the tenure system, which protects them to be free to express their ideas. Professors who take refuge in academia to enjoy comforts do not belong in the profession. Conscientious critics in academia do not neglect their most important duty, which is to teach the students to develop a critical attitude.

IS: Literary theory was imported into American colleges and universities in the 1960s. To some, its effect was devastating. What are the contributions it has granted us?

LL: If students are trained to develop a critical attitude, it is assumed that they will put in practice what they learned. There is no problem regarding criticism other than political. And as I have already stated, political criticism is essential in a democracy.

IS: When you began your career as a critic, who were your role models?

LL: I was fortunate to have had excellent role models. As an undergraduate, I had as a model Professor Roberto Brenes Mesén, a poet and diplomat from Costa Rica also known as a critic. The principal lesson I learned from him was to try to practice a criticism based on Latin American concepts, as he had done in his book *Crítica americana*. As a graduate student at the University of Chicago I also had excellent role models: Amado Alonso, Germán Arciniegas, Joan Corominas, Giuseppe Borgese were the principal. Alonso, with his book on the poetry of Pablo Neruda, opened for me new perspectives in literary criticism. Arciniegas made me conscious of the importance of Latin American history, Corominas of the Spanish language, and Borgese of the evils of fascism and the values of democracy.

IS: How about non-Hispanic role models, figures in the European and American landscape?

LL: To the Italian Borgese, already mentioned, I want to add the name of the anthropologist M. J. Herskovits, with whom I also studied. The principal influence on my development by non-Hispanics has been through readings. The non-Hispanic authors that have influenced me the most have been the Europeans Plato, Epictetus, Dante, Voltaire, Dostoyevsky, Russell, Whitehead, and Lévi-Strauss, and the Americans Henry Adams and Waldo Frank.

IS: It has been said that Latin America lacks a critical tradition.

LL: I don't agree with the idea of a lack of a critical tradition in Latin America. It is easy to deny something with which we are not acquainted. Criticism in Latin America has always existed, but for several reasons its history has not been made known outside of the region. This may be due to the fact that there are numerous nations with different histories, cultures, literatures, and, of course, critics. Critics have always existed in Latin America, beginning with Andrés Bello, and following with Domingo Faustino Sarmiento, Eugenio María de Hostos, José Martí, José Enrique Rodó, José Carlos Mariátegui, Pedro Henríquez Ureña, Alfonso Reyes, Octavio Paz, Carlos Fuentes, to name only the most important, the ones who have contributed the most in the establishment of a Latin American critical tradition.

IS: How then would you compare the role of criticism in the U.S. vis-à-vis the Hispanic, French, and Portuguese Americas? And if Latin America lacks a critical tradition, it is fair to assume that the U.S. also comes to the so-called melting pot with this "absence." Might they be able to overcome it sometime?

LL: As in the case of Latin America, in the case of Latinos in the U.S. the common belief that there's an absence of a critical tradition is the result of the lack of studies demonstrating its presence. Latino critics in the U.S. have existed since the nineteenth century. The several books published in Philadelphia by Félix Varela early during that century were all dedicated to criticism, as are those of Lorenzo de Zavala, Father José Antonio Martínez, and Mariano Guadalupe Vallejo. During the twentieth century literary criticism has been the subject of Aurelio M. Espinosa, Américo Paredes, María Teresa Babín, David Carrasco, Norma Alarcón, and a number of others.

The problem is not the lack of criticism, but the approaches used by Latino critics. Since most of the younger critics are educated in departments of English, there they learn a methodology based on European and Anglo-American criticism, since most of these younger critics are not acquainted with Hispanic letters. This trend will perhaps predominate in the future, unless the Spanish departments wake up to the existence of a Latino literature in the U.S. and incorporate its study in their programs. The excuse for not studying it is that it is written in English. However, the new trend of mainstream publishers is to publish editions simultaneously in English and Spanish. As a result of that English training, the tendency is to analyze literary works applying European methodologies and interpreting the contents of the texts based on European culture.

IS: I'm curious about Amado Alonso and want you to talk to me more about his legacy. How would you describe his style of criticism? Has it been eclipsed by more fashionable trends today?

LL: Alonso was one of the great teachers of his time. He was a philologist, a literary critic who went from his native Spain to the University of Buenos Aires as director of the Instituto de Filología. Several well-known scholars (Pedro Henríquez Ureña, Raimundo Lida, Marcos Morínigo, etc.) worked under his direction and published outstanding books on linguistics and literary criticism, making the Instituto the leading research center in Latin America. In 1941 the University of Chicago offered him a doctorate honoris causa, and he taught there that year, when I had the opportunity to study under his direction. For political reasons Alonso left Argentina and went to Mexico, where he established and directed the Nueva Revista de Filología Hispánica at the UNAM. From there he went to Harvard, where he taught until the year of his death. Alonso's criticism differed from that of his contemporaries in that he rejected the predominant positivist approach and dealt directly with the text from the perspective of the relations between its structure and its contents. Since the forties, of course, many approaches to the study of literary texts have come and gone. Alonso, however, was a pioneer of what came to be known as New Criticism.

IS: Equally, I want to hear about Germán Arciniegas. The new generation of critics seems to have little knowledge of his oeuvre.

LL: The Colombian critic, historian, essayist, diplomat, and professor Germán Arciniegas died in Bogotá in November 1999, six days before his hundredth birthday. During his long life he published hundreds of articles and more than seventy books, some of them considered classics in the history of the Latin American essay. One of his favorite themes was the cultural and historical relation between Europe and Latin America. Some of his most popular books are *América, tierra firme* (1944), *América mágica* (1955), and *América en Europa* (1975). Because of his criticism of the military and the dictators, Arciniegas had to live in exile most of his life. In the United States he lived from 1942 to 1960, as a professor at Columbia University. He is considered one of the most prestigious Latin American intellectuals.

IS: You've mentioned Octavio Paz, Alfonso Reyes, and Pedro Henríquez Ureña. Only the last had a strong presence in the American academy. He even delivered the Charles Eliot Norton Lectures at Harvard. Paz too delivered the Norton lectures, but he was more of an interloper in colleges and universities north of the Rio Grande. Could you compare for me their styles and ponder their legacy?

LL: Alfonso Reyes and Pedro Henríquez Ureña belong to an earlier school of criticism. They were members of the Ateneo de la Juventud, a group of intellectuals that rejected positivism, which had been the philosophy held by the so-called *científicos,* the advisers of the dictator Porfirio Díaz. As a result of the revolution of 1910–1920, the groups disbanded, Reyes going to Spain and Henríquez Ureña to Minnesota, where he completed a doctorate in linguistics with a dissertation that became a classic in the study of Hispanic poetry. When José Vasconcelos was named secretary of education in 1920, he recalled Henríquez Ureña, who remained in Mexico a short time before going to Buenos Aires to work with Alonso. Octavio Paz, on the other hand, represents a later generation and a different type of literary criticism, as has already been stated. In 1968, because of the events that took place in Tlatelolco, Paz resigned his ambassadorship to India and went to France, and from there went to the University of Texas before returning to Mexico. As you have said, he delivered the Norton lectures at Harvard, just like Henríquez Ureña had done earlier. The two, however, have quite different approaches to the analysis of literature, Ureña being more interested in the historical aspect and Paz in the analytic, his criticism being much more comprehensive since he includes art and other intellectual fields.

IS: Let's return to the issue of Latino criticism. Is there tension between Chicano and Latino critics? Do these two emerge from different subtraditions?

LL: As far as I know there are no tensions between Chicano and Latino critics. The committee of the U.S.–Hispanic Recovery Project at the University of Houston, of which I am a member, is made up of critics from all the Latino subgroups, and we always have harmonious meetings. The Chicano group, of course, was the first to emerge, since Chicanos have been here since 1848. The other groups are of more recent origin, the Cubans and Puerto Ricans being perhaps the next group to have emerged, followed by the Central Americans, and finally the South Americans. Of great influence in the emergence of these groups has been the size of the communities they represent.

IS: What kind of role, if any, does criticism have in the community?

LL: It could be said that Latino criticism is almost exclusively preoccupied with the community. Most of the books in literary criticism now available give emphasis to the relations of literature to the community. As a matter of fact, the Chicano novelist and administrator Tomás Rivera in 1980 read here at the University of California, Santa Barbara, a paper that we later published entitled "Chicano Literature: The Establishing of Community," in which he argues that Chicano literature has expressed the urge and desire to establish the community, myth, and language of the Chicano ethnic group. I believe that that statement could be extended to cover Latino literature.

IS: Over a long and fruitful career, you've produced hundreds of articles on Hispanic letters north and south of the Rio Grande. You've also written a history of Latin American literature and of one of its dominant genres: the short story. I'm curious, were you ever tempted to produce a *Breve historia de la literatura chicana?* And how about a similar one on Latino letters?

LL: Yes, the temptation has been great, and as a mater of fact some time ago I began to write one, which I have never finished due to the urgency to write other things. Since there are two or three histories already available, there is no urgency to write one more. And I have written long articles about it, one of them having appeared in a history of Latin American literature. And, of course, a collection of thirty-seven essays edited by you, Ilan, under the title *The Luis Leal Reader,* will be available. I also have a manuscript, almost complete, about the Chicano short story, a genre which has not been studied.

IS: Some today talk of the modality of "critics as superstars," personalities whose charisma and oeuvre is at center stage. Is this a positive development?

LL: This may be true perhaps more of Latin American critics than U.S. critics, although there have been some superstars like Edmund Wilson. But in the English-speaking world the critic is not regarded as highly as in Latin America, where it has a long tradition, beginning with Sarmiento, Rodó, Hostos, Martí, Justo Sierra, Alfonso Reyes, Paz, and Monsiváis.

IS: How, in your eyes, will the role of critics change in this century—will there be new, as of now unknown, challenges?

LL: It will be a miracle if in the future there are no new challenges. One of the characteristics of criticism is that it is in constant change. And I don't think that this is going to change in the future.

The Ventriloquist

John Leguizamo

John Leguizamo (Bogotá, Colombia, b. 1964) is in the cast of Casualties of War *(1989),* Carlito's Way *(1993),* William Shakespeare's Romeo and Juliet *(1996),* King of the Jungle *(2001), and* Moulin Rouge *(2001). His monologues are* Mambo Mouth *(1991),* Spic-O-Rama *(1993), and* Freak: A Semi-Demi-Quasi-Pseudo-Autobiography *(1998). This interview took place in Boston, Massachusetts, March 2002.*

IS: How do you choose your characters? Who are they? Where do they come from?

JL: I do one-man shows because I've always loved it. I always felt like it was the most personal, the most intimate medium that exists between film, between television. There's no other medium like it because the audience is right there, you're right there. And it's your thoughts, your feelings, the things you want to put forth. So I've always loved it. And big influences in my life have been Lily Tomlin, Eric Bogosian, and Whoopi Goldberg. They were huge influences on me because they were the ones before me. And I took a little bit from each one of them and then changed it to my way.

And I guess I always did a lot of characters, a lot of voices, because I grew up in Jackson Heights, Queens, which is like the biggest melting pot of America (at least that's what *New York* magazine said). And I grew up with all Indian people around me. All the time all my friends are Indian. And then of course we had the nice Jewish folks around the corner. Well, everybody was their little bobola, little schmuckola. And I had all those voices all the time. I wasn't just hearing voices (I do that too), but they were always around me. I always wanted to imitate it. We'd make fun of each other. It was part of the letting go of tension.

IS: Ever since you were a little boy? Have you been impersonating people since you were little?

JL: Since I was little. Because my parents had accents, I was always making fun of them. Because when you come to this country, everybody wants to be the same. You don't want any difference. You know I'd be embarrassed of my parents because they spoke like this. They had thick Spanish accents. I was kind of embarrassed when I was six years old.

IS: And how do you come to shape a show?

JL: My shows have different geneses. It depends. It depends where I'm at in my life: what the theme is going to be, what the story is going to be. And a lot of it also shapes itself. Sometimes, I don't know what I want to say. I have a big picture, but then the show kind of dictates. And subconscious stuff comes out that tells me, Wow . . . this is my issue, something I'm working through that I wasn't even aware of. And I guess *Mambo Mouth,* my first show, it was monologues. And it was a lot of costumes and props and big sets. It was expensive. And it was a neighborhood and they were slightly related. And I just did the Japanese guy because . . . it just came to me. I saw a lot of Japanese seminars and America was—Japanese were at the top of their market in business. And I just felt like Latin people should skip trying to be white and trying to be American. Just try to be Japanese, go for the gold, you know. And that was kind of an attack on, sort of Latin self-hate and racism in America. And all the things that I felt like I had to deal with and I see Latin people having to deal with.

IS: And do you have everything ready, even written down, before opening night, or does the show even after opening night keep on changing? Does it depend on the audience, how it changes? A person that sees the show, say, on day one, will see the same show on day ten? I assume it's different.

JL: It changes a lot. My shows go through a similar process. Basically, I write it all down. I have it in my head for a long time and then I write every day. And then I have collected anecdotes and then I type it all in my computer, like *niiiiiih,* like a mad nerd, you know? Until it's all like perfect and I'm just ready to show it. And then I show it to my friends. Then, when I pass that, then I go to my family.

IS: Do you get feedback from them?

JL: I ask questions. I say "Tell me—you're my friends. Be honest, you know, I can take it." Unfortunately, they listen to me and they tell me honestly what they think. And it's pretty harsh.

IS: Does the audience also shape a particular show? A single night you might get an audience that is different from another night, and does that have an impact on how that performance goes?

JL: If I get a rowdy audience, then I'm going to be wilder. I'm going to be trying to control them a little bit too. And the serious moments aren't going to be as serious, because they're not going to sit through it. And then when I've a quiet, serious audience, I'm not as rowdy. And I get kind of angry, and you're going to see a more hostile John Leguizamo. But that's all right because that's what theater is—it's whatever I'm feeling that night is right. That's what teaches you how to be a real actor. You know because you have to deal with so many different variables. And you learn that the choices are infinite, and that's when good acting starts to happen.

IS: When you are in some of these monologues and in one of them that I saw you are talking to somebody else and reacting . . . the audience doesn't hear the other voice, only yours, but one can see in your face, in your body movement, that there's another person out there. Do you see that other person? And do you see also how you are being perceived by the audience? What do you see in your head?

JL: Do I see anything? If I'm hearing voices? I'm very "method," right? Which is a good thing. I studied with Lee Strasberg for a day and then he died the next day. I did a sense memory object. And you just try to vision . . . it was all about taking things that aren't there. And you work at home with an object and you try to make it come to life. (It's going to become extremely—hey you know, I'm teaching acting here.) But you know you try to feel it and see it and visualize it. And I was doing that in Lee Strasberg's class. And you make some "aahhhhh." And Lee started going, "Try a little harder. You're not working hard enough." He had a windpipe problem. And then he perished the next day.

But it was important to me because when I go on stage, I try to prepare like that. I try to be able to see all the people I'm talking to, the places I'm in, the objects that I'm holding. I try to see it, feel it, smell it. And when I'm on my game, I'm all those people. And all those people are there and I'm in those places. I'm not aware of the audience. I'm not aware of myself. It just happens.

IS: Is there ever a problem of you disappearing and the character taking over fully? Losing sense of reality?

JL: In a good way. I can still come in and take over. I can still as myself come back. It's not like—I'm not crazy. That's the difference between crazy and creativity. They can't stop it; I have control. I could still come back and be rational. I can let it go and watch it and then come back and pull it back and be myself again, when I need to. Certainly when I do movies and I'm a character, the same character for a long time, it seeps into your life. You can't help it. Like when I did *Summer of Sam*, and I was doing all the research, I started getting paranoid at home. I couldn't sleep at night, I kept thinking people were trying to kill me.

IS: How so?

JL: You know, coming after me all the time. And it just started to seep into my life. It was creepy because I would hear noises and I would run out of bed and see what's going on. I had a lead pipe underneath my bed. I put all the alarms on every night.

IS: Do you prefer theater to cinema? To film? Is it better to have the audience? Is that what you were saying at the beginning?

JL: There's no comparison, man. The magic of theater is something. When theater is good, it is the best thing in the world. But when it sucks, it is the worst thing in the world. Which, you know, is tough, but to me theater is magic. It's like a religious event. It's an incredible vibe that happens. You don't get it in the movies. Movies, it's still a director's medium. You're not as proactive. It's kind of a passive sport. Theater is much more active. You got to go in there. The audience has to use their imagination. They have to listen. But they can participate, and what they do is going to affect the way I perform.

IS: Most of the theater that you have done has been in the form of monologues. Have you done theater of ensemble with other people, and is that different from doing the monologue?

JL: What are you trying to say—people don't want to work with me?

IS: I was asking you . . .

JL: Why . . . am I working alone? I did *Ice Age* by myself or something.

IS: But you have enough people on stage by yourself alone. But have you worked with other people in theater on stage?

JL: I've done a lot of plays before . . . It's just a different gig and I love it. I did *A Midsummer Night's Dream* and ruined Shakespeare for a lot of people at the Joseph Papp Theater with F. Murray Abraham, Elizabeth Montgomery, and Fisher Stevens. And I did *La Puta Vida*, Rey Povod's last play. And Miguel Piñero was there all the time—I was his protégé.

IS: Can you get tired of a character after playing it two, three times on stage? Do you get tired of these characters, too?

JL: Every night is so different. I don't get tired of that. I do get tired of performing, I do. But the thing that happens when I'm tired, my defense mechanisms are down and all of a sudden some new stuff takes over. And at the end of the show I go, Oh man, I'm so glad I did it. I didn't want to do it, but some new stuff just came out. You just learn every time. And I don't do the shows for that long. I never do. I've never done them for longer than about a year. I always move on.

IS: You talked about Whoopi Goldberg. And I've heard you also talk about Lenny Bruce and Richard Pryor. And you are obviously the "Latino" comedian today. What is the difference, John, between Latino humor and say African American or Jewish humor? How would you put it?

JL: That's kind of tough to say. Humor is humor. Funny is funny. And it's more like an American humor as opposed to a French humor. That's where I see the big difference, more culturally. Because you know I do my shows and there's a lot of white people laughing, a lot of black people laughing. And I watch Richard Pryor and I'm cracking up, do you know what I mean? So funny is funny. Cultural American. The difference, it's hard to say. I know things about Latin people—we gesticulate a lot and there's a lot of movement. And we're physical, and so the humor is definitely going to have a lot more physicality to it and a lot more emotion. And storytellers—we're big storytellers but also so are other cultures. But those are three factors of Latin culture. And then themewise is what becomes a difference in humor. Because we're such a family-oriented culture, whether you're Mexican, Puerto Rican, Colombian, Dominican, Cuban. Family is one of our biggest issues. My shows always are similarly about family. Or the lack of family.

IS: Was there a lot of humor in your education, in your growing up in Queens? People telling jokes, people making fun of one another at home, in the street?

JL: My friends were hilarious, man. I mean, my youth was funny. At home it wasn't as funny, but outside of my house, my friends were hilarious. We had a great time goofing on everybody, every ethnic race. We goofed on ourselves, goofed on all our limitations—

IS: In good times and in bad times. Did it matter?

JL: It was always a great time to be had. And there was such a great sense of humor that it was just so wild to me to finally realize that there weren't enough Latin comedians out there. Because I was cracking up all day long. Where's all this material—just going into the atmosphere? It could have been channeled into so many movies, plays, and tv shows.

IS: You have worked with some important directors—Spike Lee, Brian DePalma—tell me something about working with Spike Lee. You did *Summer of Sam.*

JL: He did *Freak* too.

IS: Tell me about working with Spike Lee . . .

JL: Well, I've worked with a lot of different directors. I've done, I guess over thirty movies: independent and big features, bad ones, good ones, you know the whole range and gamut of it. When you work with a great director, it's such leagues above anything else. Because first of all, they free you up and they take you to a place you haven't been before. They understand the actor. They trust themselves and they trust you. There's none of that fear. First-time directors sometimes are bad directors, I call them, are so controlling and limiting and they shut you down.

IS: They want the opposite.

JL: And then you would think a powerful director would be like that. But no, a great director is so trusting. He lets you experiment, lets you try things. Because that's where the magic happens, is when you're trying stuff you didn't expect. Especially for movies because movies have to be so spontaneous. And you want it to be so real, that you don't want anything hindering that. And with Spike, Spike knows how to shoot an actor. He puts two cameras there, one on either side, so that both actors are using their best stuff at the same time. It's not like I'll shoot you first and I'll shoot him, and by that time things get a little stale, a little prepared. No, he's right here and gives you both a chance to be as spontaneous as each other. And just frees you up. And he puts that camera in places that lets you be yourself.

IS: How about Brian DePalma or Mike Nichols?—you have also worked with them.

JL: Well they're different. Brian DePalma is much more . . . I had a great *Carlito's Way.* I did two movies with him: *Casualties of War* and *Carlito's Way. Carlito's Way* was the first time that I felt I had arrived. This is when I felt I knew how to work in movies. And Brian is much more meticulous about the shot. And it's more, you have to find yourself, finding the camera. He doesn't put it there for you; you have to find it.

But he let me do like crazy things, man. I did insane things. And just him allowing me to do that, I found myself in movies. You know, my birth as a cinema actor. And it was such an exciting moment for me. And he asked me to do *Mission Impossible.* But I couldn't get out of something I was doing.

IS: And Mike Nichols.

JL: Mike Nichols saw *Spic-O-Rama.* He wrote me this amazing letter and we started to hang out together. He had this movie, *Regarding Henry,* and I did this part that I would never do in a million years because it was so negative. And I'm conscious of what I represent as a Latin man, as a Latin actor to Latin kids and the youth. And other, white kids and black kids too. I want to give the right perspective. And this was a negative role. And I would have never done it, but it was Mike Nichols. And I met him and he's a god, and so I did this role that I would never do. And I just . . . and I was ashamed of it all; you know I've always been ashamed of it.

IS: You regret it?

JL: To some extent, yeah. I love Mike Nichols and respect him, but I still shouldn't have done it. I didn't need to do that. But I did it for whatever my reasons were at the time. They seemed right.

IS: In one of the movies that most people have seen, *Moulin Rouge,* you play Toulouse-Lautrec. It's quite a role.

JL: With Baz, doing *Moulin Rouge,* he wanted me to play this unconscious Argentinean. And I said, unconscious Argentinean? How many lines can an unconscious person have? I'm not playing that. I said what else you got? He says "Well, I've got Toulouse-Lautrec; I don't know, but we want a real English person, you're so New York." And I was like "Yeah, but you know, I could do an accent." He said, all right. And I auditioned for him for two hours. And I studied. I got an acting coach, a dialect coach, and worked to try to get rid of my New York accent, and talk this way. And then I had to get a lisp because that's what the character had, sort of a lisp. And that's what I did to try to get the part. I auditioned for two hours on my knees. I usually get all my parts over a lot of English actors.

IS: You were born in Colombia . . .

JL: Yeah.

IS: And came to the U.S. at the age of four.

JL: That's right. Are you following me around? What are you, are you stalker?

IS: Your father is . . .

JL: Puerto Rican.

IS: Was there—is there a difference in the sensibility between Puerto Rican and Colombian? I want you to start talking about the nuances within the Latino culture, of how Colombians see the world different from Puerto Ricans or Mexicans or Ecuadorians.

JL: You know that's fascinating because everybody always wants to know what the differences are. To me it's amazing how similar we are. That's what grabs me. Because I do my show—I did my show—all over America, twenty-four cities, *Sexaholix*. And you know I went to the West Coast, which is mostly Mexican. And they got it. They got all the things and they kept going, "You know I relate to that, you know I totally relate, that's exactly like my family is."

IS: Do you feel Colombian or Puerto Rican?

JL: I've gone back to both places. I don't know . . . I feel at home in any Latin country. That's what's so strange. Because I grew up in New York City. I grew up with Dominicans, Cubans, Puerto Ricans, Colombians, Ecuadorians, Chileans, Argentineans—they were all in my neighborhood. I never felt different, or an affinity to one group as opposed to another. And when I would go back to the country, like to Mexico or whatever— I just feel at home anywhere, in Latin countries.

IS: Now, in your shows there's a lot of mixing of languages, of Spanish and English, unlike some of the comedians that you were describing before as role models. You grew up in Spanish and English, bilingual.

JL: Well, English is my stepmother tongue. You know, I spoke Spanish first, until I was four. And then I had to learn English fast and catch up. And my parents, I had to mostly read stuff for them because, as I went on I advanced a lot quicker in the language. I had much more facility with it.

IS: Would you be able to perform one of your monologues in Spanish?

JL: No.

IS: Would it be different?

JL: It's hard. I can speak Spanish and I can understand it, but—

IS: Can you write Spanish?

JL: I can write Spanish, but I have a third-grade writing level and reading level. I tried to read *A Hundred Years of Solitude* in Spanish. That was my biggest mistake, because I can never read that book now because I couldn't get through the first chapter. It was like the begats of the Bible, and I just—in Spanish and like these names. Forget it, it killed me.

IS: When you use some of the Spanish words in one of the monologues, what do you do in order not to alienate the audience that might not know Spanish?

JL: It's not that I try to alienate them—

IS: Do you translate simultaneously?

JL: No, I don't translate. I don't translate. I keep it like the way I experienced it, in the way I grew up. See I grew up, I'm telling you, in Jackson Heights, I would hear Jewish people saying a lot of Yiddishisms and Italians using *capito, etestatuto,* or whatever. And I just love the sound of it. You know even if I didn't know what it meant, I loved the sound of foreign words and what people are trying to say. And you get it through their gestures. I was always hoping that that's what the audience got. That the white audience or American audience, non-Spanish-speaking audience would get the same joy that I got from hearing other foreign words. And what it sounded to me like, too, is the sound of it. Spanish sometimes has this great fun and bubbly and—it's just got this great flavor that I was hoping would be infectious.

IS: Had you not been born in New York—in Colombia and educated in New York. But say you would have ended up in, in some other—

JL: Oklahoma. I would talk like this; I wudda been a different person.

IS: But would you have become an actor? A standup comedian?

JL: Dude, I don't know.

IS: New York is in your blood.

JL: New York made me who I am, and my crazy dysfunctional family made me who I am.

IS: And it lives on stage with you.

JL: It's all the obstacles and all the strife and struggle made me who I am. And if I didn't have those things, I wouldn't be who I am. I wouldn't have to have been creative. I wouldn't have to be funny.

IS: What do you hope to provoke in your audience? When you talk about that character, for instance, of the Japanese wannabe that tells Latinos, "You're never going to make it in this country if you don't become Japanese"?

JL: *Mambo Mouth* is my angriest show. That was my first show and my angriest. And I'm proud of having that raw anger on stage. So many times comedians just get nicer and nicer, but I was at my angriest, and I was angry at a lot of things and I was still funny. And to be funny and angry to me was powerful, and I said a lot of things that offended a lot of people.

IS: And is your purpose to offend? Do you want to generate some sort of discomfort in the audience so that people—do you want to change things?

JL: I wanted people to feel the things that I felt. I want them to feel as angry and to feel all the things that go on in my head to be who I am, and that's what *Mambo Mouth* was. It was having to go through all the self-hate and all the second-class feeling that you have to grow up with; to get past that, to go another place in your life—that you have to go against all this negativity to be somebody.

IS: But hopefully also so that society might be able to see Latinos under a different light.

JL: Also, to see that we're smart and bright. We can do a lot of things. I came up at a time where the only show that was using Latin people was *Miami Vice*. You got to remember the context of where I came from and where we are now. And I was fighting a lot of resistance. I had to knock down a lot of doors. It was a tough battle that I enjoyed because I felt like a warrior, like I had to go out there and change people's opinion of what Latin people were. We were smart. We were clever. We had a lot to contribute to this culture.

Crossing the Border

Rubén Martínez

Rubén Martínez (USA, b. 1962) is the author of The Other Side/El Otro Lado: Fault Lines, Guerrilla Saints, and the True Heart of Rock 'n' Roll *(1992),* Crossing Over: A Mexican Family on the Migrant Trail *(2001), and* The New Americans *(2004). This interview took place in Boston, September 2003, as the paperback edition of his second book was released.*

IS: How many people cross the U.S.-Mexican border annually?

RM: Impossible to say. All we know is how many people are apprehended at the border by the border patrol and turned back, and then there are some estimates of how many people are living undocumented in our cities. But I would have to say about 2 million, 3 million maybe, every year.

IS: Three million people?

RM: Yes, a year.

IS: How is it that we know so little about who they are?

RM: Because we simply don't pay attention. The media doesn't know how to pay attention. It's a bias of the mainstream U.S. media. I'm talking about radio, print, TV . . . The undocumented Mexican laborer who's omnipresent in a colloquial way on the street, whether it's a day laborer or somebody painting your house, somebody nannying your children. Somebody helping with your groceries, helping you get your groceries to your car at the supermarket. So in one way there is an omnipresence of the immigrant laborer in the United States, but that doesn't get translated into the media image.

IS: Why are we so afraid to talk about it?

RM: It's a hand grenade. American consciousness historically splits right down the middle between the American that receives with generosity through the Statue of Liberty: "Give me your tired, your poor, your huddled masses yearning to be free . . ."

IS: Emma Lazarus, "The New Colossus."

RM: Exactly. And the other side is the one that simply rejects, closing borders.

IS: Yet with nostalgia for a mythical land of opportunity that is always open . . .

RM: Ellis Island on the one hand, receiving the stranger with open arms and the possibility of becoming a Horatio Alger on the streets of America, and on the other hand intense vitriolic xenophobia, which in its extreme forms has led historically to lynchings of Chinese laborers in Los Angeles and in recent times to the deaths at the hands of paramilitary groups of Mexican laborers on the U.S.-Mexico border.

IS: Is the situation with those millions of Mexicans that are crossing the border, and Central Americans too that are crossing the border every year, different from the Italian immigration or the German or the Irish?

RM: A fundamental difference.

IS: How so?

RM: The most obvious one is that the old-world European immigrants who arrived at Ellis Island in the middle of the nineteenth century and then again in the early part of the twentieth century—an ocean separated them from their homeland. Many of them talked about returning home; the first generation, the zero generation immigrant, would yearn to go back to Italy, go back to Germany. But the reality was that most of them ended up staying here. The impossibility of travel or going back, swimming against the tide of immigration coming across the ocean this way. Latin American immigrants are within reach of their homelands, especially Mexican immigrants. The U.S.-Mexican border is the longest single frontier in the world between a first-world nation and a developing world or third-world nation. This makes the relationship of the United States to Mexico—and of the Mexican immigrant laborer vis-à-vis American society overall—absolutely unique in terms of American immigration history.

IS: In a science fiction twist, imagine one year without these million Mexicans crossing the border. What would happen to the United States?

RM: The immediate impact would be going to the supermarket when strawberry season starts in March and April—there wouldn't be any strawberries. Because strawberry picking is a labor-intensive, manual labor intensive proposition, and if you didn't have the seasonal flow of undocumented—we're talking about undocumented labor, the vast majority of strawberry pickers in northern California strawberry fields . . .

IS: You have a chapter called "Strawberry Fields Forever."

RM: Everybody in California—the growers, the politicians, the labor unions, the supermarkets, the corporations—everybody knows this to be true. It is just a fact of life. But do we talk about it? No. Just like one of these open secrets, it's wink, wink. A politician can rail at election time against "illegal immigrants," but when we go to the supermarket we're all enjoying the fruits of that labor.

IS: Is it only the supermarkets? Okay, so for a year we won't eat strawberries . . .

RM: Not just the strawberries, of course. In the seasonal sense of labor, migratory flow, the immediate impact would be in foodstuffs, the produce sections in our supermarkets. But beyond that, say in my home state of California, in the skyscrapers downtown the trash would start piling up in all the offices. Drywalling, all the new developments going up—because the drywallers are mostly undocumented immigrants now—there will be nobody to tack the drywall in the developments.

IS: Mexico needs to allow those immigrants to come north . . .

RM: Oh yes. Mexico must have it that way.

IS: So both economies depend on this coming and going from people south to north.

RM: Just to mention the other side of the equation: It's crucial for the Mexican government to have the flow going northward as much as it benefits the United States. It benefits Mexico to the extent that Mexico does not have enough jobs to give to its people, and the number three source of income right now for the Mexican, the Mexican economy, is the amount of dollars sent from laborers in the United States to their family members back home. And that's after tourism and oil; then comes the Mexican laborer in the States sending money back home to their mom and dad. That's a huge contribution to the economy.

IS: You begin *Crossing Over* with the death in a car accident of a number of immigrants. Every so often the media gives us news of immigrants that have died in the desert of thirst, immigrants that are beaten down by the border patrol. Do you have an estimate of how many people are killed or die that way?

RM: It's a conservative estimate because many of the dead, their bodies will never be found. The bones are at the bottom of the Rio Grande, they're out in the middle of the desert in southern Arizona or in Texas.

But we have found many bodies over the years. The University of Houston has done a study that tallied from coroners' reports on both sides of the line some 3,000 people over the last decade, and that study is a few years old now, so we can calculate that it's probably closer to 3,500 to 4,000 people—

IS: That's more than those that died on September 11.

RM: A huge amount of people, and yet on a daily basis the media coverage given to the deaths is usually relegated to border newspapers: the *El Paso Times,* the *Arizona Daily Star.* There will be a small notice: another undocumented immigrant found in the desert looking for shade died of thirst.

IS: It isn't only the media and the politicians. In our capital, there are monuments for the Holocaust, there is a proposal to build a memorial or a monument for slavery and the place that it has in the United States. Should there be a point, not so distant hopefully, where we should have a monument, a museum, a memorial in Washington to remember all the many crossing from south to north and whose presence is at the very heart of the American dream?

RM: There won't be such a monument to undocumented Mexican laborers in my lifetime, I'm sure. We have a plethora of memory sites that celebrate immigrants throughout American history. But Mexicans are a dirty secret. It's an open secret, always with that wink for the corporate moguls and the politicians and everybody who knows that this is the way things work. They can have their cake and eat it too. It isn't something that you could acknowledge aboveboard, because to do so is to implicate yourself morally in the deaths of thousands—not just of thousands of people but the destruction of millions of people's lives, stripping the dignity from these people's lives for generation after generation after generation, because this story is not new. People have been dying and being exploited and being spit upon as greasers or spics for generations now, and there hasn't been a whole lot of change in that story because we're not willing to fess up.

IS: With the slow but obvious move of Latinos from the margins of society to the middle class, and with a sense that Latino culture eventually will become an essential part of American culture, could there be this vision that the Mexican immigrant, the South American immigrant, will play a larger role in our psyche in the way we perceive things?

RM: I don't know . . .

IS: Too optimistic?

RM: It depends what time of day you speak to me.

IS: Not now?

RM: Generally speaking, the fact that Carlos Santana has won a dozen Grammys in the last couple of years and sold a billion albums and that Ricky Martin was shaking his bonbon and then J. Lo and Ben are going out—I really don't think it makes any difference whatsoever to the lives of the millions of people in this country who are living in the shadows. Jennifer Lopez, Carlos Santana, and Ricky Martin aren't saying, Now that I have the eyes of millions, it's about time for us to address this terrible immigration policy.

IS: You *are* speaking out.

RM: This is personal.

IS: How so.

RM: I'm the son and I'm the grandson of immigrants from El Salvador and from Mexico to the United States. When I see my brothers and sisters, not just from Mexico but from Central America, from China, Korea, central and eastern Europe, when I see any immigrants' dignity stripped from them because of some exploitation in the labor situation, my own humanity is diminished as an American. Because we have these ideals here; we have the Statue of Liberty that says this, and we have the Constitution that says this—it's there on paper. Our mythology is supposed to be part of the way we live, the way we act in the world.

IS: In the end, literature has a limited impact in a society. Is your voice doomed to be lost? What can be accomplished through reportage like yours?

RM: To reach a wider audience, I would have to shake my bonbon like Ricky Martin. How many people have read this book? 20,000? Would I like to be on the Oprah Book Club? Of course. Anyway, there's nothing else that I can do.

IS: Oprah won't be interested . . .

RM: It's a messy subject, not sexy. The book begins with the mangled bodies of nine young men crushed under a truck after a chase effected by the border patrol and winding up in the hills of Temecula. Now somebody might think, oh, maybe we can turn that into a Hollywood movie, but let's face it, when we get Hollywood renditions of Latinoness, it's something completely different from this scenario. This is a little bit too gritty, and yet I can do no other thing than to write about it.

IS: Are things worse after September 11?

RM: Yes.

IS: How have things changed?

RM: Since September 11 more people are dying on the U.S.-Mexican border this year. The summer of 2003 will be the deadliest season on the border in recorded history: close to two hundred people will have died by the end of this summer, most of them in southern Arizona in a very forbidding and terrible part of the desert called the Camino del Diablo, the Devil's Road, where migrants have to cross some seventy miles of desert without a single water source. And that's where they're dying. Why are they dying? Even before September 11, and even more so since September 11, the border patrol has had a strategy of trying to close down the major crossing points, that is, San Diego, Nogales, El Paso, McAllen, Texas, trying to divert the migrant flow, keep it back. The border is two thousand miles long. Most is open. You could skip across it. The water only goes up to your knees. I was there a couple of weeks ago as a matter of fact. Even though people maybe don't cross at San Diego anymore, they cross in the mountains east of San Diego. They don't cross at Nogales; they cross in the open desert, and that's what's becoming deadly. I'm afraid that the United States, everyone, all American citizens are complicit in the deaths of the migrants to a certain extent.

IS: We are guilty, all of us?

RM: Yes. The Mexican government is guilty. And the migrants have to take some responsibility, and the smugglers have to take some responsibility too. There's plenty of responsibility to dole out here. I'm not just pointing the finger at Uncle Sam in a self-righteous way. We need to come together on this. Our is the era of globalization. Some people think that we can go it alone in a complex world like this, but even in the regionalized sense of looking at the way the world is, there's no way we can come up with an immigration policy that would be humane without involving all parties, without having a direct conversation . . .

IS: Just before September 11, though, there was this debate between the two administrations, the one of President Bush and the one of President Fox, about legalizing. The numbers would fluctuate between 3 million and 5 million undocumented immigrants in the United States, and there was even tension within the Latino community of why the Mexicans are getting this preferential treatment. But then September 11 came and all that kind of discussion vanished.

RM: Right in the paranoia of the times. Understandably so in the wake of 9/11. Nobody knew where the threat to the United States was coming from. But I can tell you one thing: if there's a threat to the United States on the U.S.-Mexican border today, the terrorists, what kind of terrorists are they? Are they guys with dishrags and leaf blowers coming across to terrorize our cities? I've been on the U.S.-Mexican border; there is not a single shred of evidence that Al Qaeda has used the border to ship missiles across or anything of the sort. There's zero evidence of that. As you said earlier, we do have some evidence on the U.S.-Canada border, but right now the U.S.-Mexican border is not a place of national security threat in terms of Al Qaeda. It's a threat to our moral standing before ourselves and the rest of the world in terms of human rights and dignity for the U.S. and for the Mexican laborers crossing that border.

IS: What is it in the border that is in Rubén Martínez, and vice versa?

RM: I grew up in—or perhaps on—it. Los Angeles is 120 miles from the border. The border splits us along racial and economic lines. East Los Angeles was Mexican, west Los Angeles was white, south Los Angeles was black. As kids we'd go down and go across the border and go to Tijuana with my family. Once again Mexicans are within reach of Mexico in the United States. An hour and a half drive from LA and we cross the border, and it would be for me like going into the land of Oz. All of a sudden the neon and the color and the streets that weren't sanitized, safe, straight lines like those in San Diego. It was a whole other world. I loved leaping back and forth over that line. It's not as if one side is better than the other. I loved both. They were just so different . . . So I grew up with the border in me. As an adult the drama of the border has just drawn me for political and moral reasons. It's a place that, after I finished this book, I told myself, I'm not going to deal with the border or immigration anymore. I've done it for twenty years. And I'm about to start work on a new book that's about the southwestern desert. And it *will* have several chapters about the border.

IS: You can't get away from it.

RM: No, I can't. It's also the landscape of the Southwest. The desert west and the issue of water—water is the only metaphor in the west.

Whether you use it as the metaphor for the migrants crossing the River Jordan into Canaan, or to talk about water and gold. When you're thirsty and lost, water is the primordial trope.

IS: In a haunting scene in *Crossing Over*, immigrants that have made it to the other side in Arkansas, Missouri, or to California, in their homes they actually replicate the way they lived—the homes, the landscape that they had in the place they left behind. It is as if they needed to move north to look for paradise. And yet they carried the little home with them. Not just Mexicans do it, of course.

RM: The Little Italys, Little Saigons, Little Moscows that we have in the United States throughout our history are testament to the need of the zero and first generation of immigrants to have that cultural hearth, to bring it with them, because to deal with the newness of America, the language issues and the different cultural rites, without having that little piece of home with you—it would be impossible. There is something in human nature about it. Mexicans are particularly adroit at establishing Little Mexicos in the modern era of immigration, precisely once again because we're so close to Mexico and because the Southwest was Mexico and still is in so many different ways. To recreate the homeland, you could do it with the snap of a finger. The first time a Mexican arrives in Wisconsin, well, there are the tortillas and all the other signage that comes with them and establishes the beginning of the migrant's new life. Which doesn't mean that they're not going to Americanize in some way; of course they are. What Americans fear about Mexicans is precisely this historical memory: oh, we vanquished them 150 years ago; they probably still hate us, and we can't trust them. Well, young Mexican migrants are as enamored of violent Hollywood flicks and McDonalds and rock 'n' roll and hip-hop as any other young immigrant, as any other young global kid these days.

IS: You traveled with different members of a Mexican family from one state to another, miles and miles time over time. You chronicle what is going on in their minds, in their souls, a tension that exists between the various members. Does it ever come to a point where you feel that you're part of that family, and do you also have the sense that you're losing your subject, that they are using *you*?

RM: I've been a journalist, but I never ever subscribed to the ideal of objectivity in journalism.

IS: Writing is subjective?

RM: Yes. It's amazing to me that people like the networks, Dan Rather, look straight at the camera and say, I'm objective. Absurd. About seventy-five years of quantum physics and literary theory have done away with the idea of objectivity. It does not exist even though American media runs on that for its moral authority. I subscribe to the idea that subjectivity reigns in my realm of writing.

On Brevity

Augusto Monterroso

Augusto Monterroso (Guatemala, 1926–2003) is the author of Movimiento perpetuo *(1972),* Lo demás es silencio: La vida y la obra de Eduardo Torres *(1978),* La palabra mágica *(1983),* La letra e: Fragmentos de un diario *(1987),* Los buscadores de oro *(1993), and* Complete Works and Other Stories *(1995). Conducted in Spanish, this interview took place in San Antonio, Texas, October 1993.*

IS: A couple of years ago, while browsing around in the Gandhi Librería, in Mexico, I found an anthology of sad stories that you and Barbara edited together. It was called, if I remember properly, *Antología del cuento triste*—a beautiful idea. Frankly, I was unaware of your work as editor, and it was a most welcome surprise. With it as an excuse, I would like to begin by exploring your career as reader. After all, what's an anthology if not a miniature, itinerant library? If I'm not mistaken, you had stories by Juan Carlos Onetti, Saul Bellow, Thomas Mann, Dorothy Parker, Flaubert, Melville, and Faulkner.

AM: My career as a literary reader began in Honduras, in elementary school. In *Los buscadores de oro* I write about how I was stirred by a handful of texts by French writers and poets, as well as books by Latin Americans. My father was Guatemalan and my mother Honduran, but I was never a Honduran citizen because we moved from place to place frequently. When I came of age, I had the right, by virtue of being Central American, to choose my citizenship, and I chose to be Guatemalan, since that's where we lived most. I was a precocious reader: I'm self-taught and have enjoyed reading since my early childhood. Much of my education I had to organize and shape; what I didn't get in school, I got at the Biblioteca Nacional de Guatemala.

IS: Your fiction always comes in small capsules, at times one sentence long, like the celebrated "The Dinosaur," included in *Complete Works* and which Italo Calvino talks about in *Six Memos for the Next Millennium*. Were you a reader of large, encyclopedic novels?

AM: Yes. I avidly read golden age volumes, in particular *Don Quixote,*

El Buscón, and *El Criticón.* I also read Shakespeare and the Latin authors, all crucial in my intellectual development. In fact, I read whatever was available at the Biblioteca Nacional, which, because of budget constraints, wasn't too much. That's where I acquired a lasting taste for the classics.

IS: How about Latin Americans like Horacio Quiroga and Leopoldo Lugones?

AM: Even though I was living in Guatemala, I discovered them much later. My readings of modern literature didn't come until I was considerably older.

IS: You must have experienced a deep abyss between the world of books and the world you lived in. After all, Guatemala then, and today, was a poor country with sharp social contradictions. Return for a moment to the young adolescent you were . . .

AM: There's definitely something valuable in what you suggest. Since I was forced, from early on, to work in order to make a living, I would divide my time between my daily job and the Biblioteca Nacional. At some point I began meeting with friends who had a similar interest in literature; together we developed a deep concern for the problems of Guatemala. As you well know, Guatemala had been suffering under the long dictatorship of General Ubico. The forties in Central America, mainly as a result of World War II, was a decade of important liberation movements. We listened to a lot of propaganda—movies and numerous publications aimed at fighting fascism. Soon the battle against fascism evolved into a struggle against dictatorship, a struggle in which I found a place, alongside other students and workers.

IS: Did the focus of your reading change immediately?

AM: Certainly. As soon as I would leave the Biblioteca Nacional, I would take to the streets and meet other writers and poets who had done different reading. Their taste, I should say, was not as detached from reality as mine. They mostly were reading the moderns, anything from Rilke to Neruda. But I never experienced a connection between politics and literature in which literature became an instrument aimed at promoting social upheaval.

IS: Indeed, your work hardly ever makes such connections.

AM: That, I guess, is due to the fact that my education was almost completely focused on literature. My thought and my literary preferences had already taken shape by the time I joined the political struggle, so I never considered literature an instrument for social change. Which doesn't mean that I didn't participate in the struggle. Let us just say that I do so physically, in the streets, at protests, in the political struggle, but completely divorced from literature. I do write stories with political echoes: for instance, "Mr. Taylor" and "First Lady." I think that, in general, my work demonstrates a concern with social dilemmas, but not with politics in any strict sense of the word.

IS: Since brevity is a crucial component of your work, particularly your fiction, I want you to define it for me. Or better, I want you to explain why your short stories and essays are so brief. Borges, Juan José Arreola, and Rubén Darío were also Latin American masters of brevity. Where does the need for compactness come from? Is it the Latin classics? It certainly couldn't be from Quevedo's *El Buscón* and Cervantes's *Don Quixote* . . . On the other hand, Quevedo's conceptual sonnets are astonishing examples of poetic and philosophical precision, don't you think?

AM: Horace preached the value of brevity. And he's a representative of many other Latin and Greek authors I could mention. His odes, satires, and epistles are all brief by definition. Most of them were not translated into verse form but into prose; I tried to imagine their poetic melody. This is where my love for brevity and concision come from. But I did read golden age writers from Spain, particularly Baltazar Gracián, who recommends brevity. I sometimes ask myself this same question you pose, and my answer once again is none other than my great love for the classics.

IS: "The Dinosaur" . . . Let me quote it from memory: "When he awoke, the dinosaur was still there."[1]

AM: It wasn't hard to write it; after all, anybody can have a bold idea. The problem was getting it published. I had many doubts about whether it should be included in *Complete Works*. My friends encouraged me to do so, for which I'm thankful. But the story has not only brought me enormous recognition; it also generated great harm. To the point that I've come to feel uncomfortable about it and might not even include it in selections of my work. People think that, since they've read "The Dinosaur," which obviously doesn't take much effort, they know my entire work. I sill have the first reviews of the book: critics hated it. Since that point, I began hearing complaints to the effect that it isn't a short story. My answer: true, it isn't a story, it is actually a novel . . .

IS: Did you ever write another one?

AM: Yes, just one other one: "Fecundity," part of *Complete Works.*[2]

IS: Allow me to differ, but that's an essay, or else an epigram.

AM: Perhaps. At any rate, scores of people say about me: "Ah, Augusto Monterroso writes those one-line stories," but it isn't true. In fact, take a look at "The Dinosaur"; it is sandwiched between two long stories, one twenty pages long, the other, eighteen. I deliberately placed it between these long stories. Making many of these would be unwise, of course. Please don't think I say it to discourage any competition. Martial said in one of his, it would cancel its true worth. As for a one-line essay, I guess you can get away with it if it's placed in a volume of essays. It's all a matter of perception.

IS: And why is "The Dinosaur" a short story?

AM: Simply because it narrates something: it has a subject and an argument. That is, something happens to so-and-so in a period of time.

IS: Did it come to you with a dinosaur early on? What about the comma?

AM: Without the comma, it would seem as if the dinosaur was the one who awakened. A friend of mine suggested inserting a comma, and I did . . .

IS: Did you place it after the first edition was completed or before it was published?

AM: No, before it was published. I was asking my friends, and one suggested that I both publish it and add the comma.

IS: Brevity . . . Even *Los buscadores de oro,* when compared to standard memoirs, is incredibly brief. Do you rewrite a lot? Are there many versions of the same tale before its final shape comes about?

AM: Yes, many.

IS: Do they get shorter as you move toward completion?

AM: Some do, but others, a few of them, get longer. It is all dictated by instinct. Instinct, in my view, is of central importance in a writer's style: it announces what needs to be eliminated, what can ruin a story by making it too short.

IS: What else, aside from instinct, is at stake in a good story? Some of your briefest stories are, in my opinion, perfect. In fact, when I was young I memorized "The Eclipse," an example of clarity and vision, a story about history and the imagination. Later on, I was ecstatic to discover that Mark Twain, in *A Connecticut Yankee in King Arthur's Court*, had actually preceded you. An outstanding story, obviously, is not the property of a single writer.

AM: It's easy to know what makes a good story, but it's difficult to articulate it. The genre has great variety with regard to the situations, forms, the spins given to different concepts. Among the golden age Spanish authors which I also read were the Arcipreste de Ita, Don Juan Manuel, as well as folktales. It was an astonishing treasury of creative talent and technique. Traditional stories are useful in that they broaden our scope by showing us what people enjoy most: simplicity. Among my own favorite stories is Melville's "Bartleby the Scrivener," which is actually a novella, as well as Flaubert's "A Simple Heart," and others by Chekhov, Maupassant, Faulkner, the Salvadorean Salvador Salazar Arrué, and others that Barbara and I included in *Antología del cuento triste*. I also love a story by Lugones, "Tzur," about a monkey that metamorphoses into a man—a tale that prefigures the best in Kafka.

IS: How about Poe, whom Julio Cortázar, as you know, adored?

AM: Although any anthology of modern short stories should include him, we didn't simply because we couldn't come up with a sad story of his. All dealt with fear and terror. As for "The Eclipse," my point of departure was indeed Mark Twain, although I didn't get it from him directly. I wrote it while a Hollywood movie on King Arthur was playing in Mexican theaters. One of the characters knew an eclipse was going to take place in Africa and that the savages would witness it. So I asked myself: What if the gringo character ended up among the Mayans? What would have happened to him? I then made up the story of a Spanish friar. But it is also well known that Columbus applied the trick in the Bahamas, during his third voyage, I believe. Since he knew about an eclipse, he was successful in scaring the natives. In other words, the seed of the story dates back to Columbus, was later reworked by Twain, revisited in a Hollywood movie, and reapplied to Guatemala.

IS: So what amount of the story is actually yours? We cannot avoid, at this point in our dialogue, the topic of originality.

AM: Originality isn't based on the construction of a certain argument, but in the style and twist a writer gives it.

IS: The history of world literature is the history of a limited number of plots, reworked time and time again?

AM: Yes. It's only possible to achieve originality through form. What Ibsen turned into tragedy was vaudeville theater; that is, he gave the same motifs a new twist.

IS: Ralph Waldo Emerson believed we're only pipelines to a Writer of Writers: the same set of ideas appears in different languages, different corners of the world, sometimes at the same time. Our creative freedom is truly limited.

AM: Borges enjoyed repeating that same idea, which goes to show you how unoriginal he was.

IS: Let's turn to the essay. Latin American letters has a strong essayist tradition, and my generation grew up reading Borges, Octavio Paz, Cortázar, and you, particularly in essays like *Complete Works, Perpetual Motion,* and *La letra e.* If you were about to edit an anthology of our best continental essays, what would your priorities be?

AM: Although, as you say, the literary essay generates a tremendous interest, many people are still unclear as to what it is and how to distinguish it from the academic essay. By this I mean that the public still needs to be educated. People tend to believe the literary essay is a form of analysis in which one discusses the salient features of a classic, say the sonnets of Sor Juana Inés de la Cruz; that is, one tries to prove one's point of view. While I personally read these types of essays from time to time, for general information and out of sheer curiosity, I've never written one of them and I don't intend to do so. It's not that I'm against them; I simply don't like to write them. The type of essay I embrace was born with Montaigne. When I arrived in Mexico in 1944, exiled, with only a sweater and a change of clothing, I had only two volumes with me, and one was a collection of essays by Montaigne. I had been reading him feverishly in Guatemala, but I never tried to imitate it; it would be extremely difficult to do so. Instead, I tried to imagine him writing in the twentieth century, in Central America. And I nurtured my love for Montaigne by reading other essayists, especially Bacon. It's interesting that any óne of Montaigne's essays could pass as scholarly desideratum; he doesn't write a page without quoting Plutarch and Ovid, without offering Greek and Renaissance bibliographical references.

IS: He wasn't a concise man.

AM: Yes, absolutely. Only time could bring brevity back to the essay form, and Borges, no doubt, is to be congratulated for accelerating the speed.

IS: When you arrived in Mexico, he had just published *Other Inquisitions*. His best work was written at the end of the thirties and in the early forties.

AM: I began reading him in the Buenos Aires magazine *Sur*, way before he would become an icon. His talent as an essayist and fiction writer was absolutely stunning. The publication of his *Antología de la literatura*, which he edited together with Silvina Ocampo and Adolfo Bioy Casares, opened a whole world to us. Essayists in Latin America have been active since Domingo Faustino Sarmiento and Esteban Echeverría. And probably earlier, with Sor Juana's *Carta Atenagórica*. But, in spite of Borges's revolution, it unfortunately doesn't have the cachet other literary genres have. That's because every age has its privileged genre. Remember that poetry also has a small readership; and yet, it's alive and well in our fin de siècle. Nowadays the novel is our privileged genre; that's OK. As I see it, the essay isn't aimed at large audiences. It might sound elitist, but it's true. Poetry reaches a wider audience because it doesn't require any previous education. If one is to understand, say, Pablo Neruda, it's enough to hear his poems. However, the essay does require some background knowledge, if nothing else to understand its literary references. If asked to compile an anthology of essays, I would include Charles Lamb, Dr. Johnson, G. K. Chesterton, George Orwell, and of course many Latin Americans. A most challenging endeavor: it would take me a couple of years to reach its final list . . . I try not to distinguish between short stories and essays in my work. As you know, my books include both, and no sharp frontier is established. But it is true that my own short stories are discussed and anthologized more frequently. Borges made an effort to confuse the border between the two and we often don't know if his essays are fiction or vice versa. In my case the division is more clear-cut.

IS: Talking of mixed techniques, in *La letra e* you also include a sample of your drawings.

AM: Many of them were done while on hold over the telephone and while at the dentist. But I've never considered myself an artist. Putting them in the books wasn't even my idea. Jaime García Terrés, presently the director of the Biblioteca Nacional de México and a good friend of mine, is known for curating outrageous exhibits. One day he thought of one with drawings made by writers. Since we had worked together for many years, he asked me for samples. He then envisioned a catalog, but someone recommended that it was better to bring out independent volumes. And so my book was born. It's a nice idea, but I've absolutely no pretensions about it.

IS: When did you begin publishing? Tell me, in particular, how *La oveja negra,* perhaps your most famous book, came into being.

AM: I was almost forty when *Complete Works* appeared—maybe thirty-eight or thirty-nine. I remember being scared. I didn't publish it of my own volition but because someone convinced me to do so. You see, I've had good friends: some like my drawings and others want my stories. My friend Enrique Gonzáles Casanova insisted that I, a Universidad Nacional Autónoma de México employee, should publish a book. He had given me my job in the first place; so when he told me to gather all the stories I had placed in various magazines and newspapers, and some more still unknown, I listened to him. Actually, it seems as if he ordered me to write the book. I truly owe my first book to him, because if he had not insisted, I would have probably never written my first book and, thus, none would have followed thereafter. The book appeared and I was terrified. What would others think? After that, I let two, three, or four years go by—actually, almost a decade. I didn't want to fall prey to repetition. I didn't even want to hear about short stories; yes, I could write tales small and large, but thinking of myself as a short story writer was something different. So I began writing essays. But again, could I consider myself an essayist? I accumulated observations and notes, I handwrote ideas for possible stories . . . Until one day I suddenly had the idea that I could put all this in fables. Neither a fully convinced short story writer, nor a committed essayist. I came upon the fable because Aesop and La Fontaine were among my favorite readings since early childhood.

IS: Shyness is of course good for brevity . . .

AM: I'm not a prolific writer. On the contrary. The intervals between my books are of five, six, up to seven years. I still experienced the same resistance to repeating myself. I always think my newest book is my last.

IS: So you have repeated yourself? Have you been able to avoid it? You fear falling into a pre-established pattern, don't you?

AM: At least with regard to form. Logic tells us that if one is already able to do something well, one should continue to pursue it. But I'm still embarrassed at doing something I've already done. In short, I enjoy experimentation; that's where I should have started. I like experimenting, and I'm somewhat opposed to our modern view of knowledge. When I feel I know something, it ceases to interest me. And I'm also afraid of taking myself too seriously. *Los buscadores de oro* is a memoir made of segments; I incorporated essays into the text, whenever I was able to. The memoir is a complex genre, particularly in Latin America. We're all modest, and we think the publication of memoirs, diaries, and letters should be the monopoly of the world's geniuses, one reserved for the great masters. When I published *La letra e,* a diary, it was at a considerable social cost: I was the target of laughter, newspaper parodies, and heavy sarcasm. I guess people thought it was presumptuous to do so; they didn't consider the diary a serious literary genre. Laughter generates fear, and fear of how others will react is added to my own caution about publishing in general.

IS: One genre we haven't discussed is the conversation, which you've embraced quite well. In fact, *Viaje al centro de la fábula* is a compilation of your conversations.

AM: Yes. We also need to educate the public about the value of this most beautiful of art forms. Few people listen today, and even fewer consider it a valuable idea to write down their dialogues. A pity, no doubt. Plato is an illustrious example, whom we should emulate more often. Learning to think is also learning to talk: to articulate one's vision of the universe. A conversation should be like a tennis match: when the ball hits the rackets and the ground, it generates a certain melody; that, I think, should be what the echo of a conversation should sound like. Echoes, of course, are repetitions, but with a different sound and feeling.

Notes

1. The authorized English translation by Edith Grossman was published by the University of Texas Press in *Complete Works and Other Stories.* The original Spanish reads: "Cuando despertó, el dinosaurio todavía estaba allí." Its perfect structure (a beginning, a middle, and an end), its suspense, its ambiguity (based on the Spanish third-person *despertó*), and Monterroso's ironic approach to narrative, have been discussed widely by critics like Irving Howe and Emir Rodríguez Monegral. In his Charles Eliot Norton Lectures at Harvard, Calvino wrote: "Borges and Bioy Casares put together an anthology of short extraordinary tales (*Cuentos*

breves y extraordinarios, 1955). I would like to edit a collection of tales consisting of one sentence only, or even a single line. But so far I haven't found any to match the one by the Guatemalan writer Augusto Monterroso."

2. The Spanish original appears in *Movimiento perpetuo* (1972). Edith Grossman's translation: "Today, I feel well, like Balzac; I am finishing this line." Ironically, this puzzling essay opens with a long epigraph from Jean Jaures's *Regarding God,* longer than the essay itself: "Between the provocation of hunger and the passion of hatred, humanity cannot think about the infinite. Humanity is like a great tree full of flies buzzing angrily beneath the stormy sky, and in that buzz of hate, the deep, divine voice of the universe cannot be heard."

An Actor Prepares

Edward James Olmos

Edward James Olmos (USA, b. 1947) has been in the cast of Alambrista! *(1977)*,
Zoot Suit *(1981)*, Blade Runner *(1982)*, The Ballad of Gregorio Cortez
(1982), Stand and Deliver *(1988)*, American Me *(1992)*, My Family *(1994)*,
and Selena *(1997). This interview took place in Manhattan, March 1988.*

EJO: Did you like *Stand and Deliver*?

IS: It bored me. It is too apologetic, moralistic. It wants to show Hispanics their indisputable place in North American society, but the script
does not know how to make the message subtle. *Zoot Suit* and *La Bamba*
indulge in a similar message, but they present it in a more subtle way.

EJO: Because of its pedagogic tone it touches many more hearts, it
reaches a larger audience.

IS: What you say is not completely unbiased. I understand that with
Stand and Deliver, in addition to acting, you have an interest that
supercedes merely the artistic. After all, you were also involved in its
production. On the other hand, I consider *The Ballad of Gregorio Cortez*
your best film . . .

EJO: I agree. In the year 2010, if in fact I leave a mark, it will be through
that film. It'll be regarded as my most mature histrionic expression. It's
interesting: maturity in acting does not always come with age. Someone
young can achieve unsuspected intonations, while a veteran, say
Lawrence Olivier or Ralph Richardson, can stumble. Giving a good performance depends on at least three factors, some over which you have
control and others over which you don't: luck, dignity, technique. If truth
be told, taking on the role of Gregorio Cortez turned out to be the acting
experience that has most impacted me. It left me unnerved and weakened.

IS: In Mexico, *Zoot Suit* is considered a classic, evidence that Mexicans know how to express their debt without reserve. As a Chicano actor, what relationship do you have with Mexico?

EJO: When I think of the word "culture," I think, I don't know why, of
The Scarlet Letter by Nathaniel Hawthorne. Here, the culture is a symbol-
stigma by which you are recognized and categorized. Culture is everything:

the color of your skin, your eyes, your weight, your gestures, the way you speak, your smile, your religion. Defining yourself culturally is a necessary mechanism, no doubt. It divides, ramifies itself, distances people in a pluralistic society. But it is also a phenomenon that affects people negatively because it invariably creates stereotypes. What is a Chicano? A Mexican who by chance (or by circumstantial or economic necessity) was born in Los Angeles, although he very well could have been born in the Soviet Union or in Asia, wherever it was possible to eat, work, live without fear, without having to live in poverty. I'm a Mexican actor . . . *de culo colorado,* like Pedro Infante or Jorge Negrete. But I have entered another sphere, one located in *el coloso del Norte.* I'm a Mexican who lives in another language. My roots, my culture, each of my gestures and my likes, are Mexican, but my citizenship is different. What is an American? A sum of differences. What is a Mexican? A mestizo, half Spanish, half indigenous. A mixture of races, a camouflage. I understand—misunderstand, perhaps—the world as a chaos because I'm a sum of cultures, a mess, a chaos. I'm a Mexican by looks, an American by passport. Being Chicano is not difficult because of that: both Mexicans and Americans are familiar with cultural confusion. Decades ago, to be a Hispanic actor was a disadvantage. They ignored our race, doubted our capacity, good roles didn't exist. That's when I thought of Hester Prynne's misery, protagonist of *The Scarlet Letter.* Today the situation is changing. Our mission as Hispanic actors in the United States is to express our unique experience, to include it in the historic mosaic of the migratory waves, culture shocks that shape, conform, and mold each other, in this heterogeneous, this dissimilar society. Each minority gets its turn: Jews, Italians, Germans, Irish, etc. We were always told that our turn was just around the corner.

IS: What type of roles were you offered when you had to be patient?

EJO: Let me tell you: drug addicts, criminals, blackmailers, the mentally insane, smugglers, delinquents, corrupt politicians, rapists, monsters from outer space. I refused them. Cinematography for me comes in two forms, which sometimes intermix: the artistic and the commercial. More than 95 percent are commercial, made for Hollywood. Today, proving your talent, at least for a minority actor in America, implies maintaining your dignity, being patient, believing. Before, it wasn't like that: the minority actor sooner or later bought into the trends in vogue, losing his individuality. Today, patience is running out, though not in a negative way: our awareness as a Hispanic minority is heightened, but the producers of the big studios in Los Angeles, it seems, are still hesitant to market products that are less superficial, which don't contain stereotypes. What's one to do? Spike Lee, Luis Valdez, and others like me have chosen, in the end, to write, to shape and produce our own films. The responsibility is ours. The means: independent films. *La Bamba, The Ballad of Gregorio Cortez, El Super, Crossover Dreams, Zoot Suit, Alambrista!, El Norte, Stand and Deliver* are all independent films, with scripts written by independent writers, and that were later adopted by the system. This elevates quality. It also teaches the public to be more selective. It's obvious that Hollywood is a river not to be ignored, but rather from which we also are to drink. Like Mexican cinema, gangsters and musicians were popular in the 1940s and 1950s, the French and Brazilian cinemas in the 1960s, the Australian cinema and spy films in the 1970s. The North American Hispanic cinema will have its turn soon—or perhaps that brilliance, that influence has already begun . . . and many haven't yet taken notice. In the 1980s and in the future, we will have our own space; we will put forth our art. Later, we will fall out of style, exactly like all the other cinematographic trends. But we will leave our mark. That is sufficient. We will be in the firmament like everybody else. The history of film, like the other arts, consists of an infinite succession of marks. My models are actors like Anthony Quinn, Martin Sheen. Two-time Academy Award winner Anthony Quinn, whose real name, Antonio Reina, brings him back to his Mexican heritage, has opened the field for himself by forgetting his roots. Quinn, for the new Chicano wave, represents all you never wanted to be; perhaps his histrionic technique is exemplar, but what is remembered? Your techniques? The roles you play? For us (for me, for Valdez, etc.) the denial is what is remembered. Perhaps I'll never attain the caliber, the fame, the influence that Anthony Quinn had and still has, but that is because I've given my attention to a more collective work, in which the star never matters more than the final product. I'm not saying that Quinn or Sheen have run their careers erroneously. Mine is not a value judgment of an individual, but a generalization. The next generation will understand, I hope, that all I've touched, that all Luis Valdez has touched (he is even more obsessed with the American dream than I am), what should have been hidden, was meant to contribute to the Chicano identity. Others, on their own, are doing the same with the Cuban American identity or the Puerto Rican identity. This "touch of distinction" has not yet been noticed, and it's possible that it will all dissipate due to all this commercialism. But as far as I can, I do everything in my power to achieve that.

IS: Do you think that Chicanos are a Mexican extremity?

EJO: When I go to Mexico, I'm a foreigner . . . I imagine my movies awaken conflicting emotions there. Some, like you for example, are happy that we are doing our thing as Hispanics in the north. Others are envious because we have abandoned the home country. In this sense, without wanting them to do so, my movies contribute to the national identity, even in an indirect way. There are some who will say that we as Hispanics, as citizens of America, will at any moment kick over the system, will realize *la revancha de Moctezuma*—Moctezuma's revenge—against the gringos . . . for their antipathy toward Mexico, for their pedantry. I doubt it: sooner or later we too will be (if we aren't yet) gringos. Why fight our compatriots?

IS: What is the difference between being under Luis Valdez's direction, a man of the theater, and Robert Young, whose presence is already legendary in the world of independent films?

EJO: Valdez puts emphasis on the physical; he wants to see and feel that the actor generates life. The physical, for him, implies concentration and a spiritual vision. He is interested in knowing that you know not where the character comes from but rather what future the character will have. He is not interested in the text, but in the subtext, what exists between the lines. Young is more interested in realism. He prefers events, facts, not mental images. He does not indicate. It's difficult to act with him. He tells you: "Don't give me a result." What is a result? His response: "I want you to be Gregorio Cortez, not that you imagine being Gregorio Cortez." He says: "Don't move me. I, through editing, will move the audience. You simply devote yourself to acting." He is aggressive, and also defiant. He made documentaries for many years, and that style still affects him.

IS: What technique do you use as an actor?

EJO: The imagination is what's primordial, but it should be based on a real event, some memory or sensation that you've had. It's Stanislavsky's technique and his three questions: Where do you come from?

Who are you? Where are you going? If the character is old, then imagine a bit of rain, overcast weather, frigid temperatures. You should see the rain, hear it. Little by little, you feel you are in that place, that it is in effect raining.

IS: It makes me think, I don't know why, of mental illness. Someone crazy thinks he is in a dungeon . . . and he ends up being in one. Clearly, the difference consists in auto-control. The lunatic does not choose to be in the dungeon, neither does he know how to escape it if he feels suffocated. The actor, on the other hand . . .

EJO: The actor might fall into a trance. To be able to act, you have to know how to fake it. Believing you are in the countryside, and maintaining, in your subconscious, the knowledge that you are imagining realities, that you are not in the countryside. A trance, I would say, is that instant when you lose consciousness of reality. Certain genres facilitate trances; others do not: in the theater, if the play is intense, you can forget reality. That can never happen in movies or in TV because the cuts, the multiple takes, the set impede that phenomenon. An actor in complete control reduces any eventuality of trance to zero. He knows how to maintain the sensation of "to be or not to be."

IS: What kind of research do you do to create a character?

EJO: Do you know how much work it takes to make others believe that Jaime Escalante or Gregorio Cortez exist? You have to know when they were born, where, what kind of childhood they had, where they were educated. The actor, when he displays his creation, sees the world through eyes that aren't his. You have to accumulate his memories in your own mind. Spencer Tracy used to say that "acting is an easy art form. All you have to do is memorize dialogue, concentrate, and not crash into walls. Learn these steps, and you will be a great actor." I would add to that: the most difficult task is not to recite dialogues, but to end them. The silences, the subtleties, facial expressions, the absences are all a difficult test for the actor. Because being in a scene without speaking, you have to continue to project your memories, but physically, not audibly. And how do you express memories through your body? That is precisely where you have to implement technique: you have to digest the character's identity, incorporate it in such a way that you can express their presence through yours. You have to imagine quite a bit. Actors like Meryl Streep or Dustin Hoffman take six or eight months to prepare their characters. We, the extras, have one or two weeks. They send them the script in advance. If they reject it, the search implies less time to prepare for the second-choice actor. Well, when the character is historic, like Cortez or Ritchie Valens, the dimensions of imagination should be restricted to the facts. You have to study, read books, watch videotapes. If the character is a creation of the writer, novelist, or playwright, then images can fly with more ease. It happens sometimes that your creation, the character, is so convincing that the person's identity you are taking on is so powerful, that you as an actor are jealous. For me, more than once have I wanted to be like el Pachuco or Gregorio Cortez. Something in them that's fabulous, adorable: their courage, spirit, integrity. But to be like them requires that you forget the set exists, that you forget the lights, the cameras. Impossible. It is here that your comparison to mental illness becomes relevant: sometimes it is more difficult ceasing to be a character than beginning to be him. Leaving the stage, for me, is more painful than entering it. It's dangerous when by day you act as a teacher and by night a policeman. You have to understand your creations will open up the drawers filled with memories in your mind, but prevent them from mixing . . . The human psyche is incredible. You have to trust your faculties: when you begin to shape the new identity, you have an infinite amount of ideas. As time goes by, you distill them, one by one. You edit some, add to others. When it comes time to perform, you have only a couple of clear ideas, of certainties; that is enough. The actor, thus, can be, in the twinkling of an eye, one and many men.

Literature and History

Fernando del Paso

Fernando del Paso (Mexico City, b. 1935) is the author of, among other books,
José Trigo *(1966),* Palinuro de México *(1977),* Noticias del imperio *(1987),*
and Sonetos del amor y de lo diario *(1997). Conducted in Spanish, this*
interview took place in Mexico City, October 1995.

IS: Since in *Palinuro of Mexico* you function not only as the novel's
author but also as a cultural commentator, I wonder if you could take a
step back for a moment and assess for me its merit and achievement.
Almost two decades after its original publication, what's your opinion
of it? What are its excesses? Would you change anything today? Have
you ever considered a revised version?

FdP: The novel does suffer from excess—excess in style, excess in references. The same can be said of my other two novels: *José Trigo* and
Noticias del imperio. But most of these excesses are deliberate. In fact, I
remember once being asked during an interview why I wasn't capable
of writing shorter, more condensed books. I answered that *Palinuro of
Mexico* could have had some 3,000 pages and that I had made a conscious effort to abbreviate it and the result was 650 pages. By nature I'm
a baroque writer, extravagant and immoderate. This is a spontaneous
drive in me. At the same time, I've gone from an extremely complicated
to a more accessible style. My third novel is notably less complex than
the second and, similarly, the second is less difficult than the first. So
I've made some progress—my artistic route has been from excessive
complexity to relative simplicity. As for what I would or wouldn't change
in the novel today, to be honest it's hard for me to say. Books are like
children: once they are born, the world is theirs and they are part of the
world, and our role shaping their lives diminishes as time goes by. They
have their own virtues and their own paths, and the only thing one can
do is witness their development and feel amazement by what they can
or cannot achieve.

IS: I have with me the Mexican edition of *Palinuro of Mexico,* published in 1980. But the book first came out in Spain, by Alfaguara, in
1977—three years earlier.

FdP: I can give you a curious explanation. The novel in manuscript was awarded the Premio Novela Mexico, sponsored by Editorial Novaro, a publishing house, as you know, dedicated to comic strips and second- and third-rate titles. Then, Editorial Novaro established this important prize, which was given first to the Mexican playwright and novelist Jorge Ibargüengoitia, second to the Spanish writer Juan Marsé, and in its third year to me. But a conflict arose when the owner realized that the mammoth-size brick that had earned the prize was too much and refused to publish it. But the jury didn't want to change its decision, and since the owner didn't want anybody else to bring out the book, a year and a half or two went by before my literary agent, Carmen Balcells, could get it away from Editorial Novara. Those are the vicissitudes that took it first to the Iberian Peninsula and only later to Mexico.

IS: I assume the critical reaction in these two countries was different. After all, the novel is, among other things, an investigation of the Mexican psyche, its past and present.

FdP: Spanish critics were a bit more generous. Both agreed, though, that the novel had an extraordinary richness, a praiseworthy poetic content, good sense of humor, but that it was an excessive book, arrogant, too ambitious, and hence, frustrating in some aspects. Its attempt to create a macrocosm was enchanting, they claimed, but it also backfired.

IS: As far as I know, the novel has been translated into French, Portuguese, German, and English. The English version by Elisabeth Plaister, of course, was first issued by Quartet in London in 1989.

FdP: Plaister's translation, with the exception of a tiny notice in the *Times Literary Supplement,* went totally unacknowledged in England. The reception was a disaster: nobody talked about it, I never got a single pence. The French edition came out earlier, in 1985, just as classes had resumed after the summer break, and it was a huge success. Translated by Michel Bibard, it won the prize for best foreign book of the year. Every single newspaper and literary supplement discussed and praised it. It's important to note that a good segment of its French readership, as far as I can tell, was young and enthusiastic—just as *Palinuro of Mexico* has remained an all-time favorite among the young in my own native country. In Portugal it also went unnoticed, but the German translation by Suzanne Lang (who took five years to complete it) was also successful. It was presented during the 1992 Frankfurt Book Fair, and not long ago, in Munich, it won the prize for best translation. Recently, the book appeared in Holland as well, where in a few months it has sold six thousand copies—a best-seller for such a small country.

IS: Just out of curiosity, did the Portuguese version circulate in Brazil?

FdP: It did, but with no reaction whatsoever. Needless to say, the Portuguese language in Brazil is quite different and thus I doubt the country is a suitable market for a dense novel translated across the Atlantic.

IS: Along similar lines, it will be interesting to see how Plaister's British translation fares with North American readers. Anyway, I'm interested in your work with translators. Were any major changes made in any of these versions? Or rather, could we talk about "variations" of the book and not of "versions"? Were translators free to manipulate the text to some extent?

FdP: I worked with all of them by mail. Elisabeth Plaister and I corresponded for a long time, and then, almost at the end of the process, she came from Portugal to visit me for a few weeks in Paris, where I was living at the time. It's only natural that it has errors and mistakes, of course, but in my opinion it's a splendid translation.

IS: Let me turn to the topic of polyglotism. In your career as a reader, knowledge of other languages, I assume, has been essential. You speak English and French, don't you?

FdP: But that's all. As a child I didn't have a bilingual education, since I went to Mexico City's public schools. My first readings of Alexander Dumas, Sir Walter Scott, Jules Verne, Eugène Sue, and Emilio Salgari were in Spanish, often in terrible translations from Barcelona and Buenos Aires. I became acquainted with Faulkner, Erskine Caldwell, and Thomas Wolfe in Spanish. My passion for a handful of dramatists also dates from these foundational years, when my spoken and reading skills in Shakespeare's and Diderot's tongues were nonexistent. Of course every so often I would come across an extraordinary translation, like the one Borges made of Faulkner's *The Wild Palms;* but these were exceptions, not the rule. I began doing some readings in French and English on my own when I turned twenty or twenty-one; but I wasn't even close to fluency. Only later, when, together with my family, I settled first in Iowa City for a couple of years, then in London for fourteen years, and finally in Paris—the whole journey a total of twenty-four years—would I master both tongues. Obviously the moment we returned to Mexico in the mid-eighties, I stopped practicing them, and, as a result, I've already forgotten a lot. I could still write a letter to the dentist or an inquiry to a foreign publisher, but I certainly couldn't write literature in either of them. No, I don't consider myself an authentic polyglot. Spanish is my mother tongue—my only language.

IS: But *Palinuro of Mexico* was written after English became a tool and not an obstacle, right?

FdP: Yes.

IS: I ask because your Spanish seems to me bookish, foreign, its syntax alien, or at least peculiar, to native speakers. This issue of writing in one's native tongue but thinking, or imagining, in another, obsesses me, and not without reason: I left Mexico in my mid-twenties, and almost right away I established a double loyalty with English. I've discussed the topic with Ariel Dorfman, Felipe Alfau, and Julián Ríos. As you will agree, Borges's Spanish has what I would describe as a Shakespearean or, better, a Chestertonian twist. His grammar, the way in which he uses adjectives and adverbs, is outlandish, bizarre. Something similar can be said of Cortázar's Spanish in *Hopscotch,* also mixed with gallicisms from his decades in France. These mannerisms, without ever losing their appeal, often become problematic: Borges's translation of Faulkner ends up turning the text into another one of his own creations. (The Argentinean writer Ricardo Piglia, in his novel *Artificial Respiration,* has a section about this most curious of Borges's reversals.) All this brings me back to the Spanish of *Palinuro of Mexico.* Would it be fair to talk about a kind of "promiscuity" between Spanish, English, and French in the novel?

FdP: Yes, no doubt. Furthermore, while rereading my third novel, *Noticias del imperio,* I've discovered a tendency to imitate English syntax, a struggle between Spanish and English, and even an inclination to anglicize and gallicize. It comes as a natural result, needless to say, of decades in Europe. Whenever I become conscious of this metamorphosis, I try to find a neutral language, and that's why, in *Palinuro of Mexico,* almost every character (Palinuro, Walter, Fabricio, and Molkas), when using dialogue, has the same tone of voice. But I'm not worried about this artificiality, this "pollution" between languages and styles. After all, literature is nothing but invention—sheer artifice. And perhaps I should add that beyond this linguistic "promiscuity," as you call it, Ilan, the novel is also permeated by a British sense of humor. Even though my English was poor when I arrived in London, I understood the nation's mood and state of mind rather quickly. This, I guess, comes back to one of your earlier questions: When I went over Elisabeth Plaister's translation, I realized that in English many things sounded far better, more original than in the Spanish original.

IS: This reminds me that Borges, when talking about William Beckford's *Vathek,* suggested that the original was unfaithful to the translation. These comments are fascinating, if only because García Márquez has little to do with English, but Borges, on the other hand, knew it far too well. Have you ever translated other people into Spanish?

FdP: Never. Or rather, never a literary text, only press releases and similar stuff. What I would love to translate is poetry, but unfortunately my knowledge of foreign languages is limited. By the way, I began my career writing sonnets, but later switched to fictional prose.

IS: Your first book, published in 1958 (at age twenty-three), is a collection of sonnets, *Sonetos de lo diario.*

FdP: Yes. Juan José Arreola brought it out in his series Cuadernos del Unicornio. And I've written a few more throughout my life, but never more than twenty altogether. Once or twice I've experimented with free verse, but the result was dissatisfying. The sonnet works best for me.

IS: Let's talk now about when and where you wrote *Palinuro of Mexico.*

FdP: In Iowa City and London. It took eight years—from 1968 to 1976, but I should add to that several more months in which I had to rectify spelling and information.

IS: How many versions did you make?

FdP: It depends on the chapter. For some I made many versions— twenty to thirty—and others just came out finished. An example: chapter 24, "Palinuro on the Stairs," which not long ago was published independently in book form, began as a brief description. I felt it was theatrical and thus decided to turn it into a dramatic piece. The chapter grew as versions accumulated, until it was clear to me that there was no resemblance between the first description and the final text. Then, when the novel was finished, I burned the manuscript. I did so because I didn't want anybody to know how I had arrived at the final product. I wanted to be the sole proprietor of a secret, which I knew I would sooner or later forget.

IS: Did the same happen with your other novels?

FdP: No. I have two boxes with the manuscript and notes of the first, and scattered segments of the third.

IS: The novel was written under the auspices of various grants and writing programs.

FdP: Early on in my career Juan Rulfo suggested that I apply to the Ford Foundation, and they sent me to Iowa. I had been working as a copywriter for a publicity agency in Mexico and abandoned all that. After that I applied for a Guggenheim Fellowship, recommended by Rulfo, Miguel Angel Asturias, and Octavio Paz, who had all read *José Trigo* and were ready to support me. Thanks to the money I got from the foundation, the book began to take shape. Then, in London, I began working for the BBC, where I was a newscaster and producer of programs on Latin America. And in 1985, the family moved again so that I could work for Radio France Internationale as a journalist, and finally I enlisted in Mexico's diplomatic service. *Palinuro of Mexico* obviously benefited immensely from my early globe-trotting, just before the family made it to France.

IS: Tell me about the role of medicine in your novel.

FdP: I originally wanted to become a doctor and began medical school, but for personal reasons had to abandon it. As the book acquired its present form—and it took a long time to do so—I realized my interest in medicine was based on my passion for its romantic aspects. I began to understand that it is nothing but a science of failure. It attempts to save a person's life and, although it succeeds at times, it is truly powerless in that it cannot explain the enigmas of the human body. Our body is a microcosm and is the only thing we truly own in life: with the body we love and hate, with the body we enjoy and suffer.

IS: Julio Cortázar used the phrase "a living cadaver."

FdP: That's exactly what we are—a living cadaver. I'm fascinated by our endless questioning of physical limitations and by the link between body and soul.

IS: Is there any doctor that, as a writer, marked your passion for medicine? Perhaps Burton's *The Anatomy of Melancholy*?

FdP: I was impressed by Burton, but, to be honest, there isn't a doctor/writer I admire. My attempt to establish a bridge between these two fields, literature and medical science, is self-made. Let me repeat that I'm interested in the history of medicine, but only as a romantic dream.

IS: Which isn't unlike the history of the novel as literary genre. After all, the novel's progress is also a chronology of failure, isn't it? I'm thinking of Cervantes and Diderot . . . In its attempt to encompass the world, the encyclopedic novel which you champion cannot but fall short of its totalizing dream.

FdP: Perhaps, but my attempt in *Palinuro of Mexico* wasn't a globalizing one. I knew my limits early on, although at times, I know, it's hard to get that impression from the text. I wouldn't describe my novel as a failure, but that, of course, is up to the critics.

IS: A challenge in *Palinuro of Mexico,* or I should say an obstacle, is the constant shifting of narrative viewpoint, oscillating from the third to the first person and back.

FdP: I didn't set out to employ that type of literary device. It happened as the manuscript developed in the most spontaneous of ways. Suddenly, I realized I wasn't creating a cast of characters but, in fact, a single protagonist with a number of facets or masks. In that multiplicity I myself, as the novel's creator, was also included, if only because the book has a high degree of autobiographical content, even though I've mixed the autobiographical aspect of it with fiction and vice versa. The all-encompassing protagonist could at times become Cousin Walter, who ends up being another aspect of Fernando del Paso—not of what del Paso once was but of what he could have been.

IS: Perhaps that explains why Cousin Walter reminds me of Henry James's protagonist in "The Jolly Corner."

FdP: But this omnipresent character can also unfold into Molkas, Fabricio, and Palinuro's other friends—Molkas representing the most vulgar, unrefined aspects of this character of characters, whereas Fabricio symbolizes his most refined side. Having said that, I should say that the secondary characters—Grandfather Francisco, Mama Clementina, Papa Eduardo, Aunt Luisa, the French botanist—are all more clearly defined and cannot be perceived as variations of the same individual.

IS: Let's then turn to the baroqueness (or neo-baroqueness) in your style, which you mentioned a while ago. When you talk about baroque prose, I cannot help but think of the differences between Mexican and Cuban literary cultures. I say this because *Palinuro of Mexico,* in spite of its multiple references to Mexican history and art, seems to me better suited alongside the works of Cortázar, Guillermo Cabrera Infante, José

Lezama Lima, Severo Sarduy, Reinaldo Arenas, and Alejo Carpentier. It is self-referential, carnivalesque, parodic, and satirical, and, at the same time, it offers a variety of levels of meaning and interpretation. Of course all this has come to be known as the trademark of Cuban writers. Mexican writers, on the other hand, are much more accessible—with the exception, obviously, of Carlos Fuentes, with whom you share more than a hyperactive style. Both countries, Cuba and Mexico, inherited from the Iberian Peninsula a highly convoluted, hybrid worldview, part Christian, part Muslim, part Jewish, and they added even more ingredients to the soup—in the case of Cuba a mulatto and Creole dimension, and in the case of Mexico a mestizo one. And these ingredients were in turn superseded by Oriental and Hindu influences. Our architecture is equally baroque: rococo, churrigueresque, plateresque, and other hybrid textures compete against each other for space and recognition in the same cathedral or monastery. They turn their objects into exaggerations, or what Borges would call "caricatures of themselves." In literature the two nations couldn't be more different.

FdP: Claude Roy, a French writer, once argued that pre-Columbian cultures were already baroque, meaning that in Hispanic and Portuguese America such tendencies were already in place even before the *conquistadores* stopped by.

IS: An interesting point.

FdP: But as you know, there are, according to Eugenio d'Ors, more than twenty different kinds of baroque style. The simplest definition of baroque is a style that tries to saturate space by abusing curves to the point of hyperbole, and you will agree with me that Coatlicue, the Aztec goddess, is indeed baroque. As for my own *barroquismo*, it's influenced by Rabelais and Joyce (who, by the way, isn't exactly a baroque writer, but at the same time isn't far from one), and by more contemporary figures like Günter Grass, Lezama Lima, and Carpentier.

IS: But again, Mexican writers are somehow allergic to excess. I mentioned Carlos Fuentes as an exception, and obviously not all of Fuentes's books—certainly two or three. He was born in 1928 and you in 1935. Perhaps earlier in your career that meant you were part of different generations, but you've turned sixty and he is close to seventy, so the age difference is negligible. Fuentes has been a magnetic figure, the center of a solar system around which other writers gravitate. He has overshadowed others.

FdP: You're right. Today I might say we belong to the same era in Mexican literature, although, to be accurate, he began much earlier than I did, and his early novels, up until *Terra Nostra,* had an impact on me.

IS: In what way?

FdP: *Where the Air Is Clear* was a revelation to me. It was a novel that revolutionized Mexican fiction in that it stationed itself in a decisively urban atmosphere—its protagonist, as you know, is Mexico City. It influenced me in its attitude and openness to other styles. We were at the time reading the same set of authors: Flaubert, whose approach to the novel we admired, as well as Joyce; and in more technical terms, John Dos Passos, Hemingway, Virginia Woolf, and Faulkner. Without them we wouldn't be who we are today.

IS: More than Fuentes influencing you, I would say the two of you maintain a transtextual, transtemporal dialogue. He of course has been a consummate adapter, rewriting—or shall I say: *stealing?*—say, a screenplay by Cabrera Infante, a short story by Adolfo Bioy Casares, a central motif in Henry James's "The Aspern Papers," and so on. But in your case one can talk about bridges reaching out to the other's work. In the last chapter of *Palinuro of Mexico* you mention, among many other literary and mass media names, Artemio Cruz. And in one of the early chapters your protagonist goes out to buy a copy of *Where the Air Is Clear.* Then, of course, there's the chapter "A Bullet Very Close to the Heart," in which you discuss the fate of Ambrose Bierce. In the eighties Fuentes published his novel *Old Gringo,* in which the spirit of your chapter, if not its words, is present. He even describes him as an "old gringo," as you had done: *viejo gringo.* Ambrose Bierce, by the way, also appears in *Noticias del imperio . . .*

FdP: Shortly after *Palinuro de Mexico* was published, I had lunch with Fuentes. At the time he told me: "Fernando, I've been told that one of your chapters deals with Bierce's experience in Mexico as he joins Pancho Villa's military forces. I don't want to read it, and I won't read it, because I'm preparing a whole novel on the same topic, on which I've been working for a while." It's a coincidence, then, but an expected one. After all, once one writer discovers a fascinating character like Bierce, who crossed the border at age seventy-something, traveled through Mexico, and was never heard of again, the topic becomes a magnet to others.

IS: You're not only a novelist but a painter, and your pictorial art has been exhibited in various countries. Occasionally *Tristram Shandy* dares to use drawings and graphic design to express what words cannot say. Cabrera Infante paid tribute to Sterne in *Three Trapped Tigers*, where to describe darkness a full page is printed in black ink, and several graphic designs are present. Others in what I've called the "encyclopedic tradition," which includes Cortázar's *Hopscotch*, Georges Perec, Umberto Eco, John Barth, and Carlo Emilio Gadda, have also made use of this practice. It strikes me as an interesting fact that you don't, in spite of your background as a painter.

FdP: I was tempted, but I chose to keep these worlds separate. My view of literature is still based on its oral tradition. A good page is one that can be read and enjoyed aloud. Its sound is what matters—one shouldn't mess around with easy tricks.

IS: As one of its many aspects, *Palinuro of Mexico* can also be approached as a political novel. One of its leitmotifs is the student massacre, in October 1968, at Tlatelolco Square. Just as the Olympic Games were about to begin, the Mexican government, as you well know, was facing heavy pressure from social forces asking for democratic change. But refusing to open up, the ruling party under the leadership of President Gustavo Díaz Ordáz ordered the army to confront the student uprising with tanks and bullets. Many thousands died, and many more were injured. Of course the Tlatelolco incident appears numerous places in Mexican literature, from Elena Poniatowska's *Massacre in Mexico* to books by José Agustín, Gustavo Sáenz, and Parménides García Saldaña. But your work has a special place on that shelf: the protagonist in *José Trigo* is killed by army squads at Tlatelolco; and Palinuro dies too, although at home, after being badly beaten in the Zócalo—or perhaps, he begins a new life in Tlatelolco. And yet, by 1968 you were thirty-three, too old to be an undergraduate at the Universidad Nacional Autónoma de México or the Instituto Politecnico Nacional, the two academic institutions where the uprising began. Thus, *Palinuro of Mexico* is, in a sense, about political nostalgia.

FdP: You're right. By 1968, still in Mexico, I had already begun writing the novel (under another title). I was married and had a petit bourgeois life. I witnessed the student uprising, but was never a participant. I've always been a left-wing intellectual, although a more moderate one in recent years. I was active during the Bay of Pigs protests against the United States. And yet, the Tlatelolco incident left a deep mark on me. Suddenly I had a new character, named Palinuro, a medical student killed in 1968, and I wanted to make use of him. Of course by then I had already read Cyril Connolly's *The Unquiet Grave* [published under the pseudonym of Palinurus], which I had received as a gift from a poet friend, Francisco Cervantes. This new character forced me to return to the Mexico City of the fifties for the novel's setting, which—it remains a curious fact to me—didn't bother any Mexican readers. The novel had begun as a re-creation of *my* adolescent years, particularly of my high school years in Justo Sierra Street. Then I realized that Palinuro needed to die in 1968, but since I didn't want to sacrifice what I had already written, I let the discrepancy in dates stand. The Justo Sierra milieu attracted me enormously, and I regretted abandoning it for a sterile atmosphere like the Ciudad Universitaria campus. But Palinuro had imposed himself as the novel's heart, and there was nothing I could do. And since my protagonist in *José Trigo* had died at Tlatelolco, I felt terrible about repeating myself. So I decided Palinuro would be beaten in 1968, and only afterwards would he die. This has created confusion among readers: critics and careful readers have misinterpreted my words, claiming Palinuro was indeed another victim during the massacre.

IS: Your reply brings up a crucial issue: the tie, no doubt problematic, between the Mexican government and the country's intelligentsia. I wouldn't want to repeat myself either, nor devote too much time to a topic that has soaked up incredible amounts of ink. Latin American writers and artists, as you know, often begin their careers as opponents *of* the government, speakers for the masses, antagonists *of* the powers that be. But sooner or later, they end up embracing the very enemy they vilified and fought in their younger days. The examples are numerous, including Octavio Paz and Carlos Fuentes. Could we also include you on the same list? After all, since the mid-eighties you've been part of Mexico's diplomatic service. And now you direct the Biblioteca Iberoamericana "Octavio Paz" in Guadalajara, funded by the government. Have you betrayed your adolescent principles? Should we, readers of today, read *Palinuro of Mexico* from a different perspective, and not, as has been done, as a form of a protest?

FdP: It's easy, at least in Mexico, to talk about "the government," "the state," as if they were nothing but abstract entities. One has friends in the government, longtime friends. Besides, valuable writers and artists, from José Vasconcelos to Jaime Torres Bodet, have worked for Mexico's government since . . . well, since time immemorial. Don't forget that our economy is shaped in such a way that the thinking person, once a commitment to art or literature is made, has limited options in order to earn a living. In my case, I'm far from earning enough money from royalties, prizes, and awards to support my family. Mine has been what I would call a succès d'estime. Also, after years in London and Paris, my decision to enter the diplomatic service became a kind of return—a return to my homeland, a return to my soul and sources. It allowed me to return to the study of Mexican pictorial art, music, and dance, and to help disseminate them. Which means that I've a clear conscience, to the extent that I represent the country's politics from a cultural perspective, not the country's politics from the political side.

IS: Finally, I've been thinking about your job as a librarian, which, in many ways, is what you do at Biblioteca Iberoamericana. Hispanic American civilization has a long tradition of literary figures becoming heads of major libraries, from our archetypal one, Borges, to Leopoldo Lugones, Alfonso Reyes, Paul Grousac, and so on. Add to this the fact that another aspect of *Palinuro of Mexico* is its cataloging of books from Hispanic, Anglo-Saxon, and French cultures. What about your personal relationship with books?

FdP: To be honest, my duties as director of Biblioteca Iberoamericana— which is small, 18,000 titles, created only in 1991—leave me little time to have one. And yet, my relationship with the book is quite close. Before opening one, I always begin by smelling a book. Old books of course smell better. In recent ones, the smell is neither pleasant nor distinct. Before leaving Mexico for England, I had some two thousand volumes of my own, which I had to store for more than two decades. I love old-fashioned hardcovers. But I've ceased to read. I don't keep up with recent publications. Instead, I devote my time to the art of rereading. Lately I've been rereading Joyce, *Don Quixote,* and the Bible, which continue to amaze me for their inexhaustible nature.

Tender Gender

Elena Poniatowska

Elena Poniatowska (Mexico, b. 1932) is the author of Massacre in Mexico *(1991),* Tinísima *(1996),* Here's to You, Jesusa! *(2001), among many books. She is a regular contributor to the Mexican daily* La Jornada. *This interview took place at the Guadalupe Cultural Arts Center in San Antonio, Texas, October 1995.*

IS: To the best of my knowledge, you are the only Mexican writer interested in what is done north of the Rio Grande by writers of Hispanic background, which has led you to discuss this production critically. Furthermore, you have translated into Spanish *The House on Mango Street* by Sandra Cisneros. Would you comment on the explosive new literary "boom" in English, principally among Latinas, and what, if any, is the reception it's receiving south of the border?

EP: I used to think nobody in Mexico knew anything about Latino writers, and especially about Chicana writers. The reason had to do with culture as well as class. For women south of the Rio Grande, literature is a subproduct of their life. Most of them are members of the middle and upper middle class, and they write because they can do it, because they have the money to do it, and because they have the time to do it—just as Emily Dickinson and Jane Austen did more than a century ago. But for a Latino north of the Rio Grande, to write is to surpass your class condition. That explains, in part at least, why Latina women in the U.S. are much more self-assertive than their counterparts in Mexico. The first one, Ilan, introduces herself thus: "Hola, mi nombre es Soila Fulanita. Soy chicana y lesbiana." The second one, instead, is rather naive: "Hola, me llamo Dulce de Gracia." No national reference is given, no gender, no ideology. Personally, I don't have anything as shocking to say about myself, and I could never be so brave. But their in-your-face attitude is crucial and should not be minimized, especially because many—though not all, of course—Latinas are lesbians. Instead, we, *las mujeres mexicanas,* are extremely careful about what we say about ourselves. We never speak about our sexual life, and I'm not sure we ever will, no matter how much things might change. The Latino's affection—and affectation—for pop items will never cease to amaze me: I'm thinking of the many colorful symbols they use in their clothing à la Frida Kahlo, the artifacts they use in their cars, used in Mexico only by taxi drivers, the condiments they bring to their cooking, their grandmother's tales, the Virgin of Guadalupe, and so on. Their novels and stories are packed with mystical and mysterious tales about the world beyond childhood themes.

IS: Opposing selves.

EP: Latinos are obsessed with recuperating their collective past, things about which we care very little. We, for instance, again as a result of our class differences, never talk about the Virgin of Guadalupe or about wrestlers like El Santo and other legendary personalities of *luche libre*. We're part of the middle class, which makes it prohibitive to dwell on such vulgar topics in public. A few of us take exception, of course, like cultural commentator Carlos Monsiváis and myself, perhaps because we love slang and jargon and street culture. But our attitude is certainly marginal. Mainstream writers in Mexico are always dealing with the problems of the middle class. And the same, by the way, could be said about painting. Since the sixties Chicano art has dealt with popular motifs and symbols; it incorporates portraits of Cesar Chavez, Ruben Salazar, even Frida Kahlo. Mexican pictorial art is more highbrow, more refined and pretentious, and thus also less accessible to the masses. Consequently, when the feminist magazine *Fem* came out with a picture of the Virgin of Guadalupe in high heels and a miniskirt, people were scandalized. But if the same idea was painted by a Chicano—and it probably has been— I trust it would be taken naturally. The gap, at least to me, is clear: Latinos are far ahead of us, sexually and culturally. They are not afraid to write about their lesbianism, as we are. Lesbianism, as I see it, is their response to the abuse millions of Mexican women undergo at the powerful hands of their husbands—south of the border, it's very easy for a wife to be beaten up by her spouse.

IS: You use the terms "Latino" and "Chicano" in their generic, masculine forms. How about male figures in this artistic constellation you're discussing?

EP: I deeply admire Tomás Rivera, author of the classic . . . *And the Earth Did Not Devour Him* and particularly Rudolfo Anaya's *Bless Me, Ultima*, Alma Villanueva, the poet Alurista. But I concentrate on women because I read them with passion. Shouldn't we all? Women hardly get the attention they deserve.

IS: Chicanos complain that, until very recently, they've been ignored by Mexico's artistic establishment and literary circle. Granted, in the last decade or so a revival has taken place, but the eclipse persists. I get the impression that it will not fade away easily.

EP: Editorial Era, my publisher, for a while made an effort to introduce in Spanish some Chicano intellectuals: Miguel Méndez and the historians Luis Leal, who is an expert on Mexican literature of the revolution, and Juan Gómez-Quiñones, and the very good looking Juan Bruce-Novoa among them. But you're right: Ignorance is rampant, and prejudice against Chicanos is dies hard. We usually address those that left us behind as *traditores,* traitors—as rude and rootless people. It's ironic, of course, because the social, political, cultural, and genealogical roots among Mexican Americans are terribly strong, probably stronger than their equivalent south of the border. Even in Tijuana and Ciudad Juárez these roots are mighty.

IS: In your conversations with Latinas, do you feel their knowledge about literary matters in Mexico is less nearsighted? Is their approach to Mexico less prejudiced than the other way around?

EP: No, I think it also suffers tremendously from reductionism and simplification. Chicanas are acquainted with Rosario Castellanos, Juan Rulfo, Octavio Paz, Carlos Fuentes, and Sor Juana Inés de la Cruz. Their culture, nevertheless, is less interested in literary paraphernalia than in finding connections with popular culture. Happily, they're getting themselves very well equipped, which means that some form of encounter is taking place. It's still too early to say what this dialogue will bring.

IS: Your English strikes me as impeccable. Yet this morning, without a hint of modesty, you told me it would be very hard to converse freely in it. How many languages do you speak?

EP: Since I was born in France, my first language is French. I learned Spanish in Mexico, but never in school. At home we spoke French, and both my mother and grandmother were hoping that I would learn Spanish on the street. Consequently, mine would not be a proper Spanish. I used to make shameful mistakes, and unfortunately I still make many grammatical errors at this advanced age, and many of them make it into my literature.

IS: Have you dared to write in a language other than Spanish?

EP: As an adolescent, I was "interned" at a nun's convent in Philadelphia and had to write papers in English. Nowadays, when asked to talk to an English-speaking audience, I'll prepare a written text in English. It won't be a translation; I'll write it directly in English. But I do get lots of help from my friends. And, as you've noticed, I have an awful pronunciation: For instance, I'll pronounce "those" as the Spanish "dos"; and "those" and "dos" sound to me identical.

IS: Does your role as a translator activate language in a different fashion than the usual retrieving of words and syntax used in fiction and nonfiction?

EP: To be a translator is to be an interpreter. Which brings forth an enormous amount of creativity. You must take a step back and allow the writer to gain full command—to allow her or him to find in your tongue what was intended in the original. Helen Lane, for example, did an extraordinary job translating *Massacre in Mexico*. My work gained new life. It reached unexpected emotions in the English version. We, of course, must talk about versions when discussing translations, because the new product is somehow linked to the original text, but if it will ever be born, it has to be adapted into the receiving culture. I find women translators to have a unique sensibility for the craft. Take the remarkable work done by Margaret Sayers Peden of Sor Juana Inés de la Cruz's *Poems, Protest, and a Dream*, for which you wrote an introduction, as well as of Octavio Paz's biography of Sor Juana, *The Traps of Faith*. The nun's spirit is revived, renewed by Sayers Peden's female flavor. Sandra Cisneros's book is—though I have translated many articles—the only one I've translated so far; so I'm a neophyte. Correction: A few years ago I also did some stories that a few writer friends asked me to translate.

IS: You're known both as a journalist and as a fiction writer. What does journalism offer that fiction doesn't?

EP: Every week I submit a column of two and a half pages to *La Jornada* and *El Nacional*. I have a commitment with a Mexican daily and keep that dose steady. I see myself mainly as a journalist. I always said to myself: "When I get older, I'll have time to write literature." As a young woman, I wanted to write my own stories, but at the same time I wanted to be useful to society—much like a boy scout. I wanted my voice to contribute something to changing the status quo. I felt it iniquitous to write about my soul, or my hair, or my family in the most personal and self-centered of ways. The tension between these two aspects will always exist: When I do too much of one, I feel I neglect the other. My guilt is rampant, and I'm always looking to find a balance. But I feel I've paid more attention to journalism on the whole. I'm always telling myself: Next year, I should do more of the other facet. Again, it's an ongoing quarrel. Perhaps this rivalry derives from the fact that I still have the feeling that writing is a social act: I want to help others. That's why I'm always interviewing people, privileging someone else's words in my work instead of my own.

IS: South of the border, you're among the courageous few ready to write biography. I wonder if any attempts have been made to write autobiography. Would hiding behind other people's voices preclude such forays?

EP: I don't know. My life, for me, isn't very interesting. At the moment I'm working on my mother's memoir. I truly care for the project. When my brother died in a car accident in 1968, my mother was very sad. He had been her only son, a sunshine kid. I suggested she sit and write her life down, which she did—in French. Hers is an extraordinary odyssey. She was born in Paris but grew up on a Mexican hacienda. She fell in love with my father when he jumped from the floor to the piano—she found that rather amusing. And yet, they were never a happy couple. So this is, in some way, an autobiography. On the other hand, I would be incapable of writing about my own journey. Perhaps I would have done it when I was younger. Young people love to think about themselves constantly. But I honestly find myself boring.

IS: It's intriguing that both biography and autobiography are incredibly popular in the United States. Enter any bookstore, and you'll find a separate section devoted to them. In Latin America, on the other hand, they would never have their own section, simply because not enough is published in the genre. Why is it that societies in Hispanic America hardly embrace these forms of writing?

EP: Perhaps because Latin American writers put so much of themselves into their books. Carlos Fuentes, for example, who still uses a typewriter and uses a single finger to type—*el dedo integral*—claims he doesn't need a psychiatrist; literature cures him of his ghosts. Similarly, I put much of myself into my work, which means that autobiography as such is unneeded. We have fiction as medicine.

IS: While we're on the subject of the attitude of Latin American writers and their role in society, I want to ask you about the impact some of your books have had and how you've dealt with the powers that be. *Massacre in Mexico* to begin with—an explosive, outspoken, destabilizing volume, if there ever was one. By means of photographs and journalistic pastiche, you created a sharp, edgy, urgent portrait of the flaws of the Mexican political system. How did the government react?

EP: I was never threatened, but Editorial Era, my publisher, was. Somebody advised them that a bomb would explode in the building. The company's head, Tomás Espresate, said: "I've been in the Spanish civil war; I've suffered bombs and bomb threats, so I'm not scared. Let them fight, but I won't back away." Nothing happened, of course. Also, a rumor was spread that my book would be confiscated by the police. Obviously the government was very unhappy with it. It showed a face the nation could not afford to show at a time when Mexico was promoting itself as a peaceful country suitable for the Olympic Games. It was not confiscated, either. All this was great publicity, of course.

IS: Censorship is the mother of literature.

EP: Everyone wanted a copy. We went through a reprinting a week. Very impressive.

IS: Were you worried, personally?

EP: Not at all. I'm very unconscious, which sometimes makes people get into a lot of trouble because of me. Usually, when bad things happen to me I don't notice them. When I would notice secret policemen waiting outside my apartment, I would ask them if they wanted a cup of coffee. Or when I would get numerous journalists taking pictures of me, I would smile rather than think I was being followed. On the subject of censorship: I've experienced it hard and wild. Even today. Often sections of my texts are cut just before the daily newspaper edition reaches the stand—even in *La Jornada,* the left-wing daily. Censorship mainly comes from within the media vehicle, be that a newspaper or a TV channel.

IS: When did the idea for *Massacre in Mexico* come about?

EP: I started doing interviews on the subject of the 1968 massacre, and nobody would publish them. So I kept them all, and my editors at Editorial Era suggested I bring them all out in book form. I subsequently made other similar books, like the one on the earthquake, but they didn't come out especially well. Somehow the material was too close to me, and I didn't work on it as much as I should have. I have been called a "new journalist," in the tradition of Tom Wolfe. But the book acquired a life of its own. I never emulated or mimicked anybody else's style.

IS: Do you write every day?

EP: Every day. In a messy study, constantly interrupted by daily life—children, grandchildren, the telephone, errands, etc.

IS: With a typewriter? Isabel Allende once told me that had she had a word processor, the outcome of *The House of the Spirits* would have been drastically different. Could you say the same about your work? Do words dance in a particular way when they come out of a word processor?

EP: In 1985, during a stay at the University of California Davis, I finally learned how to use a computer. It took me about four months, and it changed my life forever. I used to rewrite and revise a lot, and the whole process has been simplified. I'm still amazed at the quantity of paper I used to waste. My style, obviously, has changed: it's freer, less bumpy. What's interesting is that, no matter how fast technology advances, I will always have my amulets next to me. I have a small *alebrije* given to me by Rosario Ferre. I used to have a sticker of Rius's *Los supermachos*, a popular Mexican comic strip. I'm also surrounded by books, particularly Cyril Connolly's *The Unquiet Grave*, John Berger's *Ways of Seeing*, as well as *Anna Karenina*.

IS: I once heard you say that to be a woman writer in Mexico is to be part of the literature of the oppressed. Latin America has a male intellectual establishment. Things have begun to change in the last twenty years, but all too slowly. What does that entail for you?

EP: We've always been considered inferior to men. Look at Rosario Castellanos, an unhappy woman with an unhappy love life, although a writer with a sharp sense of humor and a philanthropic disposition. Likewise Elena Garro, Octavio Paz's first wife, responsible for *Recollections of Things to Come* and other novels. Over the years she has slowly lost her possibilities. She lives in a small apartment in Cuernavaca, sixty miles from Mexico's capital, surrounded by numerous cats which have taken over the rooms. Elena sleeps next to the main apartment door, almost on the threshold. But Carlos Fuentes, for instance, is cosmopolitan, travels and lectures all over the world, and does not worry about cats. So there you have it: male and female writers in Mexico fall into opposite patterns. At the same time, ever since Laura Esquivel became an instant sensation with *Like Water for Chocolate,* preceded by Isabel Allende's *The House of the Spirits,* a boom of Latin American women writers is taking place. Neither of them seems like Shakespeare to me, but they are very successful, wonderful best-sellers. Men are very jealous of them. They say, "Nowadays, to succeed one has to be a *pinche vieja,* a stupid woman."

IS: What has changed?

EP: An increasing curiosity about the way women think and feel. An increasingly diversified public interested in other views. An undiminished interest in sex . . . This explains, in part at least, the success of Esquivel, Angeles Mastretta, Guadalupe Loaeza, Sara Sefchovich, and others in Mexico.

IS: Carlos Fuentes once portrayed the writer in Mexico as "a speaker for the silent masses."

EP: Not anymore. Those silent for decades are beginning to speak out. In that respect, writers are becoming obsolete. Political activism and the wide range of media outlets is allowing people to come to terms with their own voice. The Zapatista rebels in Chiapas are but one example. So we are forced to answer the question in a more urgent and essential manner. Regardless of any political inclinations, a writer, first and foremost, has to write well. Literature is coming under attack from different media forms—movies, TV, the Internet. If we are to remain valuable, we have to find a reason to produce a type of art, an imaginary universe unavailable anywhere else . . .

Behind the News

Jorge Ramos

Jorge Ramos (Mexico, b. 1958) is the coanchor for Noticiero Univisión. His books include The Other Face of America: Chronicles of the Immigrants Shaping Our Future *and* No Borders: A Journalist's Search for Home *(both 2002) and* The Latino Wave *(2004). This interview took place in Boston, Massachusetts, October 2002.*

IS: Who's the audience for Noticiero Univisión?

JR: I would say that in this country, and that is what many people are not aware of, there are at least 30 to 35 million people who speak Spanish. Some of them of course are immigrants. Some of them are American citizens, are Latinos. And that's exactly our audience. Of course the Latino community is not monolithic. We have Cuban Americans in southern Florida, 3 percent of the Hispanic population. We have Puerto Ricans in New York, 9 percent of the Latino community. Or Mexican Americans and Mexicans in Texas and California that compose about 57 percent of our audience.

IS: And what is the age of your audience? What is the average age?

JR: In the United States the average age is thirty-six. For the Latino community it's twenty-six. Therefore, we have a young community. We have a community that in many cases does not have, of course, political representation. But in less than sixty years, there will be more than 150 million Latinos in this country. And this truly is transforming this country in ways that it would be impossible to predict.

IS: Now, no other previous immigrant group ever had network television like Univisión. The Germans, the Italians, the Jews, the Polish—

JR: Not even the Irish.

IS: And in major markets like LA, like New York City, like Miami, Noticiero Univisión is number one, even above ABC News. How does the country react to this? What is your sense of what the country is feeling about this rapid growth of Spanish language viewers?

JR: The initial reaction is complete surprise. Some people are shocked. The fact is that the most listened to radio station in New York, it's in

Spanish. The most watched newscasts in cities like Los Angeles, Houston, Fresno, and Miami, especially among those who are between eighteen and thirty-four or sometimes eighteen to forty-nine years old, they're in Spanish. And the fact is that this is a trend going on in almost every single city in the United States which has a large Latino community, in Chicago, New York, for instance, or even San Francisco. The first reaction is shock. It's difficult for television and radio executives to accept the fact that they're losing the ratings battle against Spanish-speaking radio and television stations. And then, when we're not talking about only the news media, when we're talking about just the fact that in many cities in this country—in Hialeah, in South Florida, in Pearson, in Chicago, in East LA, in Brooklyn or Queens—when you realize that sometimes you might feel discriminated against if you do not speak Spanish, then there's a sense of . . . people get upset. And they constantly criticize Latinos and immigrants. Because they are saying—it's not true—that we're not assimilating fast enough to this country.

IS: How do you respond to that criticism? How do you respond to the criticism that because Latinos have a Spanish-language television, rather than helping them in the transition of becoming American, instead it's stopping them?

JR: You have to tell the facts. I recently read a study by the University of Southern California. And Latinos are getting higher wages, are getting better education, are escaping poverty and at the same time learning English at a fast pace. Those are the facts. And on the other hand, to be able to speak Spanish in this country is giving me a fantastic option. I can read Hemingway in English and García Márquez in Spanish. I can root for Mark McGwire and Sammy Sosa at the same time. I could listen to Britney Spears—I've a fifteen year old, so I have to listen to Britney Spears—or Madonna. And at the same time I can listen to Shakira, who I truly admire a lot, or Jennifer Lopez. I could get my news from CNN or from PBS and also from TeleFutura and Univisión. Yes, I have that fantastic option. I was reading the other day an article about Rosario Ferre, the Puerto Rican writer, and she was saying exactly the same thing. If I have two hands, why do you want me to use only one? If I have two languages, why do you want to force me to speak only in English when I can also do it in Spanish?

IS: What do you think is the role that Spanish-language television in this country serves in the promotion of culture, in the perpetuation of the identity of the people? Does it help people feel closer to home? What role does Univisión play in the Latino family that speaks Spanish?

JR: You're obsessed with language, Ilan. In fact, that's clearly an understatement. But the Latino identity has a lot to do with two factors. First of all our country of origin. I've known people who are first-, second-, and third-generation Latinos in this country. And you ask them, Are you a Latino? Are you a Hispanic? They say oh no, no, no, I'm Colombian or I'm Cuban or I'm Mexican. It's important where you come from. But the second element is language. Almost in every family to speak Spanish is linked to your identity as a Hispanic or Latino. Even though we do not have a national political agenda. When I say "we," I'm saying Latinos and Hispanics, because Cuban Americans have a completely different concern. For instance, Cuban Americans are truly obsessed about Fidel Castro in Cuba. Puerto Ricans might be more concerned about social issues and the presence of the navy in Vieques. And Mexican Americans might be more concerned about issues related to immigration and Mexico. Even though we do not have a national agenda, and we do not have a national leader like Jesse Jackson, we do have certain points and certain common issues that pull us together. And one has to do, of course, with language.

IS: Why don't we have leaders like Jesse Jackson?

JR: Because the Hispanic community isn't monolithic.

IS: It's fragmented . . .

JR: Yes. It's difficult to get someone from the Cuban American community that's only 3 percent of the population to represent 20 million Mexican Americans. Once we had Cesar Chavez, but he was not Cuban enough, of course, for the Cuban American community and for the Puerto Rican community. We had Jorge Mas Canosa in Miami. But many Mexican Americans felt that he didn't represent their interests. And since Cuban Americans tend to vote more Republican than Democrat, and about 60 to 65 percent of the Hispanic population usually vote for Democrats, it was difficult for Mas Canosa to become a national leader. That's one of the main problems that we have in the Latino community. To transform our numbers, 35 million, to transform our purchasing power, more than $500 billion a year and it will be $1 trillion in the year 2010, to transform these numbers into political power, that's difficult.

IS: Do you see a future in which the differences of nationality, of ethnic and racial background within Latinos, are erased and we become a unity?

JR: At this point, I find it difficult. But every time journalists predict something, we get it wrong. I'm not going to predict that there will never be a Latino leader for all Mexican Americans, Puerto Ricans, Salvadorans, Cuban Americans. But at this point it's difficult to even detect the possibility of that happening. The problem is again, lack of political representation. We are 12 percent of the population and we only have nineteen Congressmen. In comparison, the African American community, they have thirty-nine. And they're also 12 percent of the population. We are 12 percent of the population and we don't even have one senator, one governor, or one judge on the Supreme Court. There's a long, long way to go from the numbers to the political representation. And this happens also on television. For instance, only 2 percent of all the fictional characters on English-language television in the United States are Latinos. And only 1.3 percent, for instance, of all the reports that you might watch in any newscast in English are produced by Latino correspondents. There's a long way to go from our numbers to our representation.

IS: How do you manage to solve the tension between the various groups in the language that you use as a newscaster? There's Puerto Rican Spanish that is different from Cuban or Mexican Spanish. And by being one of the cohosts of Noticiero Univisión, you, I assume, have to become this neutral Latino, a Latino for all Latinos. But you're Mexican. You are an immigrant from Mexico. Do you try to tone down your Mexican accent, certain words that you use? Do you create a neutral language, a neutral Spanish that belongs to nobody?

JR: As a matter of fact, when I first came to the United States—it was in 1983. And I arrived in Los Angeles and I got my first job about a year later. The first news director, Pete Moraga, told me: "You know you sound too Mexican." "What do you mean 'too Mexican'?" He answered: "Yes, you sound too Mexican." We have this way of speaking in Mexico in Spanish and you're, I'm sure, pretty aware of it . . .

IS: We sing the language . . .

JR: Yes: we don't talk, we sing. And it was way too much. Basically we extend certain letters like *e*—"peeerro," which is dog, or "mamááá." Instead of saying that, he taught me how to speak a neutral Spanish.

IS: He coached you?

JR: He coached me in a way in which nowadays many people when I talk to them and when I find them in the streets, they say, are you from Bolivia? Are you Colombian? Or sometimes they even say that I'm Cuban or Puerto Rican, which is fantastic. Because it's not only me, but most of the correspondents, Latino correspondents in Spanish, in television and radio. Unless they only work for local markets, they have a neutral Spanish. And at the same time we have instituted certain words that could be understood by many people. Just to say the simple word "stapler" in Spanish. Chileans say "corchetera." Mexicans say "engrapadora." "Guagua" for Cubans is a bus. For others, it's a baby. And for Mexicans it might be just an expression of . . .

IS: Barking dog.

JR: No, of a set of beautiful female twins . . .

IS: You mean "wow-wow."

JR: Exactly. It's difficult to find a neutral Spanish. Another element that makes it much more complicated is that of course we are including Spanglish in our conversations and in our newscasts. It's easier to say. Instead of saying the "green card," and try to explain that in Spanish, we only say "green card" with a Spanish pronunciation, "greencar." Or instead of saying a "social security number," which would take thirty seconds of the newscast to explain, we only say "el social."

IS: Your audience will understand it . . .

JR: The most important purpose for us is just inform in the twenty-two minutes of the newscast that we have. And we do not pretend to speak pure Spanish. We get criticized from Argentineans, from Spaniards, from Mexicans—

IS: For polluting the language.

JR: Exactly. Because—that's exactly what happens when you come from a country, from Latin America, from a region where you speak Spanish and you are immersed in a country in which most of the people, 270 million people, speak English. That's what happens.

IS: Traditionally, Jorge, one expects the host on a news hour to deliver the news without interjecting any opinion: flat, impartial, objective. You are nontraditional in that sense insofar as you have a column that is published weekly all over Latin America and in Spanish language newspapers in the U.S. where you give your own opinion about immigration, about politics, about issues of language, about social issues . . .

JR: And opinions about amnesty, for instance.

IS: How to solve the tension between the impartial news deliverer and the opinionated thinker?

JR: Probably what I do in Spanish wouldn't be admitted in English. In the 6:30 P.M. newscast, people don't expect my opinion. They expect the news. But sometimes it's expected from me to be a voice of the voiceless. There're between 8 and 12 million undocumented immigrants in the U.S. The only place one listens to their concerns is the Spanish-language media. It's impossible for them to have a voice on ABC, CBS, or NBC.

IS: So you're a spokesperson for undocumented immigrants?

JR: It wasn't planned. It simply happened. Sometimes I feel frustrated with TV. This conversation that we're having is unusual. Television is not exactly the best place for a debate or for the discussion of ideas. Radio is much better. Newspapers are much better. Books are even better. This happened gradually, in which I slowly became first a proponent, for instance, for an amnesty, for more than 8 million undocumented immigrants in this country. And then I sometimes became the voice of these 8 million undocumented immigrants. Most of them, who do not even speak English, understand that I'm also an immigrant, that I have a forum in the newscast and the newspapers and books, in which I can tell other people what I think and what's fair. And for instance, I've had the opportunity to talk three times with President George W. Bush. It's not that Bush is listening to me, but in our conversations before and after the taping of the interviews and even in our conversations, I've been able to ask him, "Do you want to be a compassionate president?" That's what he campaigned for when he was a candidate for the Republican Party. Isn't it the most compassionate thing you could do to give an amnesty or to include in a guest worker program or to include in a legalization program these 8 million people who are living in fear. I mean, what can you tell a family whose children go to a public school, and these children do not know when they come back every night if their parents are going to be home because they might be deported. I've had the opportunity to talk with some of the most important leaders in this country about issues that otherwise might be completely silenced.

IS: Americans seem overwhelmed by an ambivalence toward immigrants that goes from outright compassion to undefined repulsion.

JR: Every day one thousand immigrants cross the border legally from

Mexico to the U.S. Every year one million legal immigrants come to this country. Illegal immigration has nothing to do with politics or with the military or with law enforcement or with fences. It has to do only with economics, the law of supply and demand. Because there are people in Mexico who are making five dollars a day, who are unemployed, and because there are jobs for them in the United States, that's why they come here. If they couldn't find jobs, they wouldn't be here. It's at once interesting and saddening to notice that those who are already here sometimes, and many times, want to close the door on those who are coming behind them. And what I've noticed is that among the Latino community sometimes there's an open attitude towards immigrants because they understand that some people are coming behind them. At the same time those who are already American citizens, or those who are already legal residents of this country, reject undocumented immigrants in ways which are for me truly vicious and difficult to understand.

IS: Specifically, how do you relate to the community?

JR: One of the tenets in journalism is credibility. When I started as a newscaster, some seventeen years ago, I didn't have gray hair. I was twenty-eight years old. I had no credibility. No one believed me. At one point an executive even asked me to color my hair so it would look a little—with more gray hair, with more seriousness. What I'm bringing to this debate has to do with a certain degree of credibility. People believe what I say. And that's the most important thing that I have. People believe what I'm saying. What I'm bringing to this debate is certain facts and certain information. Instead of just screaming and allowing for this emotional debate, "Are they good or are they bad?" I'm just bringing the facts. According to the National Academy of Sciences, all immigrants, legal and undocumented, contribute more than 10 billion dollars to the U.S. economy. Yes, immigrants are needed in this country in order to maintain our high standard of living. Immigrants are needed to pay for social benefits for our rapidly aging population. Without immigrants, this nation would simply collapse. They account for 33 percent of all domestic employees. There would be no nannies. Immigrants account for 33 percent of all farmers and fishermen. There would be no food on our tables without immigrants. Immigrants account for 18 percent of all assembly line workers and for all of those who work in the service industry. In *The Other Face of America* I included a chapter called "A Day without a Mexican." What would happen? What would happen is that the economy would collapse. Basically, what I'm bringing is the understanding that immigrants are a positive element in society.

IS: Do you have political aspirations of your own?

JR: I've spent too many years as a witness to history. I was right there when the Berlin Wall fell. I've been to four wars. I've talked to almost every single Latin American president and American president in the last fifteen years. I've been a witness to history. And I'm getting tired of that, sometimes. I want to do something. I don't just want to be listening to it. And I don't just want to write about it. I want to do something about it. At one point in my life I thought that my role should have been to go back to Mexico and help with the democratic movement in Mexico, so Mexico could eventually become a truly democratic country. But that was a little quixotic. It didn't happen. And Vicente Fox did it for all of us, of course with millions of Mexicans behind him. At the same time I still feel that I should jump sometimes from being a witness to being someone who's doing something about, not only Latinos and immigrants in this country, but probably about Mexicans in Mexico. Yes, I do have political aspirations. I don't exactly know how to channel that energy toward politics, but eventually I might jump.

IS: Does that mean that your political aspirations that you just mentioned having to do with Mexico might also have to do eventually with the United States?

JR: What's interesting is that I'm becoming a completely unknown person in Mexico. After twenty years outside of Mexico, many people have no idea who I am. It would take me years to get the name recognition that I might have in the United States. It might be a better idea to stay in the United States than go back to Mexico, to a country which is a little foreign to me now. There's a song by Facundo Cabral: "No soy de aquí, ni soy de allá." "I'm neither from here, nor from there."

IS: It speaks of your own dilemma . . .

JR: I'm not completely integrated into the United States. You can even hear my thick accent in English. And at the same time when I go back to Mexico, it's a little foreign to me. To be precise, I'm from nowhere . . .

Always Running

Luis J. Rodriguez

Luis J. Rodriguez (USA, b. 1954) is the author of, among other books, Always Running: La Vida Loca: Gang Days in L.A. *(1993) and* The Republic of East L.A. *(2002). This interview took place in Boston, Massachusetts, January 2001.*

IS: You were a gang member between the ages of eleven and eighteen. And many years later, in your late thirties, you wrote a classic memoir about those days, called *Always Running: La Vida Loca*. Why did the book take so long? Or better, did it take long enough?

LR: It's hard to leave that life, and then enter a writer's life—especially since besides the gang, I had a long period of drug addictions. So I spent many years just trying to stabilize myself by working in factories, steel mills, getting married, anything. But I knew that somehow within me, I wanted to be a writer. I had started to write when I was in jail, when I was around fifteen years old. There was something purposeful in this. Writing connected to me in a meaningful way. Years later I knew this was what I wanted to do. But I had to learn how to write. I didn't know how to write. I wasn't a good student. I spoke Spanish entering the schools at age six. But even after high school, my English wasn't all that hot. I needed to go back to school as an adult. It took time to enter a writer's life: taking writing classes at night, working for newspapers, writing freelance for publications, and then getting into poetry, which attracted me. That's why it took so long.

IS: Was there a difference between Chicanos and Mexicans newly arrived, or between other Latinos, and a tension or a partnership between the different groups? At the level of gang life, what kind of role does ethnicity play?

LR: There are two things pulling at these tensions. One is community. You know, "I love my home, I love my neighborhood. We'd do anything for each other." And then the competitive nature of living in a poor, resource-scarce area, which is "Yeah, but look at this other neighborhood and this other group of people, and they're coming in and they're competing with me." We were fighting for jobs, for housing, for recognition. And the competitiveness fuels the racial animosities, but also between people who have been in this country—Chicanos and *mexicanos* who've been here for a generation or more—and the new arrivals. This comes from an assumption of scarcity that poor people tend to have in this country. We fight each other for the little bit that's there—gangs are one of the organized forms this fight takes.

IS: You talked about the different circles in our society, or different kind of activities—the corporate, the educational, the professional, etc. Each of them has its own language. Lawyers, business people use the English language in a particular way. One of the most stunning, to me, memorable aspects of your book might be—might not be the one that most people would remember that quickly. And that is that toward the end, you give a glossary of terms, of how the police are described, or how a certain turf is described. How is language modeled and remodeled by different gangs? Is that also a part of turf, of control? Do English and Spanish establish different areas of influence?

LR: Oh, it's absolutely important that people find their own language. If they're not getting it in the schools, they will create their own. And what we were creating was a street language. It was poetic; it was metaphorical—full of symbols. Sometimes the words were almost meaningless in any other context. But this language connected us. We could talk to each other. Even our own parents didn't understand us. We created nuances and codes that helped seal our relationships. Same thing with hip-hop language, or any other culture or group trying to speak to each other. Others can't get in—unless you're cool, you're with it, you understand it. This language linked us, allowed us to communicate above and below and away from the rest of the world. At the same time it brought us closer, because the more marginal we were, the more we emphasized it. Once the larger society pushes people out, eventually that becomes what those same people most identify with, what they're most proud of. You can't just keep pushing people away. While some of these people try so hard to get back into the cultural fold, there are a significant number of people who say, "Fine, I'm out, and I'm going to be something from here." In our case, we dressed outlandishly. We had the tattoos. And the tattoos spoke out, too. The body was speaking. Even if you didn't find the actual words, you could see it in our skins, our faces; you could see it in the way we stood and did things like hand signs. It's all about communicating something. And it's important for people to understand what it is that we're communicating, so that they don't get confused. Society, in turn, criminalizes all this; they call this style or talk deviance. It was more like defiance. Of course, none of this is that simple. These marginal voices are not just the worst aspects of humanity. They can actually be the best of humanity, caught within a sort of box in which you can't grow, can't imagine a way out, so you can't imagine a way in.

IS: You went from graffiti and gang life into the life of the writer. The change is about order, about living according to the rules of society. Who were the writers, which were the books, that in prison and out suggested to you that perhaps there was a story inside that should come out?

LR: In the 1960s, they were important writers like Malcolm X. His autobiography was important to me. Not so much because he was African American—he came from another part of the country—but because I could relate to what he was going through: the jails, the drugs, the need for personal and spiritual transformation. Everything seemed illogical until I read Malcolm X. After that everything fell into place. Same with Piri Thomas, the Puerto Rican writer out of Spanish Harlem who wrote *Down These Mean Streets*. Piri was on the other side of the world from me, but I knew what he was going through. I knew what the addictions were. I knew his screaming, his issue about finding voice, about how to find his place in the world. I knew the racial and social class battles he was going through. There were also writers like Claude Brown, who wrote *Manchild in the Promised Land*. I was young, a teenager, very lost, and these writers spoke to me. Then Ricardo Sanchez came out with his book *Canto y grito mi liberación*. He was one of the leading, pioneering Chicano writers—he had come out of prison, out of the streets, and he was writing his own verse, his life, his way out. And he brought in the caló, the Chicano slang—he brought in the border language. I said, "I know what these people are doing." They were showing me that there was another level of communication that didn't require bullets, that didn't require tattoos. That didn't require suicide stances. It required a language that I felt for the first time I could enter. I could begin to start communicating the same feelings I had in the streets, but now with words, with poetry, with metaphors that could then tie me into the rest of the world to help change it.

IS: What has been the effect?

LR: In movies and in today's fast kind of media, you can only deal with rather small and accessible ideas to a large audience. You can't stay with larger, more dense ideas for very long. In literature, you can stay with these ideas, you can explore them, you can delve into them. You can bring out some of the different roots and branches of certain concepts and thoughts. You can enter this realm more meaningfully, whereas in the fast media, you can do it cursorily. It might take ten films or more to understand what one book will tell you. You see what I'm saying?

IS: Yes.

LR: There's a place for those films, a place for TV. But you've got to look at the power of just being able to stay with difficult but important ideas and concepts. This is what's happened with young people who've picked up my book *Always Running*. For some time, teachers have told me this is the only book they'll read all the way through. And why would these students do this? Because there's something about their lives that they're now seeing reflected. Not just superficially—insightful, knowledgeable.

IS: Gang kids in cities like Los Angeles or Miami aren't able to read the English language. *Always Running* is in English, and it's in a straightforward, standard English, so to speak. Although it also intertwines all those words that we were talking about, of caló and Spanglish. Is that an obstacle to readers?

LR: It could be. But what I find is, especially when teachers are working with this, that the more literary the book is, the more kids will be engaged. If I used just a straightforward, simple language, there's still poetry. It's not even chronological or linear. It goes back and forth. There's a circular or spherical motion in the book. It's got plenty of literary devices, but it seems to work. I find that if young people get interested in a subject matter, they will go through the whole book regardless of the degree of difficulty. And I tell you, kids who have never read a book before are reading this, no matter how hard it may seem. Even the words they don't understand, even the sentence structures that they don't quite get, don't get in the way. They flow through it. This is what the power of good literature does, and even good poetry. And why it is, for example, that poetry is one of the most important ways that young people express themselves today, even though they've not been properly exposed to it. There's not a big educational tradition in this country regarding poetry. We have some, but not much. And yet poetry seems to be one of the ways that kids are getting out there as far as expressing, communicating.

IS: And ironically, the book has been censored in many parts of the country for a variety of reasons. And there have been discussions about it having perhaps the wrong impact, or we shouldn't expose our kids, so goes the argument, to sexual scenes or to so much violence, or to the kind of inner life that a gang member goes through. How do you understand this debate?

LR: They're debates about where the culture's going. Not necessarily a bad thing. People think that my book is starting gangs; they think my book is getting kids to be sexually active. They're saying the book is the catalyst. This is where I have this argument about the media being behind all the violence. Violence was here way before there were these kind of media. Kids being sexually active is natural to them. No book does that. Some kids get off on *Archie* comics. I mean, anything can do it. It's hormones that are causing their sexual curiosity, not books. My book does have graphic violent and sexual scenes, because it's part of the reality we went through. But reading it, you'll see it was awkward sex, confused, the kind most teenagers go through. And it wasn't about idealizing sex or violence. It was just laying it out, and our kids don't have a problem with that. But certain people—adults mostly—see this as a political issue. This is a battle they want to wage. The struggle becomes the issue of the politics behind the book—not so much the graphic scenes, but what am I saying? What am I saying to kids? I'm saying that their experiences are real, that they're valid. I'm saying you just can't deny them this; you can't dismiss what they're going through or what they're thinking. You can't push their concerns aside. I'm saying you have to look at their stories and give them the place they're due. And after reading my book, the kids are saying, "It's my story, it's my life, and nobody else is talking about it." Others may misrepresent this life—they idealize it, they glorify it, or they demonize it, but they don't get to the reality of it.

IS: The book was published in 1993 by Curbstone, a small publishing house in Willimantic, Connecticut. And it was reprinted in paperback a year later by Simon and Schuster. When the book came out, it was in the form of a letter to your son. But now your son is in jail, and could you say that the message didn't come across? Could we talk about your failure as a father, perhaps?

LR: Those are legitimate issues. I don't think I can turn away from them. But failure is not the right word. Failure is a word you use in business. You either have the results or you don't. This is not a ledger kind of thing—it's real life. These are real relationships we're dealing with. So your kid's in jail. He's not a failure and you're not a failure. You make mistakes—that doesn't make you a failure. See, when you use these business terms, people get lost. Zero tolerance becomes a business term, because we don't have tolerance for trouble. Trouble is what makes life. Trouble is what gives you a direction, and we don't go there. The wounds of your life are already aiming toward something, and we don't want to touch it. So, no, I don't see it as a failure in that sense. I see it as part of what happens when I wasn't there as a father, and I knew it, and I had to enter his life again as a father at a little bit later stage in life than I should have. That's my mistake. I will pay for that mistake. My son's paying for that.

IS: And his kids will pay for that mistake, too.

LR: But I've changed. My son Ramiro and I can now relate. We have come together as father and son. So there are other factors to take into account here. There are economic factors, for example, that are real. They're even getting worse. My son, like most youth, is caught in that. The racial barriers—he's caught in that. I was trying to give him a sense that, regardless of all that, he had a path and a purpose that he had to push through. It wasn't something he could grab right away, but even in prison we're relating. Even in prison, we're interacting, and I'm saying, "Son, I'm not going to abandon you." The law is the law. The law will put down what it has to put down. And of course I have a big issue with the way the law is working with these kids and the way they're putting them away. But regardless, this is personal ordeal. He's going to have to go through it. I want him to know, however, that when he gets out, there's a family and a community he can come home to. Unlike some kids who go through similar ordeals, but when they get through them, nobody's there. The judge isn't there that put him away, or the state's attorneys that prosecuted him—nobody's there. Sometimes family isn't there, and they're like, "What happened? What happened to the community that should see me, see my mistakes, and also see the beauty that I have and help push me in that direction, even though I'm the one that ultimately has to go there?"

IS: The only way out is through immediate human contact. Literature plays a role, but in the end it's the continuity from one generation to another.

LR: It's the elemental things that we've forgotten. Because our current culture—the industrial, capitalist, technological way that we're looking at the world—doesn't have time for strong and meaningful relationships anymore. Why were kids in schools, these Columbine kids and from other communities, shooting each other? It isn't enough to say, "They're the most troubled kids. Something's wrong with them. Their parenting wasn't good." They're not having meaningful lives even in the gated communities, even in the communities that have all the material means for them. Because it's not enough. You've got to stop, pay attention, and say, "This is my son; this is my daughter. I am your father; I am your mother. How do we relate? How do we relate for the long haul, not just for now. Not just so I can make a living and retire, and then I'm gone to Florida." You know what I'm saying? It's like there are long-range things that we're forgetting, because everything becomes short-lived. It's a clash of values. This is what we're seeing. The whole present value system of the society is clashing with the old, traditional, indigenous value systems that say you see kids, you respect them, you pay attention. You give them shape and structure and you teach them, you guide them. At the same time, you never abandon them. Here we abandon kids wholesale; we do it all the time.

IS: What can we do as a society so that the next ten years will be different?

LR: There's a certain stopping, a slowing down, that we have to do. Not this politics of convenience, not this "I'm going to get my needs met, get a tax break so that I look good." The next ten years is about what are we going to do for the long run in our communities. How do people not compete against each other, not end up willing to do anything to get over? But how do they work together, cooperate? How do they find what's common between all of us? How do we find, as a society and as a world, what links us? How can we be conscious of our relationship to everything? To the earth, first of all, because we're the first ones to destroy whatever we can, or each other in the process. How do we become aware of our links to the universe—the whole thing? These are fundamental, perennial ideas that we have to bring back. They're not new ideas or old. And we're always confronted with these issues. To me, every generation confronts similar crises. My book isn't just about the past. You read it, and it tells you . . . it's got where we need to go. It illuminates something about the future we're entering. That's what good literature does. Even though for two or three hundred years, novels have been around, and they've got plenty of local things, you'll still find some relevance in them. That's what we're looking at today.

IS: After publishing it, after a decade of living with it, are there still elements of your gang life you would like to bring forth in literature? Or is this an episode that you now, as a writer, have been able to move beyond, and in other directions?

LR: Well, obviously it's important to move beyond anything you do as a youth. You have to mature, you have to grow up, and I've left a lot of that old life behind me. I've written poems, stories, and books that have nothing to do with gang life. The other side of it, though, is you have to recognize that this life is real for many other people. Many are still going through these things—in fact, it's spreading. I go to juvenile facilities, prisons, alternative schools, and I see these youths. I say they're not any different than I was, and they're going through the same thing, although in more uncertain times. They just need some compassion, some caring, some attention, some respect. And I can still teach them. But I can only teach them because they know that I've connected to something that they're going through. I've gone through what they've been through. I'm not going to go back there, but I haven't forgotten. And I know that I can interact with them in such a way where they know, "This guy has been where I've been, and he's going where I'm going. And I need to find out more about that." Unfortunately, most people, adults around them, don't connect that way. Most of these adults, be they parents, teachers, police officers, or their bosses, are yelling at them, screaming at them, telling them what to do, denying them, or walking away from them. Where are their worldly adult mentors—where are the guides, where are the teachers? They're not always there in their lives when they most need them.

The Meaning of Brown

Richard Rodriguez

Richard Rodriguez (USA, b. 1944) is the author of Hunger of Memory: The Education of Richard Rodriguez *(1982),* Days of Obligation: An Argument with My Mexican Father *(1992), and* Brown: The Last Discovery of America *(2002). This interview took place in Boston, Massachusetts, October 2002.*

IS: In the past twenty years you've published a trilogy that encompasses *Hunger of Memory, Days of Obligation,* and *Brown.* What was your quest?

RR: I was trying to place myself in America and trying to understand who I was at a time when a lot of people were telling me who I was. The trilogy began with *Hunger of Memory* with people telling me that I was a minority, that I was disadvantaged, that I was in some sense to be pitied because I was related to Latin America. *Hunger of Memory* is a book about being of the working class. It is rejecting the whole notion of ethnicity as the basis of identity. Seeing the meaning of my education as a working-class journey into the middle class. People said when I published that book: "Well, you're ashamed of being Mexican. You're not talking about that. You're looking away from the mirror. You don't want to face the Indian in the mirror." Then I wrote a book about what it is to be Mexican living in California. And how Catholicism was for me the deepest source of connection to Mexico in a Protestant country, which America is. Although America never says that about itself, that it is Protestant. And people said: "Well, we don't care about that. We're not interested in religion. Latinos are the demographic future. We are headed toward the twenty-first century and you are Latino. You are Hispanic." And I thought to myself, Am I Latino? Am I Hispanic? What does that mean? Who is a Hispanic? What is a Hispanic? There are no Hispanics in Latin America. You have to go to Dallas, Texas, to meet a Hispanic. Which is why I began *Brown.* When I began to hear myself in a survey as being a part of population that was going to outnumber African Americans, I thought to myself, there's something wrong about the way we are imagining

ourselves. I'm not going to replace African Americans in the imagination of the United States. They are part of my imagination. They form
me. I reject the black and white America in which I'm supposed to now
play the new brown center. I see brown in a different way.

IS: *Hunger of Memory* is a book that has become controversial.

RR: Yes.

IS: For many years. And it is an autobiography that in many ways
confronts people. What were your models, Richard? What other autobi-
ographies had you read? Were you trying to emulate a particular writer,
a particular style?

RR: Yes, when I was going through the anxiety of affirmative action,
feeling that I had left so much of my working-class background behind
me by the time I got to college and then graduate school. And then the
invitations came to teach at various Ivy League schools. And I thought
to myself, Why should I be invited to go to these schools as somehow
representing the culture that I had left behind? And I had to go back and
think about the drama of social class. My father had two years of grammar school education in Mexico. My mother had slightly more. They are
simple people in intellectual terms, not in imaginative or moral terms,
but in intellectual terms. Well, no one in America talks about that drama
about what it is like to be the first in your family to go to college. We
know that there are millions of us now in America. But no one talks
about it because America doesn't talk about social class. We talk about
ethnicity. We talk about race. We talk about sex, sexual identity, but not
about class. When I started that book, I went back to England and to
Raymond Williams, Richard Hoggart, but mainly to D. H. Lawrence,
the coal miner's son, who writes about his father and the relationship
the boy has to both his mother, who is a schoolmarm, and his father,
who is a miner, and his deep ambivalence about being a member of those
two worlds. I didn't find anything like that voice in America. And in
many ways Americans still cannot read *Hunger of Memory* because they
don't understand it is not a book about being brown. It is a book about
being the son of parents who had slight education.

IS: Were there any models at that point, before *Hunger of Memory* was
published, from Latin America that were influential? Were you reading
Latin American writers?

RR: No. You've seated before you a man of Latin American ancestry whose literary inheritance is almost all through the English language. What I prefer to call the American language. I have no literary connection except much later and in different ways to Latin American writers. The great drama of my imaginative life as I was growing up was through, say, British fiction. The Victorians—Trollope, Thackeray, Dickens, Austen—they were the writers who formed my imagination. And then D. H. Lawrence, the working-class writer become the sublime writer of the earliest twentieth century. He changed my life. Now I find myself in bookstores in a section devoted to Hispanic writers. I'm not a Hispanic writer. I'm a writer who comes out of some weird hybrid of cultures. I belong as much to England and probably more to England than I do to Mexico.

IS: What does the American language mean to you?

RR: The American language is wonderful . . . It's a language that was given to us first by England, forced down our throats in many ways. But which the Americans already began to subvert. As early as the 1850s, already the Britons were saying, "Those Yanks, they don't speak English. They're speaking Indian words. They're speaking African words." And then the immigration begins, the great immigration from eastern Europe, from western Europe, from southern Europe, suddenly Italian words in the language, suddenly German words in the language. And then the takeover of this enormous swath of land in the Southwest that used to be Mexico. And with it an entire vocabulary of Spanish. Now there isn't an American who doesn't speak, by virtue of speaking this language I call "American," who does not speak Spanish; who does not speak German; who does not speak Yiddish. Somebody called me the other day a schmuck and I thought to myself, I rather like that. I know it's . . . I know what a schmuck is and I know that one should not like being a schmuck. But I like being schmuck because I like living in a world of Yiddish. And that's what it means to be American. The reason that American, this tongue that I'm using, is the language of the world right now is because it eats everything. It swallows every language.

IS: How about the complaint that one hears that that flexibility, that all encompassing nature that devours whatever is in front of it, is also destructive, that doesn't allow for other languages to exist?

RR: No, it's a tyranny. But it's a wonderful buoyant force in the world. A few years ago there was a movement to declare English the official language of the United States. And I said to the organizer, I said, that's a wonderful idea except it is totally ludicrous. There's no such thing. Americans don't speak English in the first place. In the second place, the notion of putting a little fence around American English is to destroy it. It is to turn it into French where the ancients of the academy worry about "le weekend." Or the Spaniards worry about Spanglish. The moment at which you worry about the purity of your language, you lose the intensity that American English has always had, this devouring impulse.

IS: Some people take *Hunger of Memory* to be a book against bilingual education. Is it, Richard?

RR: No, it's a book. I try to deconstruct the arguments about bilingual education. I'm not interested in whether you're going to speak the language of the British sovereign or the Spanish king. I mean, it doesn't interest me. If tomorrow Americans decided to speak Esperanto, it's fine with me. What I'm interested in in that book (and it's something that most linguists don't even want to talk about because most of them live in a middle-class world of the academy) is the difference between the working-class appreciation of language and the middle-class appreciation. And how for me as a child, the great distinction in my life was not between Spanish and English, but was between a language that was used privately, this language of whispers, this language of closed doors, this language of shut windows—Spanish—and the language which is used outside: the language of the gringo, the language of the stranger, the language of loud voices, the language of advertisements, the language of television, radio—this booming voice, this English that was shoved down my throat by Irish Catholic nuns, God bless their souls, who taught me that it was my tongue. Chew it, they said: bite it and swallow it. It's yours . . .

IS: Did your parents speak to you in Spanish? In a quiet Spanish?

RR: My father died recently, but all my life they've spoken to me in a language so complicated, because it exists within the language of family. I didn't even know sometimes whether it was Spanish or English until a stranger, a boy, would come in with me from grammar school, an Irish kid, and suddenly I would realize that my mother was speaking in Spanish. If he hadn't been there, I wouldn't have known. It would have appeared seamless to me in her voice because it was mother speaking to me. It was private language. I knew that her voice changed as soon as a stranger came to the door. Knew that we began to speak like the gringos. Her voice became tight.

IS: *Hunger of Memory,* and to a lesser extent also *Days of Obligation,* created a schism perhaps between you and the Chicano community in particular. A community that sees these books as antagonistic, as negative, as a voice that one doesn't always want to hear. What do you feel throughout all this?

RR: I'm writing now dense literary essays of a sort that probably most readers can't or have no reason to appreciate anymore. I belong to a nineteenth-century literary tradition, as much French or Spanish as it is American. And now I find myself growingly irrelevant except as I try to keep up with the pace of the pop culture by going on television as an essayist or by writing the newspaper op-ed pieces. But the essays that I love, the darkest part of the water that I swim in as a writer, is a part where I'm so deeply in conversation with myself, the essay, as Montaigne taught me, the essay of such complexity that I don't know whether there are any readers of my books now. And the other political controversy . . . I think there's a paper tiger that Chicano academics create at various schools. They teach their students: "Oh, don't be like this. This is the *pocho* you want to avoid. Don't become Richard Rodriguez. Don't travel all around the world. Don't be like him, a man who's afraid of no one. A man whose uncle was from India and whose every Christmas and Thanksgiving was filled with Hindu hymns, when Dr. Gupta, his sister used to come and sing over the turkey. Don't be like Richard Rodriguez. Live in our little, little playa where there's only *español* and we can think about the conquistadors forever. Don't dare to fall in love with cultures not your own." I don't care about such people.

IS: Who's your reader then? Do you write for a reader that was in the nineteenth century?

RR: Maybe. Every once in a while I meet this reader. Sometimes it's a Chinese girl who comes up to me in the street or e-mails me. Sometimes it's a little old lady at O'Hare Airport who, while I'm running for a plane to Cincinnati, she stops me and she remembers an essay I did on AIDS, Victorian architecture, and she has to tell me about the death of her son and I'm late. And I look in her eyes and I realize she is the reader. Where have you been all my life? I say without saying to her. And then she's gone, and I'm gone. And I don't know who they are or where they are. I don't know: they might be some loony listening to this show tonight who says who is this man? Maybe they're in Vermont somewhere with a stack of books reading Trollope, you know? I don't know.

IS: A book every ten years, Richard, a trilogy. Every ten years, is this a process that you allow yourself for self-reflection? Is it because for a word to finally be printed on the page, it has to fall exactly in the right place? Tell me about your rhythm as an author.

RR: I feel an obligation after about four or five years: I should be getting serious again. I should put away the journalism or at least put it aside on Tuesdays and Wednesdays, and start thinking in larger terms. And I do give myself that rhythm that's beginning to develop every ten years. I also think that's a lot to do. I mean a complicated essay that I write takes me many, many writings and rewritings and rewritings. People say, "Oh is that it? You know, a book of 230 pages—this is pretty thin, Richard." But for me, this is dense writing. And I don't know how to rush that process. I may be dry right now. I've called this a trilogy because I feel that I'm depleted. That I've finished with something. I no longer—I want to look away. I don't want to look toward Latin America. I don't want to look through my brown face. I don't want to think about Hispanic and Richard Nixon calling me Hispanic. I want to think about something else. I want to think about architecture. I want to think about Berlin. I want to think about Islam. And I don't know whether I can get away from this. There I am in the bookstore: Hispanic writer.

IS: Does the writing itself lead you to thoughts? Do you know the thoughts before you sit and write?

RR: No, for me it's the first. Writing leads me to thought, and thinking always is this extraordinary process of surprise, which leads, because you have to slow it down in the writing, you have to make it a seduction, because what comes to me as a surprise has to be to you a seduction. I've to get you interested. Why should you read a book about brown? What is that to you? You'd probably think it's a book about Latinos. It is a book about my Indian uncle. It's a book about Filipinos. It's a book about the fact that I'm homosexual and Catholic. The brownness for me is not a book about one color, a color. It's a book about complexity, about mixture.

IS: Is that what brown means?

RR: Oh, for me it does. But to get you there, I had to seduce you. I end up writing an essay about Rogers and Hammerstein in the middle of this book, about my love of Broadway musicals. Who will come with me? Who listens to *The King and I* anymore? Who knows what it is? You know, kids? I go to a gym where it's *thump, thump, thump*. And the blond girl is reading the *Wall Street Journal* and listening to black rap. And I say listen to this essay that I've written about Broadway musicals, come with me. *Thump, thump, thump.* She turns the pages of the *Wall Street Journal* to see how her tech stocks did yesterday, you know? I don't know how to reach her. I don't know whether she's reachable. Though I was born here, I came from the other side of the looking glass, as did Alice, though not alone like Alice. Downtown I saw lots of brown people. Old men on benches. Winks from Filipinos. Sikhs who worked in the fields were the most mysterious brown men, their heads wrapped in turbans. They were the rose men. They looked like roses. And the Palestinian communist bookie—entirely hearsay—who ran a tobacco store of pungent brown-ness was himself as brown as a rolled cigar, but the more mysterious for having been born in Bethlehem.

IS: In the American imagination—an imagination that still at the beginning of the twenty-first century lives in black and white as if Technicolor had not yet set in—the color brown is for many an in-between, neither white nor black. And Latinos again, perhaps not for Richard Rodriguez, are brown even though a vast majority of Latinos might not be mestizos. A vast majority of Latinos might be multicolor.

RR: That's right.

IS: How did Latinos become brown?

RR: In the imagination of America, which is a racial imagination, what else could Latinos be but a new third race? We were somehow between whites and blacks. That's how you see us in our picture demographically. But it's a complete fiction. It reveals the poverty of the American imagination. We come to this country not talking about blood, but talking about culture. That's how we are Latinos. Americans think of color as being blood. I'm of the black race. I'm of the white race. Suddenly there are 34, 36 million Americans who call themselves Latinos. And they are white and they are black and they are brown and they are yellow and they are red. And some of them speak Spanish and some of them don't. But they all refer to this thing called *la cultura*. It's revolutionary. And no one understands it because everyone thinks that we merely are peering our heads in to try to get in between the white and black argument. There I sit at conferences and there will be the white professor and there will be the black professor, and I'm invited to play the man in the middle. But I tell you I'm bringing a different kind of message. I'm bringing the message of brownness. I'm reminding America that from the moment the Indian saw the African and the European, American history has been brown. Because they both met within the Indian iris and within that complexity of vision where suddenly red, black, and white meet together, they create brown.

IS: Have you tried your luck at other forms of writing aside from the essay?

RR: Yes, I do, but I'm very private with my writing. In fact, I've always had a sense that I don't exist as a writer. I can't explain that, but I just do. And I see my work published. As I say, I go to that Spanish, the Hispanic section, and there it is, one little book there, or two little books. But by and large, I'm not ready to publish the novel. I've written a novel and a half. And I love the theater. I've written a play about Victorian England, of all things. And I don't know whether it's ready yet. Maybe it's something my literary executor finds in a pile of dust and says, "Oh, what a smart thing for him not to have published that little play . . ." Maybe it's brilliant. Maybe it's the best thing I've written. I'm not ready to know that yet.

IS: Many people that know you or that recognize your face, it is thanks to your work in television.

RR: That's right. That's what the thing is. This is the biggest boom box there is.

IS: Talk to me about the difference between Richard Rodriguez on screen and Richard Rodriguez writing. You appear to have given up on readers or perhaps hope to get one reader at an airport, but you haven't given up on viewers.

RR: No, viewers are—they're surprising to me. Because the show I work on, *The NewsHour with Jim Lehrer,* has a special kind of viewer. I'm not intending to flatter PBS audiences, a special kind of listener who does listen. And they put aside whatever the preconceptions this sort of unglamorous face might have, to listen to what I say. Suddenly people will come up, again, months later, they will remember rhetorically how an essay on television worked. They will be able to reconstruct it. I thought to myself, you know McLuhan nowhere says that people can respond that way. This leads me to think that there's a hunger out there, which people are looking to television to satisfy. For ideas, for feeling, for impression. That every once in a while some weird Mexican guy comes along and says something on television and people will remember it to me two years later.

IS: When describing your work on TV, you talk about your listeners or somebody that will hear something that you said more than will view something that you said or will view you. That's the realm of radio . . .

RR: Oh, I love radio. Radio is much sexier than television by far. But one of the reasons I don't say "my viewers" is that the visuals from my essays tend to get edited in Washington. I don't often see the completed essay until viewers see it. I write to a visual imagination, but I'm not the person cutting the essay. To answer your first question, that's the other difference, that television is collaborative. They keep dabbing your face so you won't shine too much. It's all this vanity that's not interesting because I'm not beautiful. If I were beautiful it would be interesting, television would be. I would look at my monitor all the time like those actresses one sees, you know, on the morning shows, kind of testing their beauty against the camera. In the absence of that, all I can offer you is this language. This is my only seduction.

IS: What are the differences between—what are the tools that you use, Richard?

RR: In television?

IS: Between writing an essay for publication and writing a piece for television. What moves inside? Do you have to tone down your ideas? Do you have to present them in a way that more people will understand it? Is there a different writer?

RR: Partly. You can't use irony on television. And I love irony. You can't even use irony in op-ed pieces in the newspaper. People are pretty puritanical. Give me exactly what you mean. What do you think of 9/11? Say it plainly. If you say anything too complicated, then the whole planet starts veering, you know. So you always have to get to the point. You have to keep it within that. I remember James Agee, who worked in the obituaries at *Time* magazine for many years, said that for a young writer it was always useful to work within the limitation of a form to feel the cage. To feel the burden of that—that I've to be a writer within this formality. Sometimes working within a six-hundred-word essay for television can be exciting because I have so little time. I have to grab you so fast. And there's almost no time for preliminaries. I have to grab you. And this is in the middle of you cooking dinner or you're scratching or you're looking at your mail. I have to find you. My entire life now is looking for you, and I don't know whether I ever will.

When I'm Puerto Rican

Esmeralda Santiago

Esmeralda Santiago (Puerto Rico, b. 1948) is the author of When I Was Puerto
Rican *(1993),* América's Dreams *(1996),* Almost a Woman *(1998), and* The
Turkish Lover *(2004). With Joie Davidow, she has coedited two anthologies of
Latino literature:* Las Christmas *(1998) and* Las Mamis *(2000). This inter-
view took place in Boston, Massachusetts, April 2002.*

IS: Why is *When I Was Puerto Rican* in the past tense? Have you ceased
to be Puerto Rican?

ES: By no means. The title is meant to be a statement of my experience as a Puerto Rican in the United States. The first thing that happened to me here, about a day after I arrived, was that I met a young girl
who spoke Spanish, and we just began chatting as girls will do, and she
said that I was not Puerto Rican—I was Hispanic or Latina. She said,
"When we're here, if you're Puerto Rican, you're Hispanic; if you're
Cuban, you're Hispanic; if you're Mexican you're Hispanic." It was a
shock to me that just by coming over from Puerto Rico to Brooklyn I had
ceased being who I was. The title is a comment on this labeling that
happens to us the minute we arrive here. It's the beginning of a process
of questioning our identity. I don't think it's necessarily one of losing it
but of thinking about it in a way that we aren't used to.

IS: What is the process that involves you in the actual shaping of a
memoir? Is there also a present and past tense between how you lived
your life and then when you start writing, how you look at it as a past
experience, as an adventure?

ES: It's an interesting thing as a memoir writer, because your life is
your work. For me when I begin to write a book, when I decide that
what I'm going to write is memoir, the first step is thinking about what
the voice is like, because the voice is what speaks to me of what the
experience that I'm going to be relating is. By its nature you cannot write
everything that happened to you. It would be dull, not to mention painful. So for me it's a question of finding the right tone from the beginning
and making decisions about what it's going to sound like. And then the

process of choice is actually one of editing. I write as much as I can possibly remember and just keep at it until I feel like I've reached the point where I have to stop. This is usually around the five-hundred-page mark. Then I begin to select what scenes will remain, what events aren't necessarily important in this book, and structure the book that way through the process of elimination and editing.

IS: Talk about self-censorship. When one writes a memoir, certain events, anecdotes that might be too painful for oneself or perhaps, and even more important, too painful for the family to know that they will appear on the page and that other people will find out . . . Are you conscious of certain things that perhaps shouldn't be known?

ES: It's not that my life is an open book or that everything about me is worth knowing or is known, but when I write the first draft, I try to be completely free and nothing is off-limits. I will write about anything, the most embarrassing, the most painful, the funniest, whatever, and the choice comes at the editing stage. At that point I decide what this is going to be, what are the major themes that have emerged in all this writing that I've allowed to flow freely.

IS: Have you had any experience of somebody, a mother, a sister, a friend that tells you, I'm not happy with that part that you tell?

ES: I've been incredibly fortunate in the response that my family has had to my books. They have been generous and, I must say, mature in the way that they read the books. I think that even more sometimes than the readers themselves, they realize that I'm writing about a time that has passed; I'm writing about who we were. My mother will be the first to say, "That's the way things were, things are not like that now." So they have this attitude of, I'm writing about the people that they were, and it reflects on the people they have become. They're proud of this work actually. They thank me. They feel like they are a part of it. I'm writing about them, and so they claim part of the process for themselves and have been nothing but complimentary and supportive all along.

IS: Your books fall into the tradition of the immigrant story, in your particular case Puerto Rico. You were born in the city but lived the first thirteen years of your life in the countryside and eventually moved to Brooklyn and started a new life. They tell us about the American dream. Who is your audience? Is it an audience made of immigrants? Are you writing for a core American audience so that that audience sees what the Latino or Puerto Rican experience is about? Are you conscious of all this?

ES: I've no desire to even imagine who's going to read my work, because that would stop me from writing. If I start imagining people reading what ends up being intimate moments in my life, I don't think I would ever sit down to write. I write for myself, and that's how my writing began, in my journals and my diaries. It was a way for me to understand what was happening to me in this country. And it's ironic that my story is thought of as an immigrant story because as Puerto Ricans, born American citizens, we are not immigrants, we're migrants. We are the same as somebody from Texas moving to Alabama. There's this irony about it and also this tension in what I'm writing because most people who aren't aware of the special relationship between Puerto Rico and the United States have formed opinions about who we are without knowing who we are. I think of my books as documents to help them understand. But I don't get to that point until I'm actually in front of an audience and look out and see who's reading and buying them.

IS: How is your book perceived in Puerto Rico? Latino authors, and Puerto Rican authors on the mainland in particular, complain that their books are not read, even acknowledged at times, in their places of origin. But your particular case is an exception. You are extremely popular in the island. You're recognized, you're a celebrity, your books have been adopted in the school curriculum. They are in libraries. But there is a reaction of a segment of the readership that says, Well, you're presenting a stereotypical portrait of the Puerto Rican, an unpleasant one, one that isn't for us—single motherhood with many children, poverty, the projects, etc.

ES: I'm a stereotype . . . I'm the child of a woman who ended up being a single mother with many children on welfare living in roach-infested tenements in Brooklyn. This is the reality. I'm not making it up, and I'm not going to pretend otherwise or in any way whitewash that to satisfy people's idea of what a Puerto Rican should be depicted like. That's up to the people who had a different life. They should write their own books, and I encourage that and want to see that because I think it's important. But as a memoir writer, I would be doing a disservice not only to myself, to my memory, to my family, but to other Puerto Ricans who share this experience by pretending that it's prettier than it was or cleaner than it was or anything other than what it was. I do feel like it's my responsibility to be as truthful and honest as I can about it. And then people will just have to arrive at their own conclusions. At the same time, that is what has made these books popular. I'm writing about real people. A stereotype is a flat picture of a person. You only see whatever you want to see: it's defined and narrowed. What I've taken is that stereotype and tried to humanize it. And tried to bring the human aspect of these people to readers that recognize themselves and hopefully will learn something about themselves. To people who have a problem with my depiction of the stereotype, the only thing I can say is, You will have to encourage and support other writers to come up with other stories, because I'm writing my truth, and I can't pretend that I had a convertible when I was sixteen. I mean, that's just not the way my life was.

IS: Is it possible to live without stereotypes?

ES: People need shorthands to get to know one another or to see each other. Unfortunately, the problem with stereotypes is that they're a negative way of knowing people. It's not a positive way. If we think of a positive way, we would call it an image. But the other side of that is, yes, I'm a stereotype, I write about having been a stereotype, but this is a stereotype who went to Harvard, who lives in a suburb, who lives a life that is not at all like the life I lived before. I've managed to go beyond that, and that is part of what my books do for people, as I understand it from the mail that I get. It allows them to see themselves reflected: I'm a single mother . . . , or I'm the child of a single parent . . . , or I live in these conditions . . . It is indeed the stereotype of Puerto Ricans, but somebody has risen above them, somebody is overcoming them. It's not what I'm presenting per se in my work but the fact that it's being presented and humanized and expanded upon. It gives people a sense of their own humanity. A stereotype takes away your humanity, but a work of art brings that humanity and makes it real, expands you, and that's why people are responding to it in a positive way.

IS: In order to go beyond the stereotype, education played a major role in your life. As you describe it in *When I Was Puerto Rican* and *Almost a Woman*, you had crucial teachers, role models that encouraged you to pursue certain talents, to explore certain areas of yourself that would open up new possibilities. You went to an important performing arts school in New York, and eventually to Harvard to a writing program.

On the other hand, often as minorities we see education as a period when we get away from our roots. We're told we're different, we're told we're tokens. Talk about the process of going through these educational institutions and how they changed your identity.

ES: I had to learn to be strong. The hardest battle that I fought as a human being, especially in my early adolescence, in those first few years that I was in the United States, was to disbelieve the stereotype, to consciously refuse to accept prejudice, racism, classism. I just had to consciously make that decision and say, This teacher may think that I'm not college material, but I will prove him wrong. Or this teacher may discourage me from wanting to study medicine, but that's too bad for him, you know.

IS: It won't stop you . . .

ES: I wasn't willing to let other people define me. That's a part of my personality. I don't know where that came from, and I can't take any credit for it, but I do think that's what allowed me to do the things that I did and allowed me to focus. Every time somebody would throw me just the tiniest little piece of rope, I would grab it, and when they didn't, I just looked for the next person who was going to throw me a little piece of rope. It was a question of taking the opportunities that I saw and going with them in a conscious and focused way and refusing, just absolutely refusing, to believe that I couldn't do the things that I wanted to do. I refused to believe it was impossible, and it didn't matter to me who told me that I couldn't do these things, because they were not me.

IS: One of the ubiquitous elements in *When I Was Puerto Rican* is your tenacity, the perseverance in spite of all odds or against all odds, the finding out that you've a path in which words are your tools. Your way into the world and your way in the world of words. What about your discovery of literature, the first readings that you made, the first writers. How did you decide to become one?

ES: My first introduction to literature was with my father, who's a poet and who loved poetry and would recite the greats of his generation. I was also fortunate to have received my elementary education up to the seventh grade in Puerto Rico, where literature and poetry were an important part of the curriculum. We were required to memorize a poem a week and recited it in front of the whole class. Most of us recited pretty much the same things to one another. The schools were poor, they didn't have great libraries, but they had the works of the greats. To hear Cervantes read aloud by somebody was not foreign in my tiny rural schools in Macún, Puerto Rico. That was something that just happened every week. When I came to the United States and I discovered the public library and I could borrow the books and bring them home, it was like a whole world opened up. I understood, yes, we lived in a tenement, we're on welfare, there're eleven people in three rooms, we don't have much, but I can open any book and learn about another world that is outside of this particular area. And that gave me courage. Knowing that other worlds existed allowed me to dream, and to be tenacious and to be persistent and to refuse to believe the negative stereotypes. So literature for me is not just something I do on the beach; it's something that I live. I lived the books that I read; I lived their lessons. I truly believe that reading saved my life. For other people, it can and will save your life if you're willing to believe it can. There are other worlds and possibilities for you.

IS: Reading and writing saved your life. What did it feel like when you first saw a book of yours in one of those libraries like the temple that you're describing?

ES: It's indescribable. As a writer, when you walk into a library, you say to yourself, Why would I even attempt to do this when there are already so many books out there? But as a reader I knew that there were no books about my experience, because I was at that library every day. There were no books about Puerto Rican girls living in Brooklyn struggling with language, a single mother, lots of sisters and brothers having dreams that people kept trying to squelch. There were no books about that. I remember my local library featured *When I Was Puerto Rican* prominently because I'm active in this library, and I was so proud of myself, because I said: a child is going to walk into this library and see this book and maybe he or she will feel less invisible in this society.

IS: Like you did . . .

ES: Yes, like I did. And see that book and he or she will find something in themselves that will allow them to become the person that they can be, and that is the best thing I could possibly imagine.

IS: With time you have become a spokesperson for libraries nationwide. You're also the author of a novel, *America's Dream*. What's the difference between writing novels and writing memoirs? Is the writer freer with fiction?

ES: No, I don't think it's that easy. It lies in the question of responsibility.

IS: Tell me.

ES: When I'm writing memoir, there are people who are alive. The only image that other people are going to have of these people is what's in the pages of this book. So I've a responsibility to be fair to those people I love and even to people I cannot stand. I have to be fair to them because it would be unfair to show my side of it because I'm the writer. I'm aware in the editing process when I'm selecting the memories that will be included in a memoir of the responsibility I have to those people.

IS: Responsibility means balance.

ES: A balance, but also I have to humanize them. It would be easy to turn your memoir into a way of getting even with all the awful people who ran through your life or all the boyfriends who you didn't like. That is easy to do. It's much, much harder to make those people human, and that's what I strive to do even with the people who are not quite so nice to me. I want to bring their humanity forward. Writing is too hard, too precious, too important.

IS: In fiction . . .

ES: In fiction you have the same responsibilities, but you're writing about yourself. All those characters are me. It was Flaubert who said, I am Madame Bovary. Well, I am América González. But I'm also Correa. I'm all my characters, and so the responsibility is to the truth within myself. And to try and be true to the ugly feelings as well as the feelings that are much more pleasant to hear about.

IS: You recently adapted *Almost a Woman* into a PBS movie for *Masterpiece Theatre*. Was it painful?

ES: It was difficult, because the second memoir, *Almost a Woman*, was much harder for me to write than *When I Was Puerto Rican*. I had forgotten, had wanted to forget, that part of my life. To write a memoir and then to relive it by writing the screenplay and selecting the scenes that would be the most interesting to watch, as opposed to what you write in a book, which has different goals, was a difficult process. Then to see it being filmed and see people who looked like me and my family portraying those scenes was painful, because I had to live those moments again, and I had to make sure that the portrayal was true to the people who first experienced them. It was a difficult process, one that allowed me to understand more about the power of words and the power of experience and how you can take an experience that seems so simple. The film is about how Esmeralda comes to New York, goes to school, graduates from high school. That's all it is . . . But between the beginning and the end there's a lifetime of experience that I share with millions and millions of people, not only Latinos, but people from all over, men as well as women. I remember sitting in a room surrounded by friends the night that the film was broadcast, realizing that 18 million people are looking at this, and saying to myself, This is the most terrifying moment of my life. I was glad that I was surrounded by friends and family, because it would have been too lonely a moment without them to support me.

IS: Could it have started the other way around, a screenplay that becomes a memoir?

ES: Well, I couldn't have written that. I don't think that I could have made those choices. I don't think that I would have made the same choices for the film.

IS: It isn't your medium, either.

ES: No, it isn't. Screenplay writers would hate me for saying this, but I don't think of scripts as a literary form. I think of them as blueprints for whole casts of talented, creative people to present their vision in a medium that they know well. For me, writing this screenplay was a frustrating experience for that reason. The first thing I had to lose was all my favorite cousins and aunts and uncles that didn't make it into the film.

IS: All that family.

ES: It just didn't fit the theme of the film. And there's also the budget and other considerations I don't have when I'm sitting all by myself in my room ready to write my stories.

Dirty Sleuth

Paco Ignacio Taibo II

Paco Ignacio Taibo II (Spain, b. 1949) is the author of Calling All Heroes: A Manual for Taking Power *(1990),* Some Clouds *(1992),* Shadow of the Shadow *(1991),* Four Hands *(1994),* Leonardo's Bicycle *(1995),* Guevara, Also Known as Che *(1990), and* Returning as Shadows *(2003). Conducted in Spanish and translated by Carrie Van Doren, this interview took place in Mexico City, September 1994.*

IS: When and how did you begin to write?

PT: When I first learned how to form my letters, the moment I acquired the use of reason. Since then, writing has been my destiny. At age eleven, I was making steps toward printing a magazine, and at thirteen, I wrote my first short story. I have been a journalist since age fifteen, an obsessive reader since five, and I managed to finish my first novel, which fortunately was never published, at twenty. I suppose that this obsession is part of a family tradition nurtured by a great uncle who was also a writer, and by my father, Paco Ignacio Taibo, a journalist, novelist, and critic according to whom the best trade of the world wasn't to be a trapeze artist or a fireman—those are no doubt the best secondary trades—but a writer. When I was five years old, my father used to come home from the newspaper for which he worked, in the middle of the night, and instead of going to bed, he would put newspapers and a towel on the dining room table and over them his Olivetti typewriter. He would then write a novel, trying to make as little noise as possible in order not to wake up the family. He would write until dawn. I would silently escape from bed and crawl beneath the table. It was clear to me that my father was doing something important, so important that I had to be a witness . . . I slept the first of my life lulled by an Olivetti.

IS: What technique do you follow?

PT: I write all day at all hours. I tend to work with music—the more rhythmic, the better. Richard Wagner and Carlos Santana, for example. My only talisman is a change of work. I'm a voracious writer. It could be that right now I have begun three novels, another three are outlined with notes, a historical essay about Mexican anarchists of the twenties, two or three reports, and a comic strip script. I go from one text to another. When I feel I'm not getting anywhere with one project, I abandon it and begin another. I tend to have a few dry spells, and when they arrive I don't fight them, but rather, I travel and dedicate myself to helping here and there in community projects.

IS: What was your first encounter with Héctor Belascoarán Shayne? Where does his physical appearance and his intellectual capacity come from?

PT: He was born by elimination, and his physical presence developed from a variety of things. He is rootless, a refugee of the middle class, madly curious, stubborn, full of humorous feeling toward his fellow Mexicans, a bit melancholic. Actually, his appearance came from an anthropologist friend, Sergio Perello, who wore the clothing of the fashion fifteen years ago. Belascoarán Shayne has become what he is over fifteen years of backwardness. I should also add that his appearance was formed from injuries and wounds throughout the novels: the loss of an eye, a slight limp, the horror of humidity that makes his bones grind.

IS: Arthur Conan Doyle, tired of his character Sherlock Holmes, once killed him, only to bring him back later on the petitioning of his readers. Belascoarán Shayne seems also to have been resuscitated in your novel *Return to the Same City*. Does he control you or vice versa?

PT: We control each other. I didn't kill him; dramatic logic killed him, the progression of facts. Then the readers protested. I decided that the saga wasn't finished and revived it. White magic . . .

IS: What is the relationship between Belascoarán Shayne and Philip Marlowe?

PT: The similarities are in the structure of the lone hero, the outsider: a vocation for solitude, a fidelity to friends (in Marlowe's case) and to certain obsessions (in Belascoarán Shayne's case). Raymond Chandler's character moves within rational histories, whereas mine is surrounded by a chaotic atmosphere, Kafkaesque and corrupt: Mexico City.

IS: To what do you attribute your huge popularity?

PT: To exoticism . . . I suppose Mexican readers find in my novels a broken mirror, a proposition that invites them not to surrender to an immoral reality.

IS: Why is detective fiction so attractive?

PT: Because of the allure of adventure, the virtues of enigma, an incredible capacity for discovering cities and ancient mysteries, a set of characters in limited situations. A good novel is a good novel, but if it has a detective plot, all the better.

IS: Before you, the Mexican detective novel didn't subscribe to the dirty realism of Chandler, Dashiell Hammett, and Ernest Hemingway.

PT: Actually, I subscribe to the ugly-dirty-fucking realism of Chester Himes and Jim Thompson, in the worst sense of the word—that of storytellers. I've added to this black humor and a Kafka-style twist in morality. I feel identified with a generation of narrators who wrote in the same years as I and see literature as subversive subversion: Manuel Vasquéz Montalbán, Jerome Charyn, J.-P. Manchette, Jean-François Vilar, Juan Carlos Martelli, Alberto Speratti, Per Wahlöö, Robert Littell, Martin Cruz Smith; likewise, with a current trend of writers of nonfiction testimonies: Rodolfo Walsh, Miguel Bonasso, Joseph Wambaugh, and Guillermo Thorndyke.

IS: Do you consider María Elvira Bermúdez, Antonio Helú, Pepe Martínez de la Vega, and Rafael Solana your Mexican precursors, all writers who wrote detective stories from the thirties to the fifties south of the Rio Grande, although in a different way? What do you think of Rafael Bernal's *The Mongol Plot*?

PT: I don't think of them as precursors. I don't owe them anything, nor do I want to maintain relations with a generation of parodists and imitators. Their books interest me little and their approximation of style is spineless. The only work that attracts me is Bernal's, which has been unfairly forgotten and which my generation has somehow revived.

IS: What do you think of Jorge Ibargüengoitia's *Las muertas* and Vicente Leñero's 1964 novel *Los albañiles*, the works of two writers who reinvigorated detective fiction without ever considering themselves practitioners?

PT: They interest me as precursors to the nouveau detectives in Mexico and the Southern Hemisphere in general. You're right: what is curious is that both authors never consider themselves part of this style.

IS: Talk to me about Carlos Fuentes's *The Hydra Head*. Also, more than your detective, talk to me about Mexico City, which was also Fuentes's protagonist in *Where the Air Is Clear*.

PT: I feel an affinity toward Fuentes, although not to *The Hydra Head*.

I like his novels dealing with this monstrous metropolis, a city that manages to obsess me. The city produces more stories in one day than Balzac would have been able to tell in numerous lifetimes. There's in this a perverse condensation of schizophrenia and horror, adorned in a mountain of myths, an incredible fountain of inspiration. Frankly, this place is shaky and full of bad vibrations and aloneness. It is surrounded by catastrophe, and people protest every day the miserable way of life they are forced to live in. But they don't leave. This place makes me sick: I can't manage to grasp its essence.

IS: What is there in you of Julio Cortázar? What influence if any did the Latin American literary boom writers have on your work—Mario Vargas Llosa, Gabriel García Márquez, and José Donoso?

PT: I like Cortázar, but something in him bothers me and keeps me away. About the rest, nothing. The first five novels of Vargas Llosa attracted me, but the rest are a bore. In fact, I feel influenced by Antonio Skármeta, Oswaldo Soriano, Eduardo Galeano, Jesús Díaz, writers of another generation in whose novels the need to locate a story in a historical context is essential.

IS: Mexico is a country where there's so much corruption that justice is obliterated. Is that the main theme of your national detective literature?

PT: Yes, that's the point. Criminality forms part of the system and is incorporated into it in a logical and coherent manner. Hence, the solution is also part of the crime. I live in a city where the police produce more deaths than all of the underworld organizations, the Mafia, and any number of marginal lunatics. Luis González de Alba, a student leader of the Tlatelolco movement of 1968, was absurdly imprisoned for four years for setting fire to a streetcar at the intersection of two streets, a place where there had never been rails, and at a time during which he was giving a lecture before thousands of witnesses on the other side of the city. To him, of course, we owe the famous phrase: "The police are always to be blamed."

Race and Mercy

Piri Thomas

Piri Thomas (New York, b. 1928) is the author of Down These Mean Streets
(1967), Savior, Savior, Hold My Hand *(1972),* Seven Long Times *(1974),
and* Stories from El Barrio *(1978). This interview took place in Berkeley, California, March 1994.*

IS: I would like to start with the topic of language. Would you reflect
on your relationship with Spanish and English? What does the Spanish
language mean to you and what does the English language mean to
you? How close or far away are you from each of them? What do you
feel for each of them?

PT: I remember with all my heart and soul the first words I learned
from Mami and Papi were all in Spanish, but as I grew up I knew that I
was not speaking Spanish from Galicia or Barcelona in Spain. I was speaking the Spanish that is spoken in Puerto Rico, which I call Puerto Rican
Spanish, because we kept our nuances and feeling and energies and
words that came from Africa, like *chévere*, which means great. We are a
mixture of all those who conquered us over the centuries, taking our
women with or without permission. We are a culmination of all that
energy, but our spirit is as free as it was born to be. We are a conglomera-
tion of manifestations.

IS: And so Spanish is the language in which you expressed your first
words?

PT: Sí, I began to go though the same process as everyone has under-
gone under the system, beginning with the Native Americans: the assimilation process. I remember in my own childhood in the thirties being in this school and I could not understand what the teacher was saying
so much, because they spoke fast sometimes and I could not catch the
words. I'd lean over to my friend, saying "José, mira, what did the teacher
say?" He would tell me and I would continue to do my homework. And
so that teacher came roaring upon me and said, "Listen, stop talking in
that language." And I said, "Well, I'm speaking my mother's language.
My mother's from Puerto Rico; I was born in this country." And she

says, "You stop talking that, you have to learn English, you are in America now. After all, how else do you expect to become president of the United States if you do not learn to speak English correctly." I thought in my young heart, "My God, this teacher has more faith than I have in my someday becoming president of the United States if I learn English well enough." And the tremendous assimilation happened to me. As a child, I first had to think in Spanish to speak in English. Then, I had to think in English to speak in Spanish, because I had forgotten the language. I had forgotten the lessons that were taught in my home where my mother taught me how to read, beginning with reading from the Bible. So I've made a determined effort to regain my inheritance back to where I came from, to learn where I had come from in order to know where I was going, to be able to then recognize my true reality, the true reality of what we are in the scheme of things. I learned that we are human beings, but that there were those who believed that there were only two kinds of people on this earth: those who ruled and those who were ruled.

IS: Spanish is also the language used by the *conquistadores* in the Americas.

PT: I'm with you totally. In fact, I said it's ironic that we who are from all the pueblos, Chile, Nicaragua, Peru, Ecuador, Cuba, Santo Domingo, Puerto Rico, all the islands, Central and South America, Mexico, are bound, blended, and held together by the language of the conqueror, whose fever for gold destroyed us physically, mentally, spiritually, and morally. They stripped away the indigenous knowledge and the religious beliefs of those they found and forced everybody into their mold, which was slavery.

IS: When you talk about regaining one's own past, one's own background and heritage, you seem to imply that the way to do it is through language. I recently talked to a couple of Puerto Rican writers who are close friends, and they were complaining that because they write in English in this country and are mainland Puerto Ricans, their work is almost totally ignored in the island because of the language issues. How about you? What is your situation? Is your work known in Puerto Rico?

PT: Let me tell you, my brother, with all sincerity I agree. I went into San Germán, I believe, where I met beautiful people. When I walked into the lobby, the walls were covered with photographs, beautiful photographs, of all the Puerto Rican brothers and sisters, writers, poets, and all the feelings, all the energies, Luis Palés Matos, Lola. I looked to the walls for a picture of all of us from the barrio and didn't find one. So I asked the brother, "Why don't we have pictures of the poets and writers, brothers and sisters, from El Barrio? Aren't we all *puertorriqueños*?" And he told me, "Well, because you don't write in Spanish." I told him "and what about these writers who wrote in French? These ones write in French, this one could speak German" and he just looked. I added: "You have to remember one of our national poets, Antonio Corretjer, who said that no matter if we're born on the moon, we are still *puertorriqueños* to our soul." And *"nadie,* nobody," I told him, "can take away my heritage, because I, Juan Pedro Tomás, was born from a Puerto Rican womb, *boricua.* Although I was born in El Norte, my soul is Puerto Rican." But things are so mixed up for Puerto Ricans. The only reason why I knew of Puerto Rico was because I sat in the corner and listened to the grown-ups speaking about places like Fajardo, Bayamón, and San Juan, among other places on the island. My beautiful child energy absorbed all that information by osmosis. I finally went to Puerto Rico when I got out of prison at the age of thirty-two. My God, as that wall of green humidity enveloped me, it was like I was entering into my mother's arms. However, soon I began to see the reality of American colonialism in Puerto Rico—a so-called commonwealth, that means common for the pueblo and wealth for the latter-day carpetbaggers who enjoy a favorable tax status with the U.S. government.

IS: Let's focus on religion.

PT: I'm a spiritual man. We all have a spirit—good, bad, or indifferent. I come from a family of different denominations. My father was a deathbed Catholic. He was only going to see a priest when he was ready to kick the bucket, but he was a good man—he didn't drink, he didn't smoke, he was a good athlete. He believed in doing unto others as you would like to be done to yourself. My lovely mother was Seventh-Day Adventist; she cooked on Friday before the sun went down and didn't cook again until Saturday when the sun went down. We went to church on the Sabbath; we were the closest thing to the children of Israel in that sense. And my aunt, Angelita, my mother's sister, she was Pentecostal, and I loved that church the best because you could express yourself there, with loud "alleluyas" and "glorias a Dios." In the others, you had to stay quiet. In the Catholic church they spoke in Latin, and I could not understand. But in the Pentecostal church, I could express myself. I began to think about God and what God was. I could not see him, but they told me I could feel him. But that changed as the years went on, and I made my inner journey, especially when I went to prison where you have plenty of time. I was determined that I was going to educate my mind. I was not going to eradicate it. I made who I was in my sense of being. I wrote it into my poetry, "To me God is a smile on the face of a child that is not being wasted. To me God is spelled G-O-O-D, good. Every child has the power force within them as well as contact with others. Everything in life has had some kind of influence on me, in one way or another." In prison, I spent time reading books on the religions of Islam, Buddhism, Confucianism. I was looking for answers in my six-by-eight-by-nine prison cell.

IS: When did literature become an answer to you, a tool for salvation? Was it in prison, as you suggest at the end of *Down These Mean Streets*?

PT: Long before prison. My mother had saved some money from the sewing machine. She worked in the sweatshops and used to bring home work from the job and work until two or three o'clock in the morning, because there was no work for my father. My father came running home one day happy, because he had hit the *bolita*, where you play *los números*— get three numbers and you win. And with that money and what my mother had saved, we moved to a foreign country called Babylon, Long Island. I went to school out there, which became a battleground for me. I was the only little coffee grain for miles around in a sea of white milk. However, I had an English teacher whose name was Mrs. Wright. She was kind to me, this beautiful white teacher, and I loved her energy flow. One day she asked the class to write a composition about anything we wished. And I wrote a composition on how much I loved her beautiful brunette hair and her hazel eyes and how I loved the way she smelled when she came over to look at my work. However, I didn't particularly care for her pronouns and adjectives and verbs because I didn't know what the hell she was talking about. Then, days later the papers came back, and she asked me to turn mine over. I'd written two and a half pages; on the half-page that was left, it said in pencil—I remember it to this day: "Son, your punctuation is lousy. Your grammar is nonexistent. P.S. We both love my wife." Signed her husband. Someone had recognized that I had a gift, an ability to express, to share feelings through words. I believe all children are born poets and that every poet is the child and what the children need is a word that will guide them towards creativity and not towards greed.

IS: Was there ever any writer while you were in Babylon or later on while you were in jail that influenced you, not in terms of the friendship that you had with her or with him, but whose book you thought was something to emulate?

PT: I loved to read as a kid. The reason I loved to read was because I was introduced by a caring teacher to a caring librarian on 110th Street in El Barrio. She allowed me to take out two books, and I would go to the fire escape and turn my blanket into a hammock and I'd just sit back reading. I'd read whatever I found. I loved adventure stories. I loved science fiction or traveling to other universes. I loved the energies of Jack London and *The Sea-Wolf* and *White Fang*—everything, the feelings. Actually, I didn't have a whole lot of time to read until I went to prison, where I found out that I could create a world in my mind that would take me away from all that if I tuned myself to books and my imagination. One night, a brother whose nickname was Young Blood knocked on my prison cell. He knocked low, and I said "Uh-huh?" And he said "Tommy, Tommy, they wrote a book with my name on it, Young Blood, you know, and, man, I want you to read it. It's by a brother man, a black brother." At that time, we were calling each other black. And he handed me the book through the bars, and it was called *Youngblood* by John Oliver Killens. He was an attorney who was also a fine writer, a beautiful black human being. I read the book; it had been read by so many people that the pages were like onion skin. When I finished reading it, Young Blood asked, "What'd you think of it, Tommy?" and I said, "Man, it was dynamite—you live it, the whole feeling." And I added, "Young Blood, you want to know something?" and he said "yeah," and I said, "I could write too." And he smiled at me and said, "Yeah, I know you can, Tommy." And that's when I began to write what would one day be known as *Down These Mean Streets*. At the time, it was entitled *Home Sweet Harlem*.

IS: Race is an issue ubiquitous in your work. In fact, few Latino writers today are brave enough to discus it in such plain, uninhibited ways as you do.

PT: Children have a spirit of discernment and the ability to perceive and to sense and to feel, and they can look at a person and see the look of contempt or the outrage or the disgust on people's faces. It is easy for children to read people like people read books. I was one of those children. So when you ask of racism and bigotry, yes, I began at the first stage of life in the barrio. As I grew older it grew harder. I remember the first time I went to the South with my friend Billy. I sat in the front of the bus, and when the bus got to the Mason Dixon line, our driver got off and a new driver got on. Immediately, he said, "All the coloreds to the back," and all the coloreds got up and went back and I just sat there. And he said, "I want all of you colored people to go to the back." And I said, "Look I'm *puertorriqueño.*" And he looked at me and said, "I don't care what kind of nigger you are," and he put his hand into his side pocket. Using the better part of my discretion and with a great nudging on my arm from Billy, because he knew we would be killed, I grudgingly but with dignity went to the back of the bus and sat for the rest of the ride staring at the back of his head, determined that I would never forget this incident. And they'd call me "nigger," and if it wasn't "nigger" they'd call me "spic." Racism was a horror to bear because most times it wasn't quite said. It was worse because they dug into your psyche with one little look of contempt, or their nose would flare as you passed them as if they had smelled dirt. So I came to my mother enraged and feeling this, saying, "Mira mami, they called me this." My mother said, "Listen to this, my son; I want you to learn this and remember it for the rest of your life. I want you to know that there's no one in this world better than you, only maybe better off, with money and so forth. You have your sense of beautiful dignity. Nobody can take that way. Only you can give it away or sell it, *¿entiendes?*" My mother said, "They don't have to kill you with hatred, my son; envy will suffice." Wisdom from my mother.

IS: I've heard you say that literature is useful to fight racism. But how effective can it be? Writers are also depressive types. Whenever they realize that words are simply words—ephemeral, transient—they fall into an impossible abyss of fatalism.

PT: Words are important because they awaken consciousness and thus can inspire action. You have to be careful how you use words because they can be bullets or butterflies. Children become what they learn or don't learn. Children become what they are taught or not taught. For thousands of years we have heard propaganda about white supremacy and "might makes right." Conquer people by might, strip away their education, their beliefs, their culture, and their land; then in two or three generations their children will be in the dark ages again. We had bright minds when we first went into their schools, because children are not born stupid. The world has no right to judge intelligence by the color of one's skin. Different colors were meant to be beautiful just like flowers come in different and beautiful colors. Birds are different colors. And this is the struggle that we have had to wage, to allow all the colors to express their humanity through literature and the other arts, to learn from each other, as people, so we are not only geographic locations, colors, sexes, or preferences. We are earthlings who share a common bond— our humanity.

IS: When *Down These Mean Streets* came out, there was an immediate uproar in terms of the sexual explicitness, and there were even some legal problems. When you were writing the subsequent books, *Savior, Savior,* and *Seven Long Times,* and *Stories from El Barrio,* did the experience of the censorship with *Down These Mean Streets* affect you in any conscious way when you were writing? Were you trying, in a sense, to be more defiant and explicit or less defiant and explicit?

PT: I didn't have too much time to think about all that. I was so elated with my gift of being able to write, even though the first book had almost killed me because it was such an outpouring—I almost suffered an emotional burnout. I could not stand the agony anymore. When I wrote *Savior, Savior, Hold My Hand,* I wrote it more gentle. And when I wrote *Seven Long Times,* I was looking at it twenty-five years later, objectively, like a scientist.

Acknowledgments

"Books and Quilts: Marjorie Agosín" was first published in the *Bloomsbury Review* 15, no. 5 (July/August 1995): 8–9. Used by permission of Marjorie Agosín and the editors of the *Bloomsbury Review*.

"Against Oblivion: Felipe Alfau" was first published in the *Review of Contemporary Fiction* 13, no. 1 (spring 1993). Used by permission of the editors of the *Review of Contemporary Fiction*.

"Beginnings: Isabel Allende" was first published in Spanish in *Imagen*, August 1988, then rendered into English and collected in *Conversations with Isabel Allende*, edited by John Rodden (2d ed., University of Texas Press, 2003). Used by permission of the editors of *Imagen*, Caracas, Venezuela.

"Salsa and Soul: Rubén Blades" aired on PBS-WGBH as part of *La Plaza: Conversations with Ilan Stavans*, January 15, 2003. Used by permission of PBS-WGBH.

"Identity and Archaeology: David Carrasco" aired on PBS-WGBH as part of *La Plaza: Conversations with Ilan Stavans*, October 25, 2001. Used by permission of David Carrasco and PBS-WGBH.

"Driven: Junot Díaz" aired on PBS-WGBH as part of *La Plaza: Conversations with Ilan Stavans*, October 18, 2003. Used by permission of Junot Díaz and PBS-WGBH.

"Life in Translation: Ariel Dorfman" was first published in the *Michigan Quarterly Review* 34, no. 3 (summer 1995): 303–12. It is reprinted in *The Inveterate Dreamer: Essays and Conversations on Jewish Culture*, by Ilan Stavans, 223–33 (Lincoln: University of Nebraska Press, 2001). Used by permission of Ariel Dorfman and the editors of the *Michigan Quarterly Review*.

"My Sax Life: Paquito D'Rivera" aired on PBS-WGBH as part of *La Plaza: Conversations with Ilan Stavans*, January 23, 2003. Used by permission of Paquito D'Rivera and PBS-WGBH.

"Poetry and Politics: Martín Espada" aired on PBS-WGBH as part of *La Plaza: Conversations with Ilan Stavans*, September 24, 2002. Used by permission of Martín Espada and PBS-WGBH.

"Onto the Diaspora: Isaac Goldemberg" was first published in *Folio*, no. 27 (1987): 141–50. Used by permission of Isaac Goldemberg.

"Shipwrecked: Francisco Goldman" aired on PBS-WGBH as part of *La Plaza: Conversations with Ilan Stavans*, February 22, 2004. Used by permission of Francisco Goldman and PBS-WGBH.

"Words and Music: Oscar Hijuelos" was first published in *Imagen* (1989): 7–8. Used by permission of the editors of *Imagen*, Caracas, Venezuela.

"The Ventriloquist: John Leguizamo" aired on PBS-WGBH as part of *La Plaza: Conversations with Ilan Stavans*, April 4, 2002. Used by permission of PBS-WGBH.

"Crossing the Border: Rubén Martínez" aired on PBS-WGBH as part of *La Plaza: Conversations with Ilan Stavans*, January 17, 2004. Used by permission of Rubén Martínez and Susan Bergholz Literary Services, New York. All rights reserved.

"On Brevity: Augusto Monterroso" was first published in the *Massachusetts Review* 37, no. 3 (autumn 1994): 393–405. Used by permission of the editors of the *Massachusetts Review*.

"An Actor Prepares: Edward James Olmos" was first published in *Gestos* 4, no. 6 (November 1988): 148–53. Used by permission of the editors of *Gestos*.

"Literature and History: Fernando del Paso" was first published in *Review of Contemporary Fiction* 16, no. 1 (spring 1996): 123–32. Used by permission of the editors of the *Review of Contemporary Fiction*.

"Tender Gender: Elena Poniatowska" was first published in the *Bloomsbury Review* 16, no. 3 (May/June 1996): 9–11. Used by permission of the editors of the *Bloomsbury Review*.

"Behind the News: Jorge Ramos" aired on PBS-WGBH as part of *La Plaza: Conversations with Ilan Stavans*, January 28, 2002. Used by permission of Jorge Ramos and PBS-WGBH.

"Always Running: Luis J. Rodriguez" aired on PBS-WGBH as part of *La Plaza: Conversations with Ilan Stavans*, April 17, 2001. Used by permission of Luis J. Rodriguez and Susan Bergholz Literary Services, New York. All rights reserved.

"The Meaning of Brown: Richard Rodriguez" aired on PBS-WGBH as part of *La Plaza: Conversations with Ilan Stavans*, February 5, 2003. Used by permission of PBS-WGBH.

"When I'm Puerto Rican: Esmeralda Santiago" aired on PBS-WGBH as part of *La Plaza: Conversations with Ilan Stavans*, September 16, 2002. Used by permission of Esmeralda Santiago and PBS-WGBH.

"Dirty Sleuth: Paco Ignacio Taibo II" was first published in the *Literary Review* 38, no. 1 (fall 1994): 34–37. Used by permission of the editors of the *Literary Review*.

"Race and Mercy: Piri Thomas" was first published in the *Massachusetts Review* 37, no. 3 (autumn 1994): 344–54. Used by permission of the editors of the *Massachusetts Review*.

Works by Ilan Stavans

Fiction
The One-Handed Pianist and Other Stories

Nonfiction
Dictionary Days
The Inveterate Dreamer: Essays and Conversations on Jewish Culture
On Borrowed Words: A Memoir of Language
Spanglish: The Making of a New American Language
The Riddle of Cantinflas
Octavio Paz: A Meditation
Bandido: The Death and Resurrection of Oscar "Zeta" Acosta
The Hispanic Condition: Reflections on Culture and Identity in America
Art and Anger: Essays on Politics and the Imagination
¡Lotería! (with Teresa Villegas)

Anthologies
The Scroll and the Cross: 1,000 Years of Jewish-Hispanic Literature
The Oxford Book of Jewish Stories
Mutual Impressions: Writers from the Americas Reading One Another
The Oxford Book of Latin American Essays
Tropical Synagogues: Short Stories
Growing Up Latino: Memoirs and Stories (with Harold Augenbraum)
Wáchale! Poetry and Prose about Growing Up Latino in America
The Schocken Book of Modern Sephardic Literature

Cartoons
Latino USA: A Cartoon History (with Lalo López Alcaráz)

Translations
Sentimental Songs, by Felipe Alfau

Editions
Encyclopedia Latina (4 volumes)
The Poetry of Pablo Neruda
The Collected Stories of Calvert Casey
Isaac Bashevis Singer: Collected Stories (3 volumes)

General
The Essential Ilan Stavans
Ilan Stavans: Eight Conversations (by Neal Sokol)

About the Author

Ilan Stavans is the Lewis-Sebring Professor in Latin American and Latino Culture at Amherst College.